John Armstrong, Jesse Buel

A Treatise on Agriculture

John Armstrong, Jesse Buel

A Treatise on Agriculture

ISBN/EAN: 9783744726030

Printed in Europe, USA, Canada, Australia, Japan

Cover: Foto ©ninafisch / pixelio.de

More available books at **www.hansebooks.com**

AGRICULTURE,

COMPRISING

A CONCISE HISTORY OF ITS ORIGIN AND PROGRESS; THE
PRESENT CONDITION OF THE ART ABROAD AND
AT HOME, AND THE THEORY AND
PRACTICE OF HUSBANDRY.

TO WHICH IS ADDED,

A DISSERTATION ON THE KITCHEN AND FRUIT GARDEN.

BY JOHN ARMSTRONG.

WITH NOTES BY J. BUEL.

NEW YORK:
HARPER & BROTHERS, PUBLISHERS.
1864.

PREFACE.

AFTER Gen. Armstrong had retired from public to private life, and turned his attention particularly to rural pursuits, he wrote the following treatise on agriculture for the Albany Argus, then conducted by the subscriber. To give it to the public in a less perishable shape than the columns of a newspaper, it was afterward published in book form. The object of General Armstrong was " to contribute his aid," to use his language, " in giving to the study and practice of agriculture a new and increased impulse throughout the state; and he supposed this could be best done by exhibiting concisely the origin and progress of the art, its present condition abroad and at home, and, lastly, the theory and practice in relation to it which have arisen out of the present philosophical attainments in Europe."

At a subsequent period, at our request, the general wrote two essays, one upon the kitchen, and the other upon the fruit garden, which were published in the second and third volumes of the Memoirs of the Board of Agriculture. As there were but few copies of either the treatise or the memoirs printed, the circulation was, of course, limited, and the supply inadequate to the demand. Now that a taste for agricultural information and agricultural improvement has become more general, and that these writings are not to be found in the market, the subscriber has been induced to unite them in one volume, and to subjoin such notes as a lapse of twenty years has, in a measure, rendered expedient, on account of the improvements which have, during that time, been made in rural economy; and, in preparing this new edition, he is persuaded that he is rendering an acceptable service to the agriculturist and to the community at large.

. J. BUEL.

Albany, June, 1839.

CONTENTS.

A TREATISE

ON

AGRICULTURE

CHAPTER I.

OF THE RISE AND PROGRESS OF AGRICULTURE.

THE origin of this art is lost among the fables of antiquity, and we have to regret that, in the present state of knowledge, we are even ignorant of the *time* when the plough was invented, and of the *name* and *condition* of the inventor.* When, therefore, we speak of the beginning of the art, we but allude to certain appearances which indicate its existence, and the employment given by it to the minds, as well as to the hands of mankind. Such were the artificial canals and lakes of Egypt. Menaced at one time by a redundancy of water, and at another by its scarcity or want, the genius of that very extraordinary people could not but employ itself, promptly and strenuously, in remedying these evils, and eventually in converting them into benefits; and hence it was, that, when other parts of the world exhibited little more of agricultural knowledge than appertains to the state of nature imagined by philosophers, the Egyptians thoroughly understood and skilfully practised *irrigation*, that most

* This invention has been attributed to *Osiris*. See Millot's Gen. Hist.

scientific and profitable branch of the art.*   Like their own Nile, their population had its overflow, which colonized Carthage and Greece,† and carried with it the talent and intelligence of the mother country.   The former of these states, though essentially commercial, had its *plantations*; and so highly prized were the agricultural works of Mago, that, when Carthage was captured, they alone, of the many books found in it, were retained and translated by the Romans.   A similar inference may be drawn from the history of Greece; for assuredly that art could not have been either unknown or neglected which so long employed the pen and the tongue of the great Xenophon.‡   It must, however, be admitted that, of the ancient nations, it is only among the Romans that we find real and multiplied evidences of the progress of the art; *facts* substituted for *conjectures* and *inferences*.   Cato, Varro, Columella, Virgil, and Pliny, wrote on the subject, and it is from their works we derive the following brief exposition of Roman husbandry.

The plough, the great instrument of agricultural labour, was well known and generally used among the Romans, and was drawn exclusively by horned cattle.   Of *fossil manures* we know that they used *lime*, and probably *marl*,§ and that those of animal and vegetable basis were carefully collected.   Attention to this subject made part of the national re-

* The best practical illustration of this opinion is found in the Valley of the Po, where " every rood of earth maintains its man."

.† The Egyptians might have sent some colonies into these countries ; but the commonly received opinion is, that the Pelasgi first settled Greece, and that Carthage was founded by a company of Phœnicians under Queen Dido.

‡ Xenophon wrote several treatises on husbandry, and gave public lectures on it at Scillonte, whither a weak and wicked government had banished him.

§ For the first part of this assertion we have the authority of Pliny ; for the latter, the practice of their colonies both in Gaul and Britain.

ligion; the dunghill had its god, and Stercutus his temple and worshippers. Their corn-crops were abundant; besides *barley* and *far*,* they had three species of *wheat*, the *robus* or red, the *siligo* or white, and the *triticum trimestre*, three months or summer wheat; they had, besides, millet, panis. zea, and rye, all of which, producing a flour conver tible into bread, were known by the common name of *frumentum*, corn or grain. Leguminous crops were frequent; the lupine, in particular, was raised in abundance, and, besides being employed as a manure,† entered extensively into the subsistence of men, cattle, and poultry. The cultivation of garden vegetables was well understood, and employ- ed many hands; and meadows, natural and artifi- cial, were brought to great perfection. Lucerne and fenu-gree were the basis of the latter; and pease, rye, and a mixture of barley, beans and pease, called *farrago*, were occasionally used in the stables as green food. Their flocks were abundant, and formed their first representative of wealth, as is sufficiently indicated by their word *pecunia*. Vines and olives, and their products, wine and oil, had a full share of attention and use. The rearing of poultry made an important part of domestic economy; nor were apiaries and fishponds forgotten or neglected.

Such was the husbandry of Rome when Rome was mistress of the world; and it was to this illus- trious period that Pliny alluded, when, speaking of the ancient fertility of the soil, he remarked, " that the earth took pleasure in being cultivated by the hands of men crowned with laurels and decorated with triumphal honours."

* Of this last there were three kinds, neither of which is now cultivated.
† The lupinus albus of Linnæus : "many other vegetables are used for this purpose, particularly the *bean*, but they do not answer as well as the *lupine ;* when this is heated in an oven, and then buried, it forms the most powerful of all manures."— T. C. L. Simonde. *Tableau de l'Agriculture Toscane.*

If we pause for a moment to glance at the civil institutions of this wonderful people, we discover how soon and how deeply it entered into their policy, not merely to promote, but to dignify agriculture and its professors.* When Cicero said that "nothing in this world was better, more useful, more agreeable, more worthy of a free man than agriculture,"† he pronounced not only his own opinion, but the public judgment of his age and nation. Were troops to be raised for the defence of the republic, the *tribus rusticus*—the country or farming class—was the privileged nursery of the legion.‡ Did exigencies of state require a general or dictator, he was taken from the *plough*. Were his services to be rewarded, this was done, not with ribands or gold, but by a donation of *land*.§

With such support from public opinion, it was not to be supposed that the laws would be either adverse or indifferent to this branch of industry ; we accordingly find the utmost security given to the labours of the husbandman ;‖ no legislative interposition between the seller and buyer; neither forced sales nor limitation of prices, and a sacredness of boundaries never disturbed ;¶ fairs and markets multiplied and protected against invasion or interruption,** and highways leading to these everywhere established, and of a character to call forth the highest praise and admiration.††

* Tanus and Numa were deified for services rendered to agriculture.
† Cicero de Officiis, l. ii.
‡ This continued till the time of Marius.
§ As much as he could plough in a day.
‖ To cut or destroy in the night the crop of his neighbour, subjected the Roman to death.
¶ Terminus was among their gods.
** Assemblies of the people on days designated for fairs, and on subjects other than those of trade, were not lawful.
†† The Appian Way yet remains the wonder and reproach of modern times.

Nor were these regulations confined to the proper territory of Rome; what of her own policy was good, she communicated to her neighbours; what of theirs was better, she adopted and practised her-self. Her arts and arms were therefore constant companions: wherever her legions marched, her knowledge, practices, and implements followed; and it is to these we are to look for the foundation of modern agriculture in Italy, France, Spain, &c.

CHAPTER II.

OF THE ACTUAL STATE OF AGRICULTURE IN EUROPE.

This is very different in different states, and even in different parts of the same state: its greater or less degree of perfection depending on causes phys-ical or political, or both. Where a state, or part of a state, from *soil, climate, manners*, or *geographi-cal position*, draws its principal subsistence from the fishery or the chase, as in the more northern parts of Europe,* agriculture will not succeed; when a state is from any cause both essentially maritime or manufacturing, as in England,† or principally

---

* Is not the author somewhat at fault here? Norway is the only country in the north of Europe where the business of fish-ing is extensively followed, and it is only in the portions of that continent, so far north as to be unfitted by climate for agricul-ture, that wild animals abound.

† The agricultural condition of Great Britain, and particularly of Scotland and of Prussia, has been greatly changed and im-proved within the last 20 years; and even Prussia has apparently commenced in earnest in enlightening her agriculture, by estab-lishing schools of scientific and practical instruction. The great Prussian school of Moegelier, under the direction of Von Thaer,

manufacturing, as in Prussia;* where public opinion has degraded manual labor, as in Spain, Portugal, and the Papal territory; or where laws villa-
nize it, as in Russia, Prussia, Poland, Hungary, &c.,
&c., it is in vain to expect pre-eminent agriculture.
These principles will receive illustration as we go
along.

I. In the Campania of Rome, where, in the time
of Pliny, were counted twenty-three cities, the traveller is now astonished and depressed at the silence
and desolation that surround him.   Even from Rome
to Trescati [four leagues of road the most frequent-
ed], we find only an arid plain, without trees, without meadows natural or artificial, and without villa-
ges or other habitation of man!   Yet is this wretchedness not the fault of soil or climate, which, with
little alteration,† continue to be what they were in
the days of Augustus.   "*Man is the only growth that
dwindles here,*" and to his deficient or ill-directed industry are owing all the calamities of the scene.‡

one of the most enlightened agriculturists of the age, aided by
the instruction in agriculture which is now given in the normal
and primary schools of that kingdom, has already produced a
wonderful improvement in Prussian agriculture. The march of
improvement in Scotch husbandry, in the present century, has
probably not been surpassed in any country; while in England,
at no time has there been greater or more wisely directed efforts
for improvement than within the last few years. Instead of
manufactures depressing, it would seem that they now operate
as the strongest stimulant to agricultural improvement, by of
fering a ready home-market for the surplus products of the soil,
both of raw materials and provisions. This also appears to be
true with regard to our country.—J. B.

·* Although great attention has been given to manufactures in
Prussia within the last half century, still it is too much to say
that she is "principally manufacturing." Agriculture is un
doubtedly, by far, the most important interest.

† The climate of Italy is now warmer than it was in the Au-
gustan age, which Buffon ascribes to the draining of great tracts
of swampy land in Germany.

‡ "Un Romain meme le plus indigent rougiroit de cultiver la
terre."—Bosc. The poorest Roman would blush to cultivate the
earth

Instead of devoting themselves to the hardy and masculine labours of the field, the successors of Cato and of Pliny are employed in fabricating *sacred vases*, *hair-powder* and *pomatums*, *artificial pearls*, *fiddle-strings*, *embroidered gloves*, and *religious relics!* They are also great collectors of pictures, statues, and medals—"dirty gods and coins"—and find an ample reward in the ignorance and credulity of those who buy them.

II. How different from this picture is that of *Tuscany!* where the soil, though less fertile,* is covered with grain, with vines, and with cattle; and where a surface of 1200 square leagues subsists a population of 950,000 inhabitants, of which 80,000 are agriculturists.† It may amuse, if it does not instruct, the reader, to offer a few details of a husbandry among the most distinguished of the present age. The plough of northern Europe, like that of this country, has the power of a wedge, and acts horizontally; that of Tuscany has the same direction, but a very different form. With the outline of a shovel, it consists of two inclined planes sloping from the centre, and forming a gutter and two ridges. This instrument is particularly adapted to the loose and friable texture of the soil. A second plough of the same shape, but of smaller size, follows that already described, and, with the aid of the hoe and the spade,‡ throws the earth, already bro-

---

* "Two thirds of Tuscany consists of mountains." Vol. viii., p. 232, *Geographique Mathematique et physique.* See also Forsyth's remarks, p. 80, where are detailed the principal causes of her prosperity. "Leopold," says he, "in selling the crown lands, studiously *divided large tracts* of rich but neglected land into *small properties.* His favourite plan of encouraging agriculture consisted, not in *boards*, *societies*, and *premiums*, but in giving *the labourer a security and interest in the soil*, in multiplying small freeholds, in extending the livelli or life leases," &c., &c.

† Tuscany, including the islands belonging to it, is stated to have a superficial area of about 8000 square miles, and, by the last census, somewhat more than 1,300,000 inhabitants.

‡ It is among the most important covenants of a Tuscan .ease,

ken and pulverized, into four-feet ridges or beds, on which the crop is sown. The furrows answer a threefold purpose; they drain the beds of excessive moisture, ventilate the growing crops, and supply paths for the weeders.

The *rotation of crops* employs two periods of different length; the one of three, the other of five years. In the rotation of *three* years the ground is sown five times, and in that of four years seven times, as follows:

1st year, wheat, and, after wheat, lupines:
2d   do.   wheat, and, after wheat, turnips:
3d   do.   Indian corn or millet.
1st year, wheat, and, after wheat, beans:
2d   do.   wheat, and, after wheat, lupines:
3d   do.   wheat, and, after wheat, lupinella: [annual clover].
4th do.   Indian corn or millet.

In the *Syanese Maremna*, where the lands want neither repose nor manure, the constant alternation is *hemp* and *wheat*, and the produce of the latter is often twenty-four bushels threshed for one sown.

It will be seen from this course of crops, that the principal object of Tuscan agriculture is wheat; of which they have two species, the one bald, the other bearded; both larger than the corresponding species in other countries of Europe; convertible into excellent bread and pastes, and probably but varieties of that *Sicilian family* which Pliny describes as yielding "*most flour* and *least bran*, and *suffering no degradation from time*." It is harvested about the middle of June, and, when the grain crop is secured, the ploughing for the second or forage crop begins; which, besides lupines, lupinella, and beans, often consists of a mixture of lupines, turnips, and flax. The lupines ripen first, and are gathered in autumn;

that one third of the ground shall be actually worked with a spade.

the turnips are drawn in the winter, and the flax in the spring.

Besides the application of *ordinary manures*, the lupine is ploughed down *when in flower;* a practice that began with the Romans: Columella says, "of all leguminous vegetables, the *lupine* is that which most merits attention, because it costs least, employs least time, and furnishes an *excellent manure.*"   The culture of this vegetable is different, according to the purposes for which it is raised; if for grain, the ground has two ploughings and twenty-five pounds weight of seed to a square of a hundred toises [about 640 feet]: if for manure, one ploughing is sufficient. Like our buckwheat, its vegetation is quick and its growth rapid; whence the farther advantage of suppressing, and even of destroying, the weeds that would have infested any other crop.   In the neighbourhood of Florence, they are in the practice of *burning the soil;* which they do by digging holes, filling them with fagots, and raising the earth into mounds over them.   The fagots are then inflamed and burned, and with them the incumbent earth, which is afterward scattered, so as to give to the whole field the same preparation.

III. " The countries," says Arthur Young, " the most rich and flourishing of Europe, in proportion to their extent, are probably *Piedmont* and the *Milanese.* We there meet all the signs of prosperity, an active and well-conditioned population, great exertions, considerable interior consumption, superb roads, many opulent towns, a ready and abundant circulation, the interest of money low, the price of labour high; in one word, it is impossible to cite a single fact that shows that Manchester, Birmingham, Rouen, and Lyons, are in a condition equally prosperous as the whole of these duchies." Their population is stated at " 1,114,000, and the territory at little more than two millions of arpons (acres). Wheat, rye, Indian corn, flax, and hemp, the vine and the olive, the caper and the cotton-tree, with all kinds of garden fruits and vegetables, are cultivated here : the soil knows no repose, and much of it yields annually and uniformly two crops of grain or three of grass."* These are the miracles of irrigation; not a drop of water is lost. Besides the permanent supplies furnished from lakes, ponds, rivers, creeks, and springs, even the winter torrent and summer shower are everywhere intercepted by drains and led to reservoirs, whence they are distributed at will to the neighbouring grounds.

In 1770 an agricultural school was established at Milan, consisting of 220 boys, who were instructed in theoretical and practical husbandry. This institution has escaped the notice of travellers; and we are unable to say whether it has or has not fulfilled the intentions of its projectors.†

IV. *Switzerland* has 1444 square leagues of surface,‡ and presents an assemblage of mountains, one rising above another, until the summits are lost in masses of snow and ice, which never melt. This short description sufficiently indicates the character of both the soil and the climate; yet, unpropitious as these are, we find a population of 1242 inhabitants to each square league! " This is, perhaps, the country of the world which presents the most happy effects of an industry always active and persevering. The traveller who climbs her mountains is struck with admiration when he beholds vineyards and rich pastures in those places which before appeared naked and barren rocks. The traces

* Geographique Mathematique, &c., article Italie.

† Since this treatise was written, we have notice of the establishment of agricultural schools in Prussia, France, Ireland, Russia, and in most of the German States; and a school, upon a very broad and liberal basis, is in contemplation in England. —J. B.

‡ The superficial area of Switzerland, as its boundaries were established by the Congress of Vienna, has been differently estimated from 14,000 to 18,000 square miles.

of the plough are perceived on the border of precipices where the most savage animals do not pass without danger; in one word, the inhabitants appear to have conquered all obstacles, whether arising from soil, position, or climate, and to have drawn abundance from a territory condemned by nature to perpetual sterility."*

V. The classical reader will remember that *Spain* was the garden of the Hesperides of the Roman writers; by which was meant the combinations of a fine climate, a rich soil, and an active, intelligent agriculture. To this state of things even the empire of the Goths was not fatal;† and that of the Moors rendered it still more distinguished. In their hands the plains of Valentia were cultivated throughout, with the utmost care and skill; and where their wheels, reservoirs, and drains of irrigation yet remain, the soil continues to yield the richest and most abundant products. In Catalonia, Navarre, Galitia, and the Asturias, many species of the ancient agriculture are yet in vigour, because "the *leases are long*, and the *landlord cannot capriciously violate them.*" The same causes are followed by the same effects in the three districts of Biscaya, Guiposcoa, and Alava. "In running over these, everything one finds is animated by the presence of liberty and industry; nothing can be more charming than the coasts, nothing more attractive than the culture of the valleys. Throughout the 30 leagues that separate Bedassos from Vittoria, every quarter of an hour we discover some well-built village or comfortable cottage."‡

* Geographique Mathematique, article Helvetia.

† It appears from Varro, *De re rustica*, and the letters of Cassiodorus, that the Goths introduced into Spain the subterranean granaries called *sillos*, and the *art of irrigation.* The former are now exclusively used in Tuscany; and Cato's precept, " Prata irrigua," &c., shows whence their knowledge of the latter was derived.

‡ Burgoing's Modern Spain, vol. i.

How different is the aspect of the other provinces!
In these not more than two thirds of the earth are
cultivated; and "it is not uncommon to travel eight
and ten leagues together without finding a trace of
human industry. In the district of Badejoz alone
is a desert twenty-six leagues in length and twelve
in breadth.* Ten of the fourteen leagues that trav-
erse the duchy of Medina Sidonia consist altogether of pasturage. There is nowhere a vestige
of man; not an orchard, not a garden, not a ditch,
not a cottage to be seen! The great proprietor appears to reign, like the lion in the desert, repulsing
by his roaring all who would approach him. But,
instead of human colonies, we encounter troops of
horned cattle and of *mares*, wandering, self-directed,
over plains to which the eye can discover no bound-
ary or barrier, and which brings to one's recollec-
tion the days when the beasts shared with man the
empire of the earth."†

"Even when the plough is used, it is little more
than a great knife fastened to a stick, that just
scratches the surface. The grain is threshed by
horses or mules driven over it, or by means of a
plank studded with nails or flint stones, and drawn
across it.‡ With even this miserable culture, the
land in Andalusia yields considerable crops ; yet are
the inhabitants too lazy or too few to gather them
together.‡ This is done by Galiegos, who are the

* Borde's Itineraire de l'Espagne, vol. iv., p. 30.
† Burgoing. Spain has been long renowned for its horses.
The Romans, in settling their pedigree and illustrating their
swiftness, called them " *the children of the winds.*"
‡ Swinburne's Travels, vol. i. A Spanish peasant, who has
earned or begged enough for the wants of the day, will refuse to
earn more, even by running an errand. Striking as this fact is,
it does not so well illustrate Spanish indolence as the following
anecdote from the same pen : In the great sedition in Madrid,
which ended in the defeat of the king and the disgrace of his
minister (the Marquis des Suillas), and in its most fervid mo-
ments, both parties retired about dinner-time to take their *nap*

labourers of Spain." We need scarcely remark, that in a state of agriculture like this, the peasantry cannot be either well fed or well clothed. "The mountaineers live principally upon roasted acorns and goat's milk, and those of the plain (from Barcelona to Malaga) on bread steeped in oil, and occasionally seasoned with vinegar."*

It is wide of our subject to examine the causes of the degradation which marks the agriculture of Spain. Well-informed writers have ascribed it to the expulsion of the Moors and Jews, to the weight of taxes and imposts, to the *mesta* or common right of pasturage, to the discovery of America and its consequences, to the effect of climate, and the ill-judged charity of bishops and convents, but principally to the great *manorial grants* and *unequal division* of the soil which followed the conquest. "We often find six, eight, ten, and even fifteen leagues of extent belonging to one master. The nobility and clergy possess nearly the whole country. One third of Spain belongs to the families of Medina Celi, D'Alba, De l'Infantado, D'Aceda, and to the archbishops, bishops, and chapters of Toledo, Compostella, Valentia, Seville, and Murcia. A great proportion of these lands remain untilled and untenanted, and those which are let in *cortijo* or farms are double or treble the quantity that can be occupied in tillage."†

VI. The agriculture of *Portugal* has been subjected to the same evils as that of Spain, to which may be superadded her connexion with Great Britain, under whose policy she has become a raiser of *fruit* instead of *grain*.

VII. *France* is probably the country of Europe

or *miridiana*, after which they returned to the combat with new vigour and enraged fury. If *habits* can thus control the *passions*, to what important uses might not a wise legislation turn them?

* See preceding note.

† Le Borde's Itineraire de l'Espagne, vol. i.

which most unites the great desiderata of an extended and profitable agriculture, fertility of soil, mildness of climate, a dense population, an enlightened government, and facility of exportation.* Within her ancient limits, she boasts a surface of more than one hundred and fifteen millions of arpens, and a population of twenty-two millions of inhabitants.† The following tables will show, in a compressed form, the nature of her soil and the uses to which it is put :‡

GEOLOGICAL TABLE.

		Arpens or Acres.
Alluvial and other rich soil	. . .	26,159,340
Chalky do.	. . . .	13,268,911
Gravelly do.	. . . .	3,261,826
Stony do.	. . . .	18,128,660
Sandy do.	. . . .	7,553,956
Stratum of clay, with a light covering of sand, called landes	. . . .	21,879,120
Granitic and other mountains	. . .	25,261,946

AGRICULTURAL TABLE.

Arable land	. . . . . .	63,600,000
Vineyards	. . . . .	4,764,960
Woods	. . . . . .	15,931,850
Natural meadows	. . . .	5,464 800
Artificial meadows	. . . .	6,332,100
Lakes, marshes, wastes	. . .	19,400,049
Total,	. . . .	115,493,759

· From the average of a number of statistical tables

---

* The natural advantages of France as to soil, climate, &c. are doubtless great ; and her agriculture, and the condition of her rural population, have been much improved since the revolution ; still, as a whole, her soil is by no means as well cultivated as that of Belgium, Tuscany, England, Scotland, and, probably, some parts of Germany.

† The population of France, by the last enumeration, was about 32,000,000.

‡ See Geographique, &c., vol. vi., art. France, p. 13, and Young's Tour through France.

made by the Abbe D'Expillyt and others, it appears
that in 1777 the agriculture of France was not only
sufficient for the subsistence of its inhabitants, but
produced a surplus for exportation;* and though it
be universally admitted that her condition in this
respect is not less prosperous *now* than it was *then*,†
still it cannot be dissembled that her husbandry has
many defects :

1. A supposed resemblance between the earth
and animals gave rise to *fallows :* because men and
horses required repose after *labour*, it was supposed
that, after *cropping*, the earth also required it. Faithful to this absurd analogy, the French landlord binds
down his tenant by lease not to crop the soil more
than *three* years out of *four*; which, in effect, is to
consign to barrenness or weeds one fourth of the
whole arable land of France yearly !

2. There is not a sufficiently fixed or steady proportion between *arable* and *pasture* land. The production of grain is the great object of culture, often
with too little regard to the nature of the soil,
and generally without any to its improvements. ·
"Where pasturage is scanty, where natural meadows are bad, where artificial are rare, and root husbandry little extended, cattle cannot be either numerous or well-conditioned; and as without these

---

* The products of agricultural labour were, in these tables,
stated at 114,552,000 L. T. Those of manufacturing labour at
128,015,000.

† The effects of the revolution of 1789 on *agriculture* are no
longer doubtful. The suppression of *tithes*, of the *exclusive
privilege*, of the *chase*, of every species of *corvee* (labour performed by tenants for landlords), of *taxes* or *rents*, and of *rights* of
commonage, was among these effects ; and if to these we add the
division of the *great landed estates of the nobility and clergy*, there
can no longer be any skepticism on this point. No truth is better established than the advantage of *small* farms over *great*, so
far as the *public* is concerned. The Roman latifundia (military
grants) destroyed Roman agriculture.

there can be no manure, so without manure there can be no abundance."*

3. The land is generally worked by *farmers hired for that purpose*, or by *renters on short leases ;†* which in neither case betters the condition of the soil; the one having no interest in improvements, and the other too small a one to justify any expense in making them.

4. A *good rotation system*, adapted to the soil and climate, is not absolutely unknown, and may be found even in whole districts (as in French Flanders), but much too rarely. We have seen *wheat* and *fallows* alternating for years, and *wheat* and *rye*, *hemp* and *rye*, and many others equally ridiculous.

5. To the eye, more than one half of France is a common, without fences of any kind, excepting garden or park walls. Can there be order, economy, or security under such circumstances? Can the *police* and the *gens' d'armes* be sufficient substitutes?

VIII. *Holland*, though essentially commercial, has, from causes rarely occurring, become also highly agricultural. To the descendants of Dutchmen, the following description of her industry, in this respect, cannot but be acceptable. It is from the pen of an excellent judge and faithful narrator.‡

* French agriculture has undergone great changes since Herbin wrote. The large estates have been mostly cut up into small ones by the events of the revolution, and are now farmed by small proprietors : the culture of the sugar-beet, and the alternation of crops, have succeeded the old system of culture ; cattle are consequently more numerous and better conditioned ; a national central agricultural society, with numerous auxiliary societies, has been established ; men of science have applied their learning to the improvement of the soil, and the government has been actively engaged in encouraging this great branch of national industry, by giving liberal bounties to those who distinguish themselves in making improvements.—J. B.

† Herbin's Statistique general de la France, vol. i., Introduction.

‡ M. Yvart, Professor of Agriculture at Elfort. See his Introductory Address to his Class in 1806.

" Their rotation of crops always begins with the culture either of some leguminous plant or profitable root, and generally with the potato, as the best preparative of the ground.   Whatever may be the grain which follows, whether wheat, rye, &c., &c., it is generally sown with *red clover*; and, where it is not, the stubble is ploughed in immediately after harvest, and a crop of turnips taken, and either consumed on the ground or housed for the winter.   A single department (that of Zealand) obtains, by the culture of madder alone, an annual profit of six millions of florins, nearly three millions of dollars; while that of Brabant boasts its twenty thousand beehives; in a word, this commendable nation, upon an extent of surface not exceeding seventeen hundred square leagues (the greater part of which has been redeemed from the ocean), counts two hundred and forty-three thousand horses, seven hundred and sixty thousand horn cattle, about a million of sheep, from ten to twelve thousand goats, four hundred and eighty-nine thousand hogs, and about three millions of poultry of every species. Their stock of manure is necessarily great, and is both well understood and well managed."

IX. Physical and moral causes operate against the existence of a productive agriculture in *Denmark* and *Sweden;* and these are, severity of climate, poverty of soil, and vassalage of tenants.* Their resources are also alike, and exist principally in manufactures and commerce, and in mines, forests, and fisheries.† The former boasts fine pasturage and cattle in Holstein.

* To give to despotism the air of freedom, the *serfs of the crown* in Denmark were liberated at the revolution, but the ex ample was neither approved nor followed.

† These remarks as to climate, soil, and productions, are applicable to Sweden, but not to Denmark.   The climate of the latter country, in consequence of the insular situation of a large part of it, is by no means as severe as its latitude might seem to indicate.   The writer of this passed the winter of 1812 at Co

X. Under the common name of Germany we include Prussia, Saxony, Austria, Wurtemburg, and Bavaria, and shall say a few words of each calculated to give a general idea of their husbandry. It was not to be expected that the great Frederic of *Prussia* (so devoted to national glory and strength) would disregard the interests of agriculture ; and the less so, as in theory he considered it " *Les mamelles de l'état,*" the paps of the state. We accordingly find him employed in draining marshes of great extent,* in filling them with industrious colonists, and in converting barren sands into fertile fields, by placing his capital in the midst of them. But, among these good works, he forgot that the *hands of the labourer, to be efficient, must be free ;* he found the peasants slaves, and left them such.

The *Saxon* peasant, on the other hand, is *free*, and protected by the laws ; he holds his farm on lease, which he sells or transmits to his children at will : and *this* is the principal cause of the flourishing state of Saxon agriculture. In Lusatia, a different legislation produces different effects; but, for some years past, the government and great proprietors have concurred in changing the *vassalage* of the peasants into a *mild* and *salutary dependance.* Saxony is remarkable for its grain products, and Lusatia for its stock ; the latter counts four hundred thousand head of sheep of the Merino race.

Geographers give to *Austria* and her dependancies 1065 leagues in circumference. In a surface of this extent there is necessarily a great variety, as well of climate as of soil ; but, in general, both

penhagen, and did not at any time see sufficient snow on the ground to make good sleighing. Much of the soil of Denmark is highly productive in wheat, rye, pasturage, &c. She has few manufactures, or mines, or forests, and, since her separation from Norway, no extensive fisheries.

* In the *Dollart,* what was lost by the sea was regained, and the marshes on the *Netz* and the *Warth,* at *Friedberg* and in *Pomerania,* were drained, and the country rendered habitable.

are favourable to agriculture. "In the districts of the Inn, of Lower Stiria, of Istria, and of Carniola, the land is of good quality, well cultivated, and very productive. In the last they have two crops in the year; sowing buckwheat on wheat or rye stubble, and millet on that of hemp and flax. They everywhere cultivate Indian corn, and in Stiria (as in Virginia) it forms the ordinary bread of the country." In Bohemia, Moravia, and Galitia,* the soil is uncommonly rich, and, under proper management, would be very productive. Austrian Silesia is less fitted for the production of grain, but excels in forage and cattle. Hungary, Transylvania, and Croatia abound in every species of agricultural produce. Their flocks and pasturage are not inferior to those of the Ukraine; and wheat, buckwheat, Indian corn, millet, rice, hemp, flax, and tobacco, yield immense harvests to very small degrees of labour. Yet is agriculture far from being in a flourishing condition! Writers on political economy ascribe this fact principally to two causes.

1st. The degradation and oppression of the labouring part of the community; and,

2d. The want of convenient commercial outlets for the produce of the soil.

We shall find in Hungary a striking illustration of the correctness of this opinion. "The *Populus Hungaricus*"—Hungarian population—is divided into four estates, the magnats, the nobles, and the clergy, who possess all the lands, and the "*misera contribuens plebs*"—the wretched contributing people—who, besides tithes, rents, and corvées, pay all the taxes. This miserable populace is composed of the burghers and the peasantry, of which there are three kinds, *slaves for life*, *temporary slaves*, and a third sort called *liberæ emigrationis*, who, as their name indicates, have locomotive powers and rights

* Geographique Math.
3

Of the condition of this people since the year 1764 (and before that period it was much worse), we may form an idea from the edict of Maria Theresa, called the *urbarium*, or law of contracts betweer. landlord and tenant, by which it is declared that corporeal punishment, inflicted by the master for insolent words or conduct, shall not exceed twenty-four strokes with a cane for a man, and the same number with a switch for a woman. Nor is the *commercial* condition of this people better than the *civil*; they are not only obliged to take from Austria many things which they could obtain in other places of a better quality and at a lower price, but they are also compelled to carry to Vienna the products of their own soil and labour, where their sale is embarrassed and their value lessened by heavy and oppressive taxes. The same remark applies to Galitia, whose natural outlet is the Vistula or the Nieper; but of these she is not permitted to avail herself, and, like her sister kingdoms, is compelled to seek the markets furnished by the Danube and Trieste. "The consequences are obvious; the tenant works only to satisfy hunger, and the landlord is satisfied with little more than '*victum et vestitum*,' "* food and clothing.

The amount of lands annually cultivated in *Bavaria* is one million one hundred and sixty-five thousand acres, which produce about six millions of bushels of grain, of which two millions are surplus. The Palatinate (one of the dependancies of Bavaria) is also very productive. The route between Heidelberg and D'Armstadt, called the *Bergstrass*, traverses one of the finest districts of Germany, and, perhaps, of Europe; where are seen extensive vineyards, vast meadows, and fertile fields, producing wheat, barley, tobacco, madder, rhubarb, turnips, &c., &c. In the year 1799, all the electoral pos-

* Geog. Math., vol. iv., article Hungary.

sessions within the circle of Bavaria, contained 199,000 horses, 160,000 oxen, 465,000 cows, 961,000 sheep, 320,000 hogs, and 378,000 goats. Yet are the Bavarians, compared with the inhabitants of the north of Germany, half a century in the rear. The people are extremely ignorant and fanatical : like the people of Rome and Lisbon, they sacrifice much time to processions and fêtes, and, like them also, are slaves of the vilest appetites. Debauchery is no-where more flagrant than in Munich.*

Wurtemburg is ranked among the most fertile and well-cultivated countries of Germany. The mountainous parts produce potatoes, oats, hemp, and flax ; the less hilly abound in wheat, spelts, rye, buckwheat, Indian corn, and barley ; and in the valleys we find tobacco, and madder, and vineyards in which the grapes of France, Cyprus, and Persia succeed perfectly. Apples, pears, &c., are of common product and of excellent quality.†

XI. It has been justly remarked, that, to know the state of husbandry in any country, you have but to examine the *instruments* employed, the *succession* of *crops*, and the *condition* of *labourers*. Tried by these tests, the agriculture of *Russia* will be found to be in a state of great degradation. The plough (called *soka*) which is commonly used is very light, of simple construction, and only calculated to enter the ground *one inch and a half;* the *harrow* consists of one or more young pine-trees (whose branches are cut off about eight inches from the stem), steeped in water to add to their weight, and tied together. With such miserable instruments, each drawn by a single horse, the farmer scratches the ground without always covering the seed, which is no doubt the reason that in dry seasons their harvests are very bad.‡

* Geog. Math., &c., art. Bavaria. Compare the productiveness of Bavaria with England ; the comparison is in favour of the former.

† Idem.   ‡ Pallas, pages 3 and 4, vol. i.

In the best soil, their *succession* of *crops* is of *eight years;* two in barley, two in oats, two in winter rye, and two in spring rye. Lands of less fertility are sown *two* years out of *three*, and mountainous tracts one year in three, when they are abandoned to weeds until rest shall have reinstated them. "To manure them would, in the opinion of a Russian peasant, make them poorer;* and therefore he suffers his dunghill to accumulate into a nuisance, while he goes on to clear and exhaust new fields." " The grains raised are rye, spelts, barley, millet, and oats, which, from want of sufficient roads and markets, are often low priced, as are also horned cattle and horses : an ox selling for a rouble and a half, a cow for one rouble, and a horse for three roubles."† To this wretchedness we must add (what, perhaps, occasions much of it), that, throughout the *civilized* part of Russia, the labours of agriculture are performed by *slaves* confounded with the soil, and bought and sold with it. In a great portion of the northern section of this vast empire, agriculture is unknown, and the chase, the fisheries, cattle, and reindeer, furnish the only means of subsistence.

XII. The climate and soil of the United Kingdoms of *Great Britain* and *Ireland* are particularly favourable to husbandry; nor is her geographical position less auspicious; placed, as she is, on the longest lirfe, and amid the most important markets of the Continent of Europe. If to these advantages be added the laborious, enlightened, and enterprising character of the nation, we cannot but expect results the most favourable to agriculture: yet is the fact notoriously otherwise. To show that this opinion is neither hasty nor unfounded, we must enter into details which may not be unprofitable.

---

* Pallas, vol. v., p. 60.
† A silver rouble is equal to five livres French, or nearly one dollar Spanish, and this is the rouble here meant. The paper rouble is one fifth the value of the silver.

The surface of England is estimated at 37,265,853 acres, which are distributed as follows:

In pasturage	18,796,458
In tillage	11,350,501
In cities, towns, villages, &c., and roads and canals	3,454,740
Lands fit for pasturage or tillage not cultivated	3,515,238
Lands unfit for cultivation	2,148,921

Of the arable land, the following annual disposition is made:

In wheat and rye	2,000,000
In pease, beans, and buckwheat . . .	2,000,000
In barley and oats	4,000,000
In fallow, or in turnips or cabbages . .	3,400,000

The lands in wheat and rye yield, on an average of ten years, *three quarters** per acre, or 6,000,000 quarters; yet is there an annual deficit in England of 1,820,000 quarters, which must be drawn from foreign markets.†

There is certainly nothing very flattering in this view of English agriculture; but it may be said to be one of statists and politicians, and probably underrated. Let us see, then, what their most eminent agriculturists, as Young, and St. Clair, and Dickson, and Marshal, say on this subject: "*A very small portion of the cultivated parts of Great Britain is, to this day, submitted to a judicious and well-conducted system of husbandry, not, in fact, more than four counties* (Norfolk, Sussex, Essex, and Kent); *while many large tracts of excellent soil are managed in a way the most imperfect and disadvantageous.*"‡

---

* Twenty-four bushels.—J. B.

† The sufficiency of the harvests in England to supply the wants of her population depends on the character of the seasons. When these are favourable, she imports very little foreign grain; and, in proportion as they are unfavourable, she is obliged to resort to supplies from abroad. For the last twenty years her average annual importation of breadstuffs has been much less than the deficit here given.

‡ See the Introduction to Dickson's Practical Agriculture, 2d vol., quarto.

Nor is her management of cattle better. "Considering the domestic animals in a general way, we find each species, and almost every race, capable of great improvement, and, with few exceptions, the sheep much neglected. In some districts are whole races of cattle capable of improvement, within a reasonable time, in the three great objects which they are expected to yield, viz., milk, flesh, and labour."[*] We now add *some* of the causes to which this defective husbandry has been ascribed: "to enumerate all would be impossible, from their number and complication."[†]

"1st. The *commons*, or unenclosed grounds, which in many places amount to near one half of the whole arable land, and which are submitted to the most absurd and ruinous system of culture."[‡]

"2d. The *terms*, amounting to personal servitude, under which many of the lands are held."

"3d. The *shortness of leases* given by corporations, civil and religious, and by individuals, and which seldom exceed *three, five,* or *seven* years, excepting in the counties of Norfolk, Sussex, Essex, and Kent, where, with great advantage to both landlord and tenant, they are frequently extended to twenty-one years."

"4th. The *tithes in kind*, paid by the farmers to the church; a tax highly vexatious in its character and oppressive in its effects: and,

"5th. The *poor tax*, which has become enormous, and of which the yeomanry pay three fourths. Of this tax it has been truly said, that it is a powerful instrument of depopulation; a barbarous contrivance for checking all national industry."[§]

* Marshal, vol. iv., p. 575.*
† Dickson's Practical Agriculture.
‡ Idem.
§ Young's Tour through Ireland, vol. ii., p. 302.

---

* Since Marshal, Dickson, and Young wrote, England has done more to improve the breeds of cattle and sheep, except the fine woolled, than any other nation or country.—J. B.

To these causes, assigned by British writers, may be added the *increase* of *population* common to every nation of Europe, and which, in Great Britain, is beyond all proportion greater than the progress of agriculture ; the *augmentation* of *cattle*, which occasions that of pasturage, and the diminution of tillage ;* the *establishment* of great *farms* at the expense of *small* ones, and the *multiplication* of *parks* and *pleasure grounds* ; and, lastly, *attractions of great cities*, and the *continual draughts* made upon the agricultural population for the army and navy, and for commerce and manufactures.†

CHAPTER III.

THEORY OF VEGETATION.

VEGETABLES may be regarded as the intermediate link in the great chain of creation between animals and minerals. The latter grow by mere chymical affinity, and by additions, sometimes analogous to and sometimes foreign from their own nature ; while plants, like animals, have an organization that

---

* Mr. Hume quotes with approbation an author who complains of the decay of tillage in the reign of Elizabeth, and who ascribes it to the increase of pasturage, in consequence of the restraints imposed on the exportation of grain, while that of butter, cheese, &c., was free. The history of Europe, if read with an eye to public economy, furnishes abundant proof that the greatest obstructions to agriculture have arisen from the interference of government.

† Our author's account of the agriculture of England evidently relates to the state of things in that country some fifty years ago ; and, with this understanding, it is interesting as showing more strikingly the extent of the improvements of every kind which have been made since.

enables them to receive their food, digest and as-
similate it to their own substance, reproduce their
species, and maintain an existence of longer or
shorter duration. Thus far the learned are agreed,
but at the next step they differ.

What is this food that gives to plants their development, and maturity, and powers of reproduction? Lord Bacon believed that *water* was the
source of vegetable life, and that the earth was
merely its habitation, serving to keep plants upright, and to guard them against the extremes of
heat and cold. Tull, on the other hand (and, after
him, Du Hamel) pronounced *pulverized earth* the
only pabulum of plants, and on this opinion built his
system of husbandry. Van Helmont and Boyle opposed this doctrine by experiments: the former
planted and reared a cutting of willow in a bed of
dry earth, carefully weighed, and protected against
accretion by a tin plate, so perforated as to admit
only rain and distilled water, with which it was occasionally moistened. At the end of five years the
plant was found to have increased *one hundred and
sixty-four pounds*, and the bed of earth to have lost,
of its original weight, only *two ounces*. Boyle pursued a similar process with gourds, and with a similar result. Notwithstanding the apparent conclu-
siveness of these experiments, their authority was
shaken, if not subverted, by others made by Mar-
graff, Bergman, Hales, Kirwan, &c., &c. The first
of these showed that the rain water employed by Van
Helmont was itself charged with saline and other
earthy matter; Bergman demonstrated this by analysis, while Kirwan and Hales proved that the earth,
in which the willow cutting was planted, could absorb these matters through the pores of the wooden
box which contained it, and that a glass case could
alone have prevented such absorption. Hunter,
finding that oil and salt entered into the composition of plants, concluded that these formed their

principal food, and accordingly recommended, as the great desideratum in agriculture, an *oil compost.* Lord Kaimes attempted to revive the expiring creed of Lord Bacon; but finding, from Hale's statics, that one third of the weight of a green pea was made up of carbonic acid, he added *air* to the watery aliment of the English philosopher, but entirely rejected *oil* and *earth*, as too gross to enter the mouths of plants, and *salt* as too acrid to afford them nourishment. Quackery, which at one time or other has made its way into all arts and sciences, could not easily be excluded from agriculture. Hence it was that the Abbé de Valemont's *prolific liquor*, and De Hare's and De Vallier's *powders*, &c., &c., were believed to be all that was necessary to vegetation, and found the more advocates as they promised much and cost little. But before the march of modern chymistry quackery could not long maintain itself; and from the labours of Bennet, Priestly, Saussure, Ingenhouz, Sennebier, Schæder, Chaptal, Davy, &c., &c., few doubts remain on this important subject. These will be presented in the course of the following inquiry.

I. Of *earths*, and their relation to vegetation.

Of six or eight substances which chymists have denominated *earths*, four are widely and abundantly diffused, and form the crust of our globe. These are *silica, alumina, lime,* and *magnesia.* The first is the basis of quartz, sand, and gravel; the second of clay; the third of bones, river and marine shells, alabaster, marble, limestone, and chalk; and the fourth of that medicinal article known by the name of calcined magnesia. In a pure or insulated state,[*] these earths are wholly unproductive; but, when decomposed and mixed,[†] and to this mixture is added

* See Gisbert's experiments on *pure earths* and *their mixtures.* See also Davy's Elements, p. 156.

† In this respect nature has been neither negligent nor niggardly, if (as Fourcroy asserts) the purest sand be a mixture of

the residuum of dead animal or vegetable matter,* they become fertile, take the general name of *soils*, and are again specially denominated after the earth that most abounds in their compositions respectively. If this be silica, they are called *sandy*; if alumina, *argillaceous*; if lime, *calcareous*; and if magnesia, *magnesian*. Their properties are well known: a *sandy* soil is loose, easily moved, little retentive of moisture, and subject to extreme dryness; an *argillaceous* soil is hard and compact when dry, tough and paste-like when wet, greedy and tenacious of moisture; turns up, when ploughed, into massive clods, and admits the entrance of roots with great difficulty. A *calcareous* soil is dry, friable, and porous; water enters and leaves it with facility; roots penetrate it without difficulty, and [being already greatly divided] less labour is necessary for it than for clay. *Magnesian*, like calcareous earth, is light, porous, and friable, but, like clay, when wet, takes the consistency of paste, and is very tenacious of water. It refuses to combine with oxygen or with the alkalies is generally found associated with granite, gneiss, and schist, and is probably among the causes of their comparative barrenness.†

quartz, alumina, and sometimes of calcareous matter. *Speculative geology* is romance, and does not merit the name of science; yet is science obliged to borrow her theory of soils. The alternation of heat and cold, moisture and dryness, *decomposed* the mountains of primitive, secondary, and tertiary formation; rains, and the laws of gravity, brought these broken parts from places of more to those of less elevation; where, by mechanical mixture and chymical combination, the present substrata were formed. But these were yet naked and unproductive, when the Cryptogamia family (mosses and lichens) took possession of them, and in *due time* produced that vegetable matter which made the earth productive and the globe habitable !

* Dead animal and vegetable matter, in the last stage of decomposition, give a black or brown powder, which the French chymists call *terreau* or *humus*, and which Mr. Davy calls an *extractive matter; this* is the fertilizing principle of soils and manures.

† The opinion is general among the chymists of Europe, that

In these qualities are found the *mechanical relations* between earths and vegetables. To the divisibility of the former it is owing that the latter are enabled to push their roots into the earth; to their *density*, that plants maintain themselves in an erect posture, rise into the air, and resist the action of winds and rains; and to their *power* of *absorbing* and *holding* water, they owe the advantage of a prolonged ap plication of moisture, necessary or useful to vege table life. But, besides performing these important offices, there is reason to believe that the earths con tribute to the *food* of vegetables. This opinion rests on the following considerations and experiments :

1. If earths do not contribute directly to the food of plants, then would all soils be alike productive; or, in other words, if air and water *exclusively* sup ply this food, then would a soil of pure sand be as productive as one of the richest alluvion.

2. Though plants may be made to grow in pound ed glass or in metallic oxydes, yet is their growth in these neither healthy nor vigorous : and,

3. All plants, on analysis, yield an earthy pro duct ;* and this product is found to partake of the earth that predominates in the soil producing the analyzed plant. This important fact is proved by De Saussure.

FIRST EXPERIMENT.

Two plants (the pinus abies) were selected, the one from a calcareous, the other from a granitic soil, the ashes of which gave the following pro ducts :

	Granitic soil.	Calcareous soil.
Potash	3.60 . . .	15
Alk. and mu. sulphates	4.24 . .	15

magnesian earth is not only barren itself, but the cause of barren ness in other soils in which it may abound, unless saturated with carbonic acid. See Bosc, Tenant, and Davy.

* Davy says this never exceeds one fiftieth of the whole pro duct.

Carbonate of lime	. 46.34 . . .	63
Carbonate of magnesia	6.77 . . .	00
Silica	13.49 . . .	00
Alumina . . .	14.86 . . .	16
Metallic oxydes . .	10.52 . . .	00

SECOND EXPERIMENT.

Two rhododendrons were taken, one from the calcareous soil of Mont de la Salle, the other from the granitic soil of Mont Bevern. Of a *hundred* parts, the former gave fifty seven of carbonate of lime and five of silica; the latter, thirty of carbonate of lime and fourteen of silica.

THIRD EXPERIMENT.

This was made to determine whether vegetables, the product of a soil having in it no silica, would, notwithstanding, partake of that earth. Plants were accordingly taken from Reculey de Thoiry (a soil altogether calcareous), and the result was a very small portion of silica.

These experiments, says Chaptal, leave little, if any doubt, that vegetables derive the earthy matter they contain from the soil in which they grow.*

II. Of *water*, as an agent in vegetation.

Seeds placed in the earth at a temperature above the freezing point, and *watered*, will develop; that is, their lobes† will swell, their roots descend into the earth, and their stems rise into the air. But without humidity they will not germinate; or, if deprived of humidity after germination, they will perish. When germination is complete and the plant formed, its roots and leaves are so organized as to

* Schæder maintains the doctrine, that the earths found in plants are created there by the process of vegetation. His essay on this subject was crowned by the academy of Berlin in 1801. His experiments were the first to determine the different quantities of silica found in different kinds of grain.

† Moisten a bean in warm water, and detach the skin that covers it, and it readily divides into two parts; these are called lobes.

absorb water. The experiments of Hales prove, that
the weight of plants is increased in wet and diminished in dry weather; and that, in the latter, they
draw from the atmosphere, by means of their
leaves,* the moisture necessary for their well-being.
Du Hamel, and, after him, Sennebier, has shown,
that the filaments that surround the roots of plants,
and which have been called their hair, perform for
them in the *earth* the office which leaves perform in
the atmosphere; and that, if deprived of these filaments, the plants die.

It would be easy, but useless, to multiply facts
of this kind, tending to establish a doctrine not contested, but which, after all, does not assert that water
makes any part of the food of plants. On this point
two opinions exist; the one, that this liquid is a
solvent and conductor of alimentary juices; the
other, that it is itself an aliment, and, at the same
time, a purveyor of vegetable food. The first opinion is abundantly established. Water, when charged with oxygen, supplies to germinating seeds the
want of atmospheric air; and, saturated with animal
or vegetable matter in a state of decomposition, or
slightly impregnated with carbonic acid, very per-
ceptibly quickens and invigorates vegetation. The
second opinion is favoured by some of De Saussure's
experiments. On these Chaptal makes the following remark, which expresses very distinctly an approbation of the doctrine they suggest: " The enormous quantity of hydrogen, which makes so large a
part of vegetable matter, cannot be accounted for
but by admitting, in the process of vegetation, the
decomposition of *water*, of which hydrogen is the
principal constituent; and that, though there is nothing in the present state of our experience that directly establishes this doctrine, yet that its truth

* Bonnet's experiments show, that it is the under surface of
the leaf that performs this function. The upper surface has a
different office.

ought to be presumed from the analysis of plants and the necessary and well-known action of water on vegetation."

III. Of *air*, and its agency in vegetation.

A seed deprived of air will not germinate ; and a plant placed under an exhausted receiver will soon perish. Even in a close and badly ventilated garden, vegetables indicate their situation; they are sickly in appearance and vapid in taste. These facts sufficiently show the general utility of air to vegetation : but *air* is not now the simple and elementary body that the ancient chymists described it to be. Priestley first,* and Lavoisier after him, analyzed it, and found that, when pure, it consisted of about 70 parts of azote, 27 of oxygen, and 2 of carbonic acid. In its ordinary or impure state, it is loaded with foreign and light bodies; such as mineral, animal, and vegetable vapours, the seeds of plants, the eggs of insects, &c. Is it to this *aggregate* that vegetation owes the services rendered to it by air? And, if not, to *how many* and to *which* of its regular constituents are we to ascribe them? This inquiry will form the subject of the present article.

All vegetables in a state of decomposition give *azote;* and some of them, as cabbages, radishes, &c., in great quantity. This abundance, combined with the fact that vegetation is always vigorous in the neighbourhood of dead animal matter, led to the opinion that azote contributed largely to the growth of plants; but experiments, more exactly made and often repeated, disprove this opinion, and show that in any quantity it is unnecessary, and that, in a certain proportion, it is fatal to vegetation.

In *hydrogen gas* plants are found to be variously affected, according to their local situation ; if in-

* See Priestley's Experiments and Observations on different kinds of Air begun in 1767.

habitants of mountains, they soon perish; if of plains, they show a constant debility; but if of marshy grounds, their growth is not impeded.

Carbonic acid is formed and given out during the process of fermentation, putrefaction, respiration, &c., and makes 28 parts out of 100 of atmospheric air. It is composed, according to Davy, of oxygen and carbon, in the proportion of 34 of the former to 13 of the latter. It combines freely with many different bodies; animals and vegetables are almost entirely composed of it; for the *coal* which they give, on combustion, is but *carbon* united to a little oxygen, &c. Priestley was the first to discover that plants *absorb carbonic acid;* and Ingenhouse, Sennebier, and De Saussure have proved that *it* is their *principal aliment.* Indeed, the great consumption made of it cannot be explained by any natural process excepting that of vegetation. On this head we cannot do better than digest the experiments of the last of these chymists into a few distinct proportions :*

1. In pure carbonic acid gas, seeds will swell, but not germinate. 2. United with water, this gas hastens vegetation. 3. Air, containing more than one twelfth part of its volume of carbonic acid, is most favourable to vegetation. 4. Turf, or other carbonaceous earth, which contains much carbonic acid, is unfavourable to vegetation until it has been exposed to the action of atmospheric air, or of lime, &c. 5. If slackened lime be applied to a plant, its growth will be impaired until the lime shall have recovered the carbonic acid which it lost by calcination. 6. Plants kept in an artificial atmosphere, and charged with carbonic acid, yield, on combustion, more of that acid than plants of the same kind and weight growing in atmospheric air. 7. When plants are exposed to air and sunshine, the carbonic acid of

* Recherches chymiques sur la vegetation, chap. ii.

the atmosphere is consumed, and a portion of oxygen left in its place. If new supplies of carbonic acid be given to the air, the same result follows; whence it has been concluded, that air furnishes carbonic acid to the plant, and that the plant furnishes oxygen to the air. This double function of absorption and respiration is performed by the green leaves of plants.* 8. Carbon is to vegetation what oxygen is to animal life; it gives support by purifying the liquids and rendering the solids more compact.

IV. Of *light, heat,* and *electricity,* and their agency in vegetation.

When deprived of light, plants are pale, lax, and dropsical; restored to it, they recover their colour, consistency, and odour. If a plant be placed in a cellar, into which is admitted a small portion of light through a window or cranny, thither the plant directs its growth, and even acquires an unnatural length in its attempt to reach it.† These facts admitted, no one can doubt the agency of light in vegetation; but, in relation to this agency, various opinions exist; one, that light enters vegetable matter and combines with it; another, that it makes no part either of the vegetable or of its aliment, but directly influences substances which are alimentary;‡ and a third, that, besides the last effect, it stimulates the organs of plants to the exercise of their natural functions.§

Without doing more than state these opinions, we proceed to offer the results of many experiments on this subject. 1st. That *in the dark* no oxygen is produced, nor any carbonic acid observed; on the contrary, oxygen is absorbed and carbonic acid produced. 2d. That plants exposed to *light*

* This was a discovery of Sennebier.

† It is by a knowledge of this fact that gardeners bleach chicory, cellery, &c.

‡ See Fourcroy, vol. viii.   § See Chaptal on Vegetation.

produce oxygen gas in water. 3d. That *light* is essential to vegetable transpiration; as this process never takes place during the *night*, but is copious through the *day;* and, 4th. That plants raised *in the dark* abound in watery and saccharine juices, but are deficient in woody fibre, oil, and resins; whence it is concluded that saccharine compounds are formed in the *night,* and oil, resins, &c., in the *day.*

When the weather is at or below the freezing point, the sap of plants remain suspended and hardened in the alburnum;* but, on the application of *heat,* whether naturally or artificially excited, this sap is rendered fluid, is put into motion, and the buds begin to swell. Under the same impulse, through the medium of the earth, the roots open their pores, receive nutritive juices, and carry them to the heart of the plant. The leaves being now developed, begin and continue the exercise of their functions, till winter again, in the economy of nature, suspends the operation of the machine. Nor is the action of heat confined to the circulation of vegetable juices; without vapour (its legitimate offspring), the fountain and the shower would be unknown; nor would the great processes of animal and vegetable fermentation and decomposition go on. Without rain or other means of ameliorating the soil, what would be the aspect of the globe? what the state of vegetation? what the situation of man?

The universal diffusion of *electrical* matter, found in the air and in all other substances, furnishes a presumption that it is an efficient agent in vegetation. Nollet and others have thought that, artificially employed, it favoured the germination of seeds and the growth of plants; and Davy " found that corn sprouted more rapidly in water *positively* electrified by the voltaic battery than in water *negatively* electrified."† These opinions have not es-

---

* Knight's Observations, &c. † Davy's Elements.

caped contradiction, and *we* do not profess to decide where philosophers disagree.

V. Of *stable manures*, and of *lime, marl*, and *gypsum*, and their agency in vegetation.

We have already said that vegetables in the last stage of decomposition yield a black or brown powder, which Davy calls "*a peculiar extractive matter of fertilizing quality*," and which the chymists of France have denominated *terreau*.* This vegetable residuum is the simple mean employed by nature to re-establish that principle of fertility in the soil which the wants of man and other animals are constantly drawing from it. It was analyzed by Hessenfratz, who found it to contain an oily, extractive, and carbonaceous matter, charged with hydrogen; the acetates and benzoates of potash, lime, and ammoniac; the sulphates and muriates of potash, and a soapy substance, previously noticed by Bergman. Among other properties (and which shows its combustible character) is that of absorbing from atmospheric air its oxygen, and leaving it only azote. This was discovered by Ingenhouse, who, with De Saussure and Braconnet, pursued the subject by many new and interesting experiments, the result of which is,

1. That the oxygen thus absorbed deprives the terreau or extractive matter of part of its carbon, which it renders soluble and converts into mucilage; and,

2. That the carbonic acid formed in the process combines with this mucilage, and with it is absorbed by the roots of plants.

If we put a plant and a quantity of slackened lime under the same receiver, the plant will perish, because the lime will take from the atmospheric air all the carbonic acid it contains, and thus *starve* the plant. Vegetables placed near heaps of lime in the

---

* De Candolle and Macaire call it *humus*, and Dance and others *geine*.—J. B.

open air suffer from the same cause and in the same way ; but though lime in *large* quantities destroys vegetation, in *small* quantities it renders it more vigorous. Its action is of two kinds, mechanical and chymical; the first is the mere division of the soil by an interposition between its parts, the second, the faculty of rendering soluble vegetable matter, and reducing it to the condition of terreau.

The *mechanical* agency ascribed to lime belongs also to *marl* and to *ashes*, and in an equal degree; but their *chymical* operation, though similar, is less.*

Gypsum is composed of lime and sulphuric acid. Mayer was the first to present to the public a series of experiments upon it in its relation to agriculture. Many chymists have followed him, and a great variety of opinion yet exists with regard to its mode of operation. Yvart thinks that the action of gypsum is exclusively the effect of the sulphuric acid, which enters into its composition; and founds this opinion upon the fact that the ashes of turf, which contain sulphate of iron and sulphate of alumina, have the same action upon vegetation as gypsum. Laysterie, observing that plants whose roots were nearest the surface of the soil were most acted upon by plaster, concludes that gypsum takes from the atmosphere the elements of vegetable life, and transmits them directly to plants. Bosc intimates that the *septic* quality of gypsum (which he takes for granted) best explains its action on vegetation; but this opinion is subverted by the experiments of Davy, who found that, of two parcels of minced veal, the one' mixed with gypsum, the other left by itself, and both exposed to the action of the sun, the *latter* was the first to exhibit symptoms of putrefaction. Davy's own belief on this subject is,

---

* Vegetable ashes are *lime* combined with an earthy saline matter.

that it makes part of the food of vegetables, is received into the plant, and combined with it. The last opinion we shall offer on this head is that of the celebrated Chaptal. "Of all substances," he says, "gypsum is that of whose action we know the least. The prodigious effect it has on the whole race of trefoils (clover), &c., cannot be explained by any *mechanical* agency, the quantity applied being so small; nor by any *stimulating* power, since gypsum, raw or roasted, has nearly the same effect; nor by any *absorbent* quality, as it only acts when applied to the leaves. If permitted to conjecture its mode of operation, we should say that its effects being greatest when applied to the *wet* leaves of vegetables, it may have the faculty of absorbing and giving out water and carbonic acid, little by little, to the growing plant. It may also be considered as an *aliment in itself;* an idea much supported by Mr. Davy's experiments, which show that the ashes of clover yield gypsum, though the clover be raised on soils not naturally containing that substance."

CHAPTER IV.

OF THE ANALYSIS OF SOILS, AND OF THE AGRICULTURAL RELATIONS BETWEEN SOILS AND PLANTS.

WE have seen that the earths have a threefold capacity; that they receive and lodge the roots of plants, and support their stems; that they absorb and hold air, water, and mucilage, aliments necessary to vegetable life; and that they even contribute a portion of themselves to these aliments. But we have also seen that they are not equally adapted to these offices: that their parts, texture,

and qualities are different; that they are cold or
warm, wet or dry, porous or compact, barren or
productive, in proportion as one or the other may
predominate in the soil; and that, to fit them for dis-
charging the various functions to which they are
destined. each must contribute its share, and all be
minutely divided and intimately mixed. In this great
work nature has performed her part; but, as is usual
with her, she has wisely and benevolently left something for man to do.

This necessary interposition of human industry
should obviously begin by ascertaining the *nature
of the soil*. But neither the touch nor the eye, however practised or acute, can in all cases determine
this. *Clay*, when wet, is cold and tenacious; a description that belongs also to magnesian earths:
sand and *gravel* are hard and granular; but so also
are some of the modifications of lime: *vegetable
mould* is black and friable, but not exclusively so:
for schistous and carbonaceous earths have the same
properties.

It is here, then, that chymistry offers herself to obviate difficulties and remove doubts; but neither the
apparatus nor processes of this science are within
the reach of all who are interested in the inquiry,
and we accordingly subjoin a method less compre-
hensive, but more simple, and sufficiently exact for
agricultural purposes, and which calls only for two
vases, a pair of scales, clean water, and a little sulphuric acid.

" 1st. Take a small quantity of earth from different parts of the field, the soil of which you wish to
ascertain; mix them well together, and weigh them;
put them in an oven heated for baking bread, and,
after they are dried, weigh them again; the difference will show the *absorbent power of the earth*, or
the quantity of water which it contained. When
the loss of weight in 400 grains amounts to 50, this
power is great, and indicates the presence of much

animal or vegetable matter; but when it does not exceed twenty, the absorbent power is small, and the vegetable matter deficient.*

"2d. Put the dried mass into a vase, with one fourth of its own weight of clear water; mix them well together; pour off the dirty water into a second vase, and pour on to the residuum in the first vase as much clean water as before; stir the contents, and continue this process until the water poured off is as clear as that poured on the earth. What remains in the first employed vase is *sand*, *silicious* or *calcareous*.

"3d. The dirty water collected in the second vase will form a deposite, which, after pouring off the water, must be dried, weighed, and *calcined*. On weighing it *after* this process, the quantity lost will show the portion of *animal* and *vegetable mould contained in the soil:* and,

"4th. This calcined matter must then be carefully pulverized and weighed, as also the first deposite of sand, but without mixing them. To these apply, separately, sulphuric acid, and what they respectively lose in weight is the portion of *calcareous* or *aluminous earths* contained in them. These last, again, may be separated by soap ley, which dissolves them."†

Here, then, is the light we wanted. By knowing the disease, we find the cure. Clay and sand qualify each other; either of these will correct an excess of lime; and magnesian earth, when saturated with *carbonic acid*, becomes fertile.

But entirely to alter the constitution of a soil, whether by mechanical or other means, is a work of time, labour, and expense, and little adapted to the pecuniary circumstances of farmers in general.

---

* See Davy's Elements.

† This method of analyzing soils is that described by M. Bosc, member of the Institute of France, &c., and recommended to French agriculturists.

Fortunately, a remedy cheaper, more accessible, and less difficult, is found in that *great diversity* of habits and character which mark the vegetable races. We shall, therefore, in what remains of this chapter, indicate the principal of these, as furnish ing the basis of all rational agriculture.

1st. *Plants have different systems of roots, stems, and leaves, and adopt themselves, accordingly, to different kinds of soils:* the tussilago prefer clay, the spergula sand; asparagus will not flourish on a bed of granite, nor muscus Islandicus on one of alluvion. It is obvious that *fibrous-rooted* plants, which occupy only the surface of the earth, can subsist on comparatively stiff and compact soils, in which those of the leguminous and cruciform families would perish, from inability to penetrate and divide.

2d. *Plants of the same or of a similar kind do not follow each other advantageously in the same soil.* Every careful observer must have seen how grasses alternate in meadows or pastures where nature is left to herself. At one time timothy, at another clover, at a third redtop, and at a fourth blue grass prevails. The same remark applies to forest trees; the original growth of wood is rarely succeeded by a second of the same kind; pine is followed by oak, oak by chestnut, chestnut by hickory. A young apple-tree will not live in the place where an old one has died; even the pear-tree does not thrive in succession to an apple-tree, but stone fruit will follow either with advantage. "In the Gautinois," says Bosc, "saffron is not resumed but after a lapse of twenty years; and in the Netherlands, flax and colzat require an interval of six years. Pease, when they follow beans, give a lighter crop than when they succeed plants of another family."*

---

* The ill effect of a succession of crops of the same kind was not unknown to the Romans. We have proof of this in the following passage of Festus: "Restibilis ager fit qui continuo

3d. *Vegetables, whether of the same family or not, having a similar structure of roots, should not succeed each other.* It has been observed that trees suffer considerably by the neighbourhood of sainfoin and lucerne, on account of the great depth to which the roots of these plants penetrate; whereas culmiferous grasses do them no harm.

4th. *Annual or biennial trefoils prevent the escape of moisture from sandy and arid soils,* and should constantly cover them in the absence of other plants;* while *drying and dividing crops,* as beans, cabbages, chicory, &c., &c., *are best fitted to correct the faults of stiff and wet clays.*

5th. *When plants are cultivated in rows or hills, and the ground between them is thoroughly worked, the earth is kept open, divided, and permeable to air, heat, and water, and, accordingly, receives from the atmosphere nearly as much alimentary provision as it gives to the plant.* This principle is the basis of drill husbandry.

6th. *All plants permitted to go through the phases of vegetation (and, of course, to give their seeds), exhaust the ground in a greater or less degree; but, if cut green and before seeding, they take little from the principle of fertility.*

7th. *Plants are exhausters in proportion to the length of the time they occupy the soil.* Those of the culmiferous kinds (wheat, rye, &c.) do not ripen, if sown in the fall, under ten months, and during this period forbid the earth from being stirred; while, on the other hand, leguminous plants occupy it but from three to four months, and permit frequent ploughings. This is one reason why culmiferous

biennio seritur farreo spico, id est aristato, quod, ne fiat *solent, qui pradia locant, excipere.*"

* The "sterilis tellos medio versatur in æstu"—the bare earth turned up in midsummer—of Virgil, shows the opinion he entertained of a husbandry that left the fields without vegetation.

crops are greater exhausters than leguminous; another is, that the stems of culmiferous plants become hard and flinty, and their leaves dry and yellow, from the time of flowering till the ripening of the seed, losing their inhaling or absorbing faculties, circulating no juices, and living altogether in their roots, and on aliments exclusively derived from the earth; whereas leguminous or cruciferous plants, as cabbages, turnips, &c., &c., have succulent stems, and broad and porous leaves, and draw their principal nourishment from the atmosphere. The remains of culmiferous crops also are fewer and less easily decomposed than those of the leguminous family.

8th. *Meadows, natural and artificial, yield the food necessary to cattle, and, in proportion as these are multiplied, manures are increased and the soil made better.* Another circumstance which recommends meadows is, that, so long as they last, they exact but little labour, and leave the whole force of the farmer to be directed to his arable grounds.

9th. *Grasses are either fibrous or tap-rooted, or both The remarks already made in articles 1, 2, and 3, apply also to them.* Timothy, redtop, oat-grass, and rye-grass, succeed best in stiff, wet soils. Sainfoin does well on soils the most bare, mountainous, and arid; lucerne and the trefoils (or clovers) only attain the perfection of which they are susceptible in warm, dry, calcareous earth.

10th. *The ameliorating quality of tap-rooted plants is supposed to be in proportion to their natural duration;* annual clover (lupinella) has less of this property than biennial (Dutch clover), biennial less than sainfoin, and sainfoin less than lucerne.

11th. *Any green crop ploughed into the soil has an effect highly improving;* but for this purpose lupines and buckwheat (cut when in flower) are most proper.

12th. *Mixed crops* (as Indian corn and pumpkins,
5

and pease and oats) *are much and profitably employed,*
and *with less injury to the soil than either corn or oats
alone.**

CHAPTER V.

OF PRACTICAL AGRICULTURE, AND ITS NECESSARY IN-STRUMENTS.

WE begin this part of our subject with a few remarks on the instruments necessary to agriculture,
which may be comprised under the well-known
names of the plough, the harrow, the roller, the
threshing-machine, and the fanning-mill.

I. Of the *Plough.*

It is among the inscrutable dispensations of Prov-
idence, that the arts most useful to man have been
of later discovery, of slower growth, and of less
marked improvement than those that aimed only
at his destruction. At a time when the phalanx
and the legion were invented and perfected, and
when the instruments they employed were various
and powerful, those of agriculture continued to be
few, simple, and inefficient.

Of the Greek plough we know nothing ; and the
general disuse of that described by Virgil and Pliny
furnishes a degree of evidence that experience has
found it incompetent to its objects. With even the
boasted lights of modern knowledge, scientific men

---

* The good effect of these mixtures was known to the ancients, from whom the practice has descended to us. What a
picture of fertility and abundance have we in the 22d chap., 18th
book, of Pliny's Natural History : " Sub vite seritur frumentum,
mox legumen, decinde olus, omnia, eodem anno, omniaque ali-
ena umbra aluntur." Under the vine is sowed grain, shortly afterward pulse, then garden vegetables, all in the same year, and
sheltered and cherished by each other's shade.

are not agreed upon the form and proportions most proper for this instrument.   As in other cases, so in this, there may be no *abstract perfection;* what is best in one description of soil may not be so in another; yet, as in all soils the office of the plough is the same, viz., to *cleave* and *turn over the earth,* there cannot but be some definite shape and proportions better fitted for these purposes, and, at the same time, less susceptible of resistance, than any other.

This beau ideal, this supposititious excellence, in the mechanism of a plough, has been the object of great national as well as individual research.   In Great Britain, high prizes have been established for its attainment; and in France, under the ministry of Chaptal, 10,000 francs, or $2000, were offered for this object by the agricultural society of the Seine. In both countries the subject has employed many able pens; those of Lord Kaimes, of Mr. Young, of Mr. Arbuthnot, of Lord Somerville, and of Messieurs Duhamel, Chateauvieux, Bosc, Guillaume, &c.   It is not for us, therefore, to do more than assemble and present such rules for the construction of this instrument as have most attained the authority of maxims.

1st. The beam, or that part of the plough which carries the coulter, and furnishes the point of draught, should be as near that of resistance as possible ; because the more these are approached, the less is the moving power required. Even the shape of the beam is not a matter of indifference. In the old ploughs it was generally straight, but a small curve is now preferred; because it has the effect of strengthening the coulter by shortening it.

2d. The *head* of the plough is the plane on which it moves.   This should be concave, because that form offers fewer points of friction, and, of course, less resistance.   Between the beam and the head is an angle, on which depends the principal office of the plough; the making, at will, a deep or a shal low furrow. If you wish a deep furrow, diminish the angle, and vice versa: but this angle should in no case exceed from 18 to 24 degrees.

The resistance made to the plough being produced less by the weight of the earth than by the cohesion of its parts, it is evident that the head should be shod with iron, and rendered as smooth as possible. This remark applies equally to the soc and to the mouldboard.

3d. The *soc*, in its widest part, should be larger than the head. It has different shapes in different countries. In some is given to it that of an isosceles triangle; in others, that of the head of a lance; in Biscay, that of a crescent; and in Poland, of a two pronged fork. But, whatever be its shape, it should be well pointed and polished, enter the earth with facility, and cut it easily.

4th. To the *mouldboard* some workmen give the shape of a prismatic wedge; others make the upper part convex and the lower concave: while many make it entirely flat. In stiff soils, the *semi-cycloid* is the form to be preferred; and in loose, friable soils, the *semi-ellipsis*.* The iron mouldboard has great advantages over the wooden, particularly when it, the shear, and the soc, form one piece, as in the ploughs of Mr. Cook.

It is a general opinion, that a heavy plough is more disadvantageous than a light one; because the draught of the former, being greater, will be more fatiguing to the cattle; but the experiments of the agricultural society of London establish a contrary doctrine, and show that, in light grounds, the labour is more easily and better performed with a heavy than with a light plough.

5th. The *coulter* is a species of knife inserted in the beam, and so placed before the soc as to cut the sod. It is susceptible of being raised or depressed at will.

6th. The handles of the plough ought to be made

* See Arbuthnot on Ploughs.

of some kind of heavy wood, that they may operate as a counter weight to the head, the soc, and the mouldboard.

To these remarks we subjoin two sets of experiments, made with the most approved French and English ploughs, that of Guillaume and Small's *Rotheram plough improved*, which furnish a means of comparison between the best ploughs of Europe and those of this country.

The resistance (stated in these tables) was measured and ascertained by a *dynonometer*, a machine indispensable to those who would make correct observations on the relative advantages of different ploughs.

THE FRENCH PLOUGH. *Resistance in pounds.*	THE ENGLISH PLOUGH. *Resistance in pounds.*
1st experiment . . 200	1st experiment . . 360
2d " . . . 240	2d " . . . 380
3d " . . . 200	3d " . . . 480
4th " . . . 220	4th " . . . 460
5th " . . . 220	5th " . . . 400
	6th " . . . 400
Divided by 5)1080	7th " . . . 420
	8th " . . . 386
Average . . 216	9th " . . . 440
	Divided by 9)3720
	Average . . 413

II. *The Harrow.*—This is of different kinds; the triangular and the square, the single and the double. But, of whatever form, its uses are the same; to smooth the field after ploughing, to break and pulverize the clods, and to cover the seed. These uses sufficiently indicate the propriety of employing two in succession; one of heavy frame, with few and long teeth, like the Scotch break; the other of lighter construction, with more and shorter teeth. Our own experience leads us to believe that the common harrow covers the seed too much, because small seeds will not vegetate at a depth greater than three inches.

III. *The Roller* is a cylinder of heavy wood, turning on gudgeons or on an axle, and placed in a frame, to which is attached a shaft; it is of different dimensions, but need not exceed that which may be drawn by one, or, at most, by two horses or oxen. This instrument is indispensable in good husbandry, yet it is rarely used in ours. Its offices are threefold; to render loose soil more compact, to break the clods on stiff ones, and, on both, to compress the earth after seeding, so that it be everywhere brought in contact with the grain. It is also usefully employed in reinstating the roots of meadow grasses, loosened and raised by the alternate freezing and thawing of the ground, and, with a similar view, may be passed over winter crops early in the spring.

Its clod-breaking and pulverizing property is much increased by surrounding the roller with narrow bands of iron, two inches broad, three inches thick, and six inches apart; or by studding it with iron points resembling harrow teeth, and projecting three or four inches.

IV. *The Threshing-machine* is of English invention, and may be well enough adapted to the taste and circumstances of rich amateurs, but not at all to those of farmers in general. Our objections to it are three: the first cost, which is great; the quantum of moving power employed, which is equal to that of six horses; and the number of hands required to attend it, which is not less than four.* We have seen, in France, a machine for the same purpose, but of much simpler structure, called the "*Rouleau de depiquer*," which is only a *fluted cylinder;* yet, simple and cheap as this was, it could not

* This opinion of the value of the threshing-machine will, we presume, meet with but little favour among our wheat farmers.

maintain itself against the more ancient instruments, the flail and the horse. Still it is to be hoped that new experiments may succeed better, and abridge the manual labour usually given to this branch of husbandry, and that the mechanical genius of our own country, which is not inferior to that of any other, may be the first to combine *power* and *cheapness* in this machine.

This hope is probably suggested by the description of a new invented threshing machine now before me, and which I may be permitted to transcribe from the letter of the inventor. " The machine I have built is three feet wide. One horse will thresh, with much ease, as much wheat as can be laid on it by one man (the straw to be taken away by another), say from *fifty* to *one hundred bushels in a day*, and the saving of grain will pay for the labour; for I think that, with good attendance, not a particle of grain can escape with the straw. The expense of the machine will be from *fifty* to *seventy dollars*, exclusive of the moving power, which is a wheel about ten feet diameter on an upright shaft, to which a lever is fixed to hitch the horse. Within this main wheel a small one should be made to work, about two feet diameter, on a shaft carrying a drum four feet wide. With this simple gearing, and drawn by a horse that walks well, the machine will give about eighteen hundred strokes in a minute, and, if fully attended, will, without hard labour for the horse, thresh *a bushel every three* or *four minutes.*"

V. *The Fanning-mill.* Other things being equal, the cleanest wheat is most easily preserved, and, on manufacture, gives the best flour and in the largest quantity. These considerations offer inducement enough for the employment of this machine, which, besides doing its business well, saves a great deal of time. It is too well known to require description.

CHAPTER VI.

OF MANURES; THEIR MANAGEMENT AND APPLICATION.

THE principle of fertility (the result of animal and vegetable decomposition) is, as we have seen, susceptible of solution, and in this form becomes the aliment of that artificial vegetation which is the work of man, and which leaves so little on the earth to compensate for the great deal which it takes from it. In a course of years, therefore, there will be an actual loss or subtraction of matter, useful or necessary to the growth of plants, and which can only be re-established by manures of vegetable or animal origin. The most approved methods of preserving and applying these must therefore be among the objects most important to the agriculturist; and that the reader may better understand the reasons of the practice we mean to recommend, we begin the discussion with Kirwan's analysis of stable manures.*

			Charcoal.	Lime.	Clay.	Sand.	Fixed Salt.	Carbureted hyd., carb. acid, and water.
105 lbs of	Cow dung	give	3.75	1.20	0.15	2. 4	0. 6	92.80
	Horse dung		10. 2	1.50	0.50	3. 0	0.21	89.77
	Sheep dung		25. 0	10.28	29. 0	29. 0	0.72	68.00

* Tull and Du Hamel's doctrine, that frequent ploughings and sowings superseded the necessity of manure, is no longer held by any well-instructed agriculturist. The maxim of Oliver de Serris is much better founded. " Le bien labourer, le bien fumer, est tout le secret de l'agriculture." Till well and manure well is the whole secret of agriculture.

The elementary parts of these manures, as exhibited in this table, sufficiently indicate the mode of *preserving them.* When dropped in the fields and in small parcels by cattle, they exhibit no signs of fermentation, nor undergo, in that state, any degree of chymical decomposition ; but, when brought together, and frequently wetted and subjected to the action of atmospheric air, they are speedily dissolved and give out much gaseous matter. To prevent the escape of these soluble and volatile parts, two things are necessary : 1st, that the dung be collected in a reservoir of convenient size, and walled and paved with stones ; and, 2d, that a layer of sand or earth be occasionally spread over the surface of the dung. The former will prevent filtration, and the latter retain the gaseous matter so useful in vegetation, and, at the same time, augment the quantity of manure. To prevent an excess of moisture, which always retards, and sometimes prevents decomposition altogether, the reservoir should be covered.

The *application* of manures is a subject of more difficulty, and has given occasion to some dispute. The controverted points are,

1st. Whether short or long dung, or, in other words, whether dung thoroughly rotted, or that which has but begun to rot, is most advantageous.

2d. Whether dung used superficially, or ploughed deep into the ground, is most profitable.

3d. Whether extraneous matters admitted into the dungheap are useful or otherwise.

4th. Whether stable manures are best applied directly or indirectly to wheat crops.

5th. At what time manures are best applied ; and,

6th. In what quantity.

We shall discuss these points separately and briefly ; and,

1st. Which is to be preferred, long or short dung ?

The discordance in practice, as well as in opinion,

prevailing on this question, induced some scientific men to institute a series of experiments, having for their object a full and regular solution of it. With this view, parcels of dung (long and short) were taken from the same stables on the same day, and applied to crops of the same kind growing on the same fields. The result perfectly conformed to theory, and was similar in all the experiments. Those parts of the field to which the short dung was applied gave the best crops the *first* year; but those on which the long dung had been laid gave the best crops the *second* and *third* years; a fact which authorizes the conclusion, that, if we wish to obtain *one* great crop, the rotted dung is best; but when we look to more permanent improvement, the long dung is to be preferred.

2d. Which is the better practice, to spread manure on the surface, or lay it deeply under the ground?

In favour of the former practice it has been contended, that the distribution of the dung could be more equally made on the surface with a spade than under ground with a plough;* and for the latter, that all tap-rooted plants, entering far into the earth, require it to be laid deep; while those with fibrous roots will be sufficiently benefited by its exhalations. Both modes, however, are obviously bad. We have seen in the preceding article that dung, to become the aliment of plants, must undergo a decomposition; and that, to the production of this, the *combined* action of *air* and *water* is indispensable. But, if the manure be buried deeply, this action cannot reach it, and the dung remains a caput mortuum. On the other hand, if spread super-

---

* The English are said to have a machine attached to the drill that goes before and distributes the manure at the necessary depth. In planting potatoes we make a bed of dung for the plant. Why not apply the same reasoning and the same practice to all seeding of the ground?

ficially, the rains dissolve and carry away many of its juices, while the sun and the wind evaporate the rest. These considerations lead to the true rule on this head, which is *to lay it three or four inches below the surface of the soil.* At this depth, if short dung, its action will be most vigorous in all directions; and if long dung, a greater depth will, as already suggested, completely destroy all action.

3d. Are extraneous matters, as horns, hoofs, bones, shells, feathers, leaves, weeds, &c., &c., to be admitted into the dung-heap?

There is, perhaps, nothing in either theory or practice so obviously right, that it may not be disputed. The principal objection made to these matters is, that they do not decompose equally; and that those ingredients of the heap which are slowest in decomposition, retard others, which, if left to themselves, would be more forward in this process. This objection is without weight; for we have seen that long or unrotted manure, though its effect be prompt, is, upon the whole, more favourable to culture than that which is rotted. The difference of time in decomposition is therefore no evil, and the augmentation of the mass is a great good; besides that, some of these offals are the most powerful manures. Horns and hoofs are compounded of albumen and gelatine; bones, of the phosphate and carbonate of lime and gelatine; shells, of carbonate of lime and animal matter; and feathers and hair, of albumen, oil, &c., &c. Applied to the roots, they forward the growth of fruit-trees more than any other species of manure.

4th. Whether stable manures are best applied, directly or indirectly, to *wheat* crops?

The practice, on this head, is different in different places. In France, as in all other countries where fallows are in use, the dung is applied directly to the wheat crop; while in England, where the rotation system is established, it is applied to the sum-

coal, are nearly the same, and resemble those of lime and marl. They powerfully attract and hold moisture and carbonic acid, and they hasten the decomposition of stable manures, or other vegetable or animal product. Their action is most favourable on wet and cold soils, and as a top-dressing to natural meadows and turnip crops.

The practice of *paring* and *burning the surface of the earth* has been much used, and warmly recommended by the Irish; and in their land of bogs, as in the marshes of Holland, where infertility arises from excess of vegetable matter, it may be useful; but to burn the surfaces of sandy, gravelly, or even of dry clay soils, would be to lose sight of all sound theory.

Soils in general may be divided into two kinds, *sand* and *clay*. The defect of the one is want of cohesion between its parts; that of the other, an excessive or superabundant cohesion. But vegetable matter is, as we have seen, a remedy for both; and to accumulate this is the constant endeavour of every enlightened agriculturist. Yet are we advised to destroy this vegetable matter by fire, and to substitute for it a small portion of ashes, as more favourable to vegetation than the soil itself! But in what will these ashes differ from those found in our chimneys, and of which enough may be had? In nothing, excepting that they may possess somewhat more alkaline salt;* a circumstance which, if the subsoil be not charged with oily and animal matter, will be more injurious than useful.

---

* De Saussure's experiments prove, that the stems of trees (other things being equal) produce less of this salt than the branches, the branches less than the twigs, and the twigs less than the leaves. M. Perthuys has formed a table of the relative alkaline products of plants and trees. By this table it appears that the leaves and stems of Indian corn give to the quintal eight pounds thirteen ounces, those of oak one pound five ounces, and those of pine five ounces.

But, besides the consideration of getting so little, and that little of such equivocal character and
use, what do we lose by the process? If we approach these little kilns, we find them emitting a
black smoke, which cannot be entirely consumed;
and our eyes and noses are assailed by some stimulating and ammoniacal matter, which is fast escaping, and which so far alters the atmospheric
air in the neighbourhood as to render it difficult of
respiration. Need we add that *this* is the animal,
oily, and gaseous matter essential to the vegetable,
and highly, important to vegetation? It may be
that the ashes obtained may give one or two good
crops of turnips; but even the advocates of this
practice admit that, "*it ruins the land for an age;
and hence it is that in England, tenants are restrain-
ed from paring and burning, especially towards the
close of their lease.*"*

Clay burning is a different operation, and made
with different views; not for the production of ashes or salts, which may operate chymically, but
merely (by the application of heat) to alter the texture of the soil; to give to it an artificial division
and porosity; to render what was cold warm, what
was wet dry, and what was compact granular.
But a small degree of heat will not produce these
effects; for, unlike the stems and roots of plants,
clay is not itself combustible; and, to bring it to the
brick state, the heat applied must be long, continued, and great: hence it follows, that the practice
becomes objectionable on the score of *expense*, and
the more so as *burned clay* has no possible advantage over the much cheaper substances of sand,
gravel, and pounded limestone. The operation of
all is merely *mechanical*, and exactly in proportion
to the quantity used.

Our partiality for *green crops* ploughed into the

* See Cobbett, part second, p. 168, "*Year's Residence in the
United States.*"

ground as manure has been sufficiently indicated, and it is now only necessary that we mention the *plants* best calculated for this purpose. At the head of these we place *buckwheat*, as well on account of *cheapness* as *effect: cheapness*, because the price of the seed, which is the only additional expense, is below consideration ; and *effect*, because this plant, while growing, is, from its umbrageous form, a great improver of the soil, both by stifling weeds and preventing evaporation ; and, when ploughed into the ground, none decomposes more rapidly, nor has any a more powerful effect in keeping the earth loose and open to the action of light, heat, air, and moisture, all of which are indispensable to vegetation. "I know no plant," says Rozier, the great French agriculturist, "that furnishes a better manure, or which is sooner reduced to vegetable mould, than buckwheat." When cultivated with this view, the usual quantity of seed ought to be increased, and the time of sowing hastened, so as to enable you to have two crops of manure the same season, and *before* the sowing of wheat.

The *lupine* (one of the leguminous family) has been long and profitably employed as a manure in Spain, Italy, and the southern province of France. Columella directs that "it be sown in September, about the equinox, so that it may attain, before winter, a growth that will enable it to resist *wet* and *frosty* weather, which it particularly dreads." I need not remark that these directions are not calculated for this climate, and that the seed-time for the lupine *here* is the 20th of May. The properties which recommend it as a manure are nearly the same as those which belong to buckwheat. It is a quick grower, and has numerous, large, and succulent leaves. While growing it subsists principally upon the air, and, when buried, decomposes entirely and rapidly.

The *pea tribe* has the next place in this list : but,

though not better adapted to the end than buck-wheat or lupine, it is more capricious than they, and requires a soil of better staple and more prepara-tion. The seed is also more expensive. Of this tribe the *yellow vetching* (lathyrus pratensis) is the species to be preferred.

Turnips have been cultivated in England with the same view, but the practice has yielded to another and better (which, however, is not suited to our climate), *feeding them off in the winter* and *on the field.*

CHAPTER VII.

OF TILLAGE, AND THE PRINCIPLES ON WHICH IT IS FOUNDED.

Tillage has three objects: 1st, the raising of plants, whose seeds, stems, or roots may be neces-sary or useful to man and the animals he employs; 2d, the improvement of the soil, by laying it open to those atmospheric influences which increase its fertility; and, 3d, its destruction of weeds or plants which rise spontaneously, and are either altogether unfit, or fit only in a small degree, for the nutrition of men and cattle, and which, if left to themselves, would stifle or starve the intended crop.

In fulfilling either or all of these objects, it is evi-dent that the surface of the earth must be broken and divided into small parts, so that it may furnish a bed and covering for the seeds sown, enable the plants to push their roots into the soil, and draw from it a portion of their subsistence.

To accomplish this leading intention, the division of the soil, various *means* have been employed. Fossil, animal, and vegetable manures, as well by their mechanical action as by their chymical properties, promote it; as do sand, pounded limestone, and water, as in the culture of the rice; but it is to the *spade* and the *plough* we must look for that degree of efficiency, without which the earth would have remained a desert, or would become one. Of these, where the scale of labour is small, as in *garden* culture, the former is to be preferred; but, in *farming*, the greater expedition of the latter gives it a decided advantage. Our remarks, therefore, will be confined to the operations of this instrument; and particularly to such as have given occasion to differences in opinion among practical farmers.

1st. *At what season of the year, spring, summer, or fall, is ploughing best performed, in relation to division and improvement of the soil, and the destruction of weeds?*

The more scientific opinion is in favour of *fall* ploughing; because to the action of air and moisture it adds that of *frost*, whose septic or dividing quality is second only to that of the plough itself. In clay soils this preparation should never be omitted; because on those the action of frost is greatest, and because one ploughing of *this* kind may save two in the *spring*, when time is everything.* In this operation, however, we must not forget to *ridge* as well as *plough;* and care must be taken that our furrows have sufficient declination to carry off surplus water. With these precautions, clay ground will be ready early in the spring for another ploughing; and the decomposition of the sod and weeds turned down in the fall will be nearly, if not altogether, complete.†

* The *marsh bean* grows best on a *fall ploughing;* and *oats,* well harrowed, will, on such ploughing, give a good crop without other culture.

† Without water there is no *decomposition,* and much water checks and prevents it.

In dry and warm soils these advantages are less; but still the time gained for spring work is a sufficient inducement to a practice that economizes, not merely labour, but the productive powers of the earth also, by soonest enabling us to shade the soil with a growing crop.*

2d. *What number of ploughings, preparatory to a crop, is necessary or proper?*

The Romans were in the practice of multiplied ploughings. This appears as well from the precepts of Cato as from the opinion of Columella, that " tillage, which does not leave the earth in a state of dust and render the use of harrows unnecessary, has not been well performed." Tull and his disciples carry the doctrine still farther, and believe that frequent ploughings enable us to dispense with even the use of manures. This, however, is extravagant: it is certain that the plough can do much, but it is equally certain that there is much it cannot do.

Agriculture, like other business having profit for its object, is a subject of calculation; its labour must be regulated by its end; and the moment the expense of this transcends the profit, it may be *improvement*, but it ceases to be *farming*. When, therefore, we hear of *six* ploughings preparatory to a wheat crop, we conclude either that the plough will soon stop, or that it belongs to one of the dilettanti, who thinks it beneath him to count the cost. In our own practice, we find that spring crops of the cereal gramina succeed best on one fall ploughing, well ridged and furrowed, and with one cross-ploughing in the spring; and that spring and summer crops of the

---

* Those who have any doubts about the importance of *shade*, have but to look at the effects of a brush-heap, or other collection of small bodies admitting air, heat, and moisture, during the spring or summer months. Under such collections he will find a much more vigorous vegetation than in the uncovered parts of the field: the cause of this effect is that the brush prevents *evaporation*.

leguminous and cruciform families form the best possible preparation for winter crops, and render unnecessary more than one additional ploughing. After all, any proper answer to this question must necessarily be qualified by considerations of soil, weather, season, crop, and culture ; influences which cannot but exist in all cases, and over which we have no control. Wheat, for instance, requires more *preparatory* ploughing than rye, and rye more than oats. Clay ground demands more tillage than calcareous earth, and calcareous earth more than sand. Wet or dry weather makes frequent ploughings, according to circumstances, either useful, injurious, or impracticable ; and the shade of a horse-hoed crop is, perhaps, in itself, of more importance to that which succeeds, than would be the fallowing of a whole summer.

3d. *What depth of ploughing is most to be recommended ?*

This question, though less complicated than the last, requires, like it, an answer qualified by circumstances. *Tap-rooted* plants require deeper tillage than others : *fall ploughings* may be deeper than those of *spring*, and *spring* than those of *summer*. If the vegetable soil be deep, deep ploughings will not injure it ; but if it be shallow, such ploughings will bring up part of the subsoil, which is always *infertile, until it receive new principles from the atmosphere.* " They who pretend," says Arthur Young, " that the underlayer of earth is as proper for vegetation as the upper, maintain a paradox, refuted both by reason and experience."

Where, however, it becomes part of your object to increase the depth of the surface soil, deep ploughing is indispensable ; and in this, as in many other cases, we must submit to present inconvenience for the advantage of future benefit. But even here it is laid down as a rule, that, " *in proportion as* *you deepen your ploughings, you increase the necessity for manures."**

"From six to eight inches may·be taken as the ordinary depth of sufficient ploughing."† And,

4th. *Of the different modes of ploughing (level or ridge ploughing), which is to be preferred?*

This question admits no *absolute* answer. We have already suggested the use of the latter mode in stiff, heavy, wet clays; and, in our opinion, all ground in which clay predominates, whatever be the culture, should be made to take this *form:* because it powerfully tends to drain the soil, and carry off from the roots of the growing plants that superfluous water, which, left to itself, would seriously affect both the quality and the quantity of their products.‡ In sandy, porous, and dry soils, on the other hand, *level* ploughing is to be preferred; because ridging such soils would but increase that want of cohesion which is their natural defect.

A *loamy soil*, which is a medium between these two extremes, ought, in a dry climate, to be cultivated in the *flat* way, that it may the better retain moisture; and in a wet climate, in *ridges*, that it may the sooner become dry.

---

* Young.   † Idem.

‡ It has been objected to *ridge* ploughing that it accumulates the good soil on the crowns of ridges, and impoverishes the sides and furrows. These objections are obviated by narrow and low ridges, which alternate every crop with the furrows.

CHAPTER VIII.

OF A ROTATION OF CROPS, AND THE PRINCIPLES ON WHICH IT IS FOUNDED.

To this branch of our subject we invite particular attention; because, in our opinion, it forms the basis of all successful agriculture. Whatever pains we take, whatever expenses we incur, in collecting instruments of husbandry, in accumulating and applying manures, and in tilling the earth, all is to little purpose, unless to these we superadd a *succession of crops, adapted to the nature of the soil, to the laws of the climate, and to the physical character and commercial value* of the article raised. Pease will vegetate on wet cotton, and wheat in pure sand; Indian corn will grow in high northern latitudes, and the apple may be found near the equator. We have seen sainfoin struggling in wet clay, and aquatic plants on the top of an arid mountain; but all indicated the violence done to nature, and presented only specimens diminutive in bulk and deficient in quality. The influence of markets on the value of produce is as little to be denied as that of soil and climate. In the neighbourhood of great cities *table* vegetables are of much more value than wheat or rye; but, remote from markets, wheat and rye have the advantage, because, being more valuable in proportion to bulk and weight, they bear better the expense of transportation.

With this general view of the subject, we proceed to examine, 1st, the practice of Europe; and, 2d, the rotation best-adapted to our own soil, meridian, and markets. And,

1st. *Of the practice of Europe.*

It was long since discovered* that the soil, when left to itself, was never either exhausted, or tired, or idle ; but that, however stripped or denuded by man and the animals he employs, it hastens to cover itself with a variety of plants, of different and even opposite characters ; that some of these have a ten-- dency to render the earth more compact, while others have the effect of opening and dividing it ; that some, from peculiar structure of roots, stems, and leaves, derive most of their nourishment from the earth ; while others, differently formed, draw it principally from the atmosphere ; and, lastly, that in these voluntary products there is a continual and nearly regular succession of plants differently organized. These observations, carefully made and no longer doubted, and others leading to the same or similar conclusions, first suggested the useful- ness of taking nature as our guide, and of conform- ing our *artificial crops* to the rules which obviously governed her *spontaneous productions.* The effect was such as was expected, and for more than half a century the rotation system has formed the true test of agricultural improvement in every variety of soil and climate. Whenever it has been adopt- ed, the art is found in a state of prosperous progres- sion ; whenever neglected or rejected, it is either stationary or retrogade. Yet, in the face of a fact, carrying with it such conclusive evidence, the bulk of agriculturists continue to resist this cheap and obvious means of improvement, and pertinaciously adhere to a system (that of fallows) which con- demns to annual sterility one fourth part of the earth ; and which prefers four months' unproductive labour to abundant harvests and nutritious crops !

---

* Virgil, who was a philosopher as well as a poet, appears to have thoroughly understood this branch of natural history : " *mutatis quiescunt fœtibus arva."* The true repose of the earth is in a change of its productions.

But from this display of folly let us turn to one of wisdom.

On the rotation system, the whole *arable* part of a farm is divided into four, six, or eight fields, and subjected to a course of crops denominated, according to the number of these divisions, the short, the medium, or the long course. In constructing these courses, however, whether long, middling, or short, the utmost attention is paid to the nature of the soil, viz., in all soils more wet than dry, more compact than porous, more hard than friable, the course is made up of the following plants: *Wheat, oats, buckwheat,* the *graminal grasses, beans, vetchlings, clover, cabbages,* and *chicory.* In soils of an opposite character, dry, porous, and friable, the plants from which to choose are *rye, spelts, barley, potatoes, turnips,* * *lupines, Indian corn, clover, sainfoin,* and many of the pasture grasses. In loams, which are nearly an equal mixture of sand, clay, and decomposed vegetables, the choice of plants is much enlarged ; embracing what is more peculiarly proper for both sand and clay, and having, besides, the following plants from which to select : *Rice, millet, sorghum,* or African millet, *lucerne, indigo, cotton, hops, tobacco, madder, hemp, flax,* &c., &c. The following cases will sufficiently illustrate the principles on which they rest, viz., *Never to select for a crop plants not adapted to the soil ; and never, in any soil, to permit two crops of the same species or kinds to follow each other.*

2d. *Of the rotation best adapted to our own soil, meridian,* and *markets.* ·

Previously to entering upon this subject, it may not be amiss to glance at the practice hitherto prev-

---

* We here speak of the white turnip. The *Ruta Baga,* or Swedish turnip, is classed by French agriculturists among the products of strong, substantial clay soils. In the next chapter we shall speak of the culture of some particular plants, and among these, of the Swedish turnip.

alent among us. What this was in 1801 may be
seen in the answer of an English gentleman and
traveller (Mr. Strickland) to certain queries of the
British Board of Agriculture in relation to the state
of husbandry here. After remarking that New-
England was not a *corn country,* and had little to do
with the *plough,* and that New-York was then, and
would continue to be, the granary of America, he
proceeds to divert his British readers with the following details: " The usual course of crops in this
state (New-York), is, first year, maize (Indian·
corn); second, rye or wheat; third, flax or oats; and
then a repetition of the same as long as the land
will bear anything; after which it is laid by to rest.
A Dutchman's course on the Mohawk is, first year,
wheat; second, pease; third, wheat; fourth, oats or
flax; and, fifth, Indian corn. In Dutchess county
the rotation is, first, wheat; second and third, pasture without seed; and, fourth, Indian corn, or flax,
or oats, or mixed crops." Jersey, Pennsylvania,
Delaware, and Maryland may be classed together,
from a resemblance of climate, soil, and mode of
culture; and here we have, "first year, Indian corn;
second, wheat; third and fourth, rubbish pasture.
Clover is, however, beginning to be introduced in
some such course as the following: First, wheat·
second, Indian corn; third, wheat; fourth and fifth,
clover."

Two exceptions are noticed, however, to this
system: 1st. In the German settlements in Pennsylvania, where, from more attention or more skill,
"the wheat crop averages *eighteen* bushels to the
acre, where *twenty-five* bushels are frequent, and
instances of *thirty* not wanting: and, 2d. In the peninsula of Maryland and Delaware, where the rotation of Indian corn, wheat, and rubbish pasture has
reduced the average produce to *six* bushels per
acre; in some instances not more than *two* bushels
are obtained, and *much is so bad as to be ploughed up
again.*"

" In Virginia the usual crops are Indian corn and wheat alternately, as long as the land will produce them; and, in parts where tobacco is cultivated, several crops of it are taken in succession, before any grain is sown. No one states the average of that extensive flat country in Virginia, lying below the head of tide-water, at more than *five* or *six* bushels; and in those fertile and beautiful valleys among the mountains, in which ignorant cultivators have not yet resided sufficiently long to have entirely exhausted the soil, the produce may not be less than *twelve* bushels the acre."

These specimens of agricultural skill will not be adduced as proof of the favourite national position, that "*we are the most enlightened people on the face of the globe;*" and the less so, as a lapse of eighteen years has not entirely weaned us from ancient habits; for neither on the Maryland peninsula, nor in Eastern Virginia, is there any material alteration in their mode of culture, excepting what may have arisen from the fact that, having no more fresh land to exhaust, they are now obliged to recur to *old field*, and are, of course, annually suffering the new and increased penalties of former improvidence. On the western shore of Maryland, in the northern parts of Delaware, and in Pennsylvania, New-Jersey, and New-York, the state of things is better; clover has been substituted for (what Mr. Strickland calls) rubbish pasture, and the root husbandry is encroaching on summer fallows; which we regard as a decisive step towards a regular and judicious rotation of crops.

After this brief statement of the past and present state of home agriculture, let us anticipate the future. We cannot believe that, favoured as we are with a temperate climate, a productive soil, an inquiring, reflecting, and independent yeomanry, and civil institutions which favour and protect all the developments of industry and genius, we shall long remain behind the serfs of Tuscany, the tenants of England, or the peasants of Flanders. But, to rival these, we must follow their example; we must multiply the means of subsisting cattle; because these will, in their turn, give manures, and manures will quicken and invigorate the soil for the production of articles of the greatest value and the highest price. It is on this simple basis that we offer the following tables of rotation of crops, adapted to our own circumstances :

Medium course in sandy soils : 1st year, potatoes dunged; 2d, rye, with turnips after harvest consumed on the fields; 3d, oats and clover, or barley and clover; 4th, clover; 5th, wheat, with turnips after harvest consumed on the field ; and, 6th, pease, or lupines, or lentils. We have, by this course, *eight* crops in *six* years, and five of these ameliorating crops.

Medium course in loamy soils : 1st year, potatoes dunged ; 2d, wheat, with turnips as in the preceding course ; 3d, Indian corn and pumpkins ; 4th, barley and clover; 5th, clover ; 6th, wheat and turnips as before. In this course we have *nine* crops in *six* years, five of which are ameliorating crops.

Medium course in clay soils ; 1st year, oats with clover ; 2d, clover ; 3d, wheat ; 4th, beans dunged ; 5th, wheat ; 6th, the yellow vetchling.

CHAPTER IX.

OF THE PLANTS RECOMMENDED FOR A COURSE OF CROPS IN THE PRECEDING CHAPTER, AND THEIR CULTURE.

THESE are wheat, rye, barley, Indian corn, oats, buckwheat, pease, beans, turnips, potatoes, cabba-

ges, clover, and chicory : but we shall take them in
the order in which they stand in the proposed rotation of crops ; and,

  I. *Of the potato.*

This plant is a native of America, and, like other
valuable things, has had violent enemies and zealous
friends.   When first introduced into France, it was
subjected to the imperfect methods of analysis of
that day, and, being supposed to yield some deleterious matter, was even proscribed by the government   But time, which rarely fails to do justice to
the injured, has re-established the character of the
potato *there;* and with the increased reputation
of being the "*manna of the poor,*"* of standing as an
article of food next to bread,† and far before cabbages, carrots, or turnips;‡ and yielding, by the
acre, a crop of greater profit and more nutritive
matter than either wheat or barley.§ Nor is this
its whole praise ; for, besides its value as food, it is
of all vegetables that which, from the number,
shape, and size of its roots, forms the best preparation for subsequent crops.‖ ' Of this valuable plant
botanists count more than *sixty varieties* and *twelve
species*, which, for agricultural purposes, may, however, be reduced to *three;* the red, the white, and
that called by the French the *quarantaine*, or forty
days' potato.   The last is the least prolific ; but

---

* Dictionnaire de l'Industrie, art. Pomme de terre.

† By the experiments of Vaugelin and Percy, 80 parts out of
100 of bread are nutritive; of the potato, 25, or nearly one
fourth.

‡ "Six chilogrammes de pommes de terre equivaloient 50
chilogrammes de navet."—Yvart.   Six kilograms [the kilo-
gram is 2 lbs. 3 oz. 5 dr. avoird.] of potatoes are equal to 50 kil
ograms of carrots.

§ 200 bushels, a medium crop per acre of potatoes, are, at 3*s*
per bushel, equal to seventy five dollars ; and a medium crop
of wheat, 15 bushels per acre, at even 16*s*. per bushel, is but
30 dollars ; difference per acre, $35.

‖ Parmentier of the French Institute.

may, notwithstanding, deserve the preference with cultivators near great cities, since, besides being the first in the market, they may be made to give a second crop. The other two are supposed to affect different kinds of soil; the red preferring clay, and the white sand or loam. Of the former there is a variety more productive than any other of either species, and which is known, and, we think, degraded, by the name of the *hog potato*. Of this variety, without any peculiar care, we have raised one hundred and eight bushels on one quarter of an acre.

Two ways are employed to propagate the potato; 1st, by sowing the seed; and, 2d, by planting the root. By the former method we obtain new varieties or revive old ones; but, as it requires three years to bring these to perfection, it follows that the other method, which continues the species you plant, and in the perfection in which you plant them, is alone resorted to for a crop. The product is small, or great, or enormous, according to the fertility of the soil and the labour bestowed upon its cultivation. We have never seen a larger product from the acre than four hundred bushels; but there are records of high authority which give much larger crops; and from which, in justice to our subject, we offer the following extracts:

"At Altingham, in England, a sandy soil gave 700 bushels per acre. At Kirklatham, a similar soil gave 580 bushels; and a blach rich loam, 1166 bushels."*

We need hardly remark, that such immense products were procured only by the most careful and well-timed cultivation, which we shall now proceed

* See vol. xiii., p. 114, of the British Annual Register. Some persons have imagined that, by cutting the flowers of the potato, the crop may be increased, and analogy forms the opinion. The procreative powers of the plant are thus diverted from the apple and concentrated in the bulb. ·

to indicate under three different heads : 1st, the preparation of the soil ; 2d, the choice of plants and mode of planting ; and, lastly, the treatment of the growing crop.

1st. Of the preparation of the soil.

Give your field intended for potatoes a good fall ploughing, and in ridges if the soil be clay. Leave it rough and open to the influences of the frost during the winter, and as early in the spring as you discover in it the marks of vegetation, harrow and roll it. When the weeds show themselves a second time, carry out your manure, cover the fields with it, and plough it under. If the quantity of manure be insufficient to cover the whole surface, apply it to the furrows only ; and if, as may happen, it be even insufficient for this purpose, then furrow both ways, manure the angles of intersection, and set your potatoes in them.

2d. Of the choice of plants and mode of planting.

Some economists begin by paring the potato, and planting only the skins ; others, less saving, cut the potatoes into slices, leaving a single eye to each slice ; and a third class, almost as provident as the other two, are careful to pick out the dwarfs, and reasonable enough to expect from them a progeny of giants. These practices cannot be too much censured or too soon abandoned, because directly opposed both by reason and experience. In other cases we take great pains, and sometimes incur great expense, to obtain the best seed. In the cultivation of wheat we reject all small, premature, worm-eaten, or otherwise imperfect grains ; in preparing for a crop of Indian corn we select the best cars, and even strip from these the small or ill-shaped grains at the ends of the cob ; so also in planting beets, carrots, parsnips, and turnips, the largest and finest are selected for seed. The reason of all this is obvious. Plants, like animals, are rendered most perfect by selecting the finest individuals of the species from which to breed. Away, then, with such miserable economy; and, instead of planting skins, or slices, or dwarfs, take for seed the best and largest potatoes, those having in them the most aliment for the young plants;* place them in your furrows ten or twelve inches apart, and cover them carefully with earth.

3d. Of the treatment of the growing crop.

As soon as the potatoes begin to show themselves weeds will also appear; a good harrowing will then save much future labour, and the injury it does the potato will be little or none. In a short time another weeding will become necessary; but your crop having now obtained some inches in height, you can no longer safely use the common harrow; but, instead of this, the small one of triangular form, so made as to accommodate itself to the width of the intervals. This labour may be occasionally repeated, if necessary, until the potatoes begin to flower, when the *horse-hoe* must be substituted for the harrow. The effects of this instrument (the horse-hoe) are to extirpate the weeds, to divide and loosen the soil, and to throw over the potatoes an additional covering of earth.

The harvesting and preserving of potato crops are processes well known in this country. With regard to the latter, however, we would suggest whether stacking potatoes on the surface of the soil, and with a narrow base, is not a better mode than burying them in the ground. Fifteen bushels will be enough for one stack, which must be well covered with straw and earth, and trenched around its whole circumference, to carry off dissolving snows and rain-water.

II. *Of rye.*

* The interior of the potato forms the *fecula*, which subsists the young plants.

This grain, though of the same family with wheat, is less valuable. A bushel of rye weighs less, and gives less flour, and of worse quality, than a bushel of wheat. Still there are circumstances which, as an object of culture, may give it the preference; 1st, it grows well in soils where wheat cannot be raised; 2d, it bears a much greater degree of cold than wheat; 3d, it goes through all the phases of vegetation in a shorter period, and, of course, exhausts the soil less;* 4th, if sown early in the fall, it gives a great deal of pasture, without much eventual injury to the crop; and, 5th, its produce, from an equal surface, is one sixth greater than that of wheat. These circumstances render it peculiarly valuable for poor soils and poor people, for mountains of great elevation, and for high northern latitudes.†

Its use, as food for horses, is known as well in this country as in Europe. The grain and straw, chopped and mixed, form the principal horsefood in Pennsylvania; and in Germany, the postillions are often seen slicing a black and hard rye bread, called *benpournikel*, for their horses; and the same practice prevails in Belgium and Holland.

Its conversion into whiskey is a use less approved by reason and patriotism.

The species of this grain cultivated here are two, the *black* and the *white*; for spring rye, though often mistaken for a *species*, is but a variety produced by time and culture, and restored again to its former character and habits by a similar process.‡

---

* We have seen a field bear rye several years in succession without manure, and the last crop was much the best. This fact is one of those which tend to discredit theory.

† Without rye the northern part of Russia would be scarcely habitable.

‡ Spring rye, sown in the fall, will give a tolerable crop: winter rye, sown in the spring, a very bad one: which shows that the nature of the plant requires a slow rather than a quick vegetation.

According to the course of crops detailed in our last chapter, potatoes, in a sandy soil, precede rye. The ploughing, harrowing, and manuring given to *that* crop, will therefore make part of the preparation necessary for *this*. After harvesting the potatoes, crossplough the ground, and sow and harrow in the rye; taking care, as in all other cases, that the seed be carefully selected and thoroughly washed in lime-water, as the means best calculated to prevent the *ergot;* a disease to which it is most liable, and which is supposed to be occasioned by too great humidity.*

Rye is not exempt from the attacks of insects, but suffers less from them than either wheat or barley. Whenever the straw of winter rye becomes yellow, shining, or flinty, and circulates no more juices, nature gives the signal for harvest, and no time should be lost in obeying it. "*Cut two days too soon rather than one day too late,*" was among the precepts of Cato; which, if adopted here, would save much grain, terminate the harvest about the 10th of July, and give abundant time to turn down the stubble and sow the crop next in succession.

III. *Turnips.*

These are said to be natives of the seacoast of the north of Europe, where they are found growing spontaneously. There are eight species and many varieties; but, as they have all the same character and uses, and require nearly the same treatment, we shall only speak of the *white* turnip and the *yellow.*

Two methods of cultivation have been pursued, according to the plan either of turning them down as manure, or of consuming them on the field or in the stable by sheep or cattle. In the first case, the harrow is used instead of the plough; and, even upon light, porous soil, is a pretty good substitute. The

* See Tessier on the Diseases of Plants.

seed is sown after the harrow, and too frequently left to its own protection. In the other case, the plough is first used, and after it the harrow; a method much to be. preferred, as the difference of crops will more than pay the difference of labour, the only advantage claimed by those who advocate and adopt the first method.

Our own practice is to plough in the stubble, harrow the ground lightly, and sow the turnip-seed in the quantity of two pounds to the acre. This allows something for insects and something for waste. When the plants are generally above ground, give them a light covering of ashes, which, by quickening the growth of the plants and leaching on their leaves at the same time, better protects them against the fly than any other means practicable on a large scale with which we are acquainted.* When the plants attain the height of four inches, we set the horse-hoe to work, running a furrow the whole length or breadth of the field, and returning with another at the distance of three feet from the former, and so continuing the work till the whole is laid off into beds of that width. What we lose by this method is only the seed buried by the horse-hoe; what we gain is the manure created by the young plants ploughed in between the beds, and the advantage of being able to weed and work those left standing for the crop. This part of the labour, which immediately follows the horse-hoeing, is expeditiously performed by two men travelling in the furrows, one on each side of a bed, and employing themselves in thinning and hand-hoeing the surplus plants. These operations of ploughing and weeding may be performed a second, and even a third time, with advantage.

* On a small scale, water in which potatoes have been boiled is believed to be very useful in protecting cabbage, turnips, and other plants from the attacks of the fly. We are in a course of experiments which will determine how far this remedy may be relied on.

If we determine to plough in the crop as manure, we should do it while the ground retains a temperature favourable to the decomposition of the plants, and before the frost has diminished the volume or altered their juices. If, on the other hand, we decide on feeding off the crop on the ground, it is but necessary to turn in our sheep upon it, under such restrictions as will limit their range and prevent waste ; and, indeed, that nothing may be lost, hogs should be made to fol'ow the sheep. If, however, feeding in the stables be thought more advisable (and it certainly better economizes both food and manure), the turnips should be drawn, topped, and stacked ; interposing between each layer of them one of coarse hay or other barn-rubbish, and capping the whole with a few bundles of clean long straw. Though less nutritive than either potatoes, carrots, or cabbages, the turnip is found to be particularly useful to stall-fed cattle, correcting, by its aqueous qualities, the heating effects of corn, oats, or rye meal.

Our acquaintance with the yellow turnip (or ruta baga) is but beginning. Mr. Cobbett's experiments have, however, been very successful, and tend much to recommend the plant in preference to the white or common species. That, of the two, it is the more compact, the heavier, the more nutritious, the less apt to become stringy, and the more easily preserved, are facts not to be contested. In both France and England it is rising in reputation, and perhaps only wants time to get into general use here. To this article we will but add an extract from the work of M. D'Edelcrants (of Sweden) on the ruta baga.

" Its root is milder and more saccharine than that of the other species, particularly when boiled. Its flesh is harder and more consistent; which better enables it to withstand frosts, and to keep from one year to another. Its leaves extend horizontally, and may be stripped off from time to time, as wanted for forage, without injuring the product of the root; which, on good soil, gives to the acre, in Sweden, 350 quintals; and, even on poor soil, a good crop. We sow half a pound of seed about the beginning or middle of May, which will give plants enough to fill an acre. Transplanting is performed about the last of June or first of July. To set out and water 5 or 600 feet in a day is the task of one man*or of two women. Qne or two hoeings augment the product much. The harvest is made about the first of November, and the turnips are covered in ditches, or dry caves or cellars for winter use."

IV. *Of Barley.*

It is probable that bread was first made from this grain. The Jewish scriptures speak only of *barley loaves;* the gladiators among the Greeks were called *barley-eaters;* and Columella says (like our Indian corn and beans in the Southern states) that barley was the food of the *slaves.* Among the Romans it was first employed as a food for man, and afterward for cattle.* The same qualities which recommended it then, have since diffused it more generally than any other grain; it is found to be better-adapted to different soils and climates; less subject to the attacks of insects, and more easily preserved. In times of scarcity it is a good substitute for wheat, and at all times yields the beverage known under the name of beer, ale, or porter. It is, besides, a food on which cattle do well, and horses arrive at their greatest possible perfection.†

The *species* of this grain most in request are two Hordeum Distichum (two-rowed barley) and Hor-

---

* This use grew out of the belief of its nutritive and invigorating qualities.

† See Buffon on the horse of Arabia. Vol. xxii., p. 195.

deum Cæleste (naked barley). The former is preferred in England, and, as we believe, in France. M. Parmentier ascribes to it all the good qualities of the other species, and much greater productiveness.*

Of the latter species, the nations of the north who are most in the habit of using barley as the basis both of food and drink, speak highly.† But among us, who cultivate it only for the last purpose, this species has less credit, and is even considered the worst from a belief that, after being dried, it malts imperfectly or with difficulty.

Though not so nice in relation to soil as either wheat or rye, still barley prefers a loose, warm, and moist, though not wet, soil, and even grows remarkably well in sand (where we have sowed it), in succession to turnips, either ploughed into the ground or consumed on the field.

Other things being equal, the spring crops which are first sowed give the best and largest products. The moment, therefore, that your soil is sufficiently dry, begin ploughing, and at a depth not less than six inches, since the roots of barley enter the earth more deeply than those of any of the other cereal graminæ. If the soil be well pulverized [as it ought to be after turnips], a second ploughing would be a waste of time and money : proceed, therefore, to sow your barley broadcast,§ and cov-

* He states it to be *double as much.*

† " Hordeum cæleste Norvegis gratissimum, quoniam cerevisiam generosam, præbeit." The naked barley, most grateful to the Norwegians, as affording to them their generous beer.— Mitterpacher, Elemen. rei rust., page 312.

‡ The Romans had two maxims on the subject of expense, which it would be wise in us to adopt : " Those profits are to be preferred which cost the least ;" and again, " Nothing is less profitable than very high cultivation." " Nihil minus expedire, quam agram optime colere."

§ Mr. Young's experiments show that there is something in the constitution or habits of this grain to which the drill or row husbandry is not accommodated. Even isolated grains weeded and hoed, did not do better than the same number in broad cast.

er it with a short-toothed harrow. The last operation will be to sow and roll in your clover-seed, destined to become the next crop in succession.

V. *Of Clover.*

The Trifolium Agrarium of Linnæus is found growing spontaneously in many places, as is sufficiently indicated by the names given to it; as Dutch clover, Spanish clover, clover of Piedmont, clover of Normandy, &c., &c.* It is about two centuries since it first became an object of agricultural attention as *forage*, while its *ameliorating effects on the soil*, produced by its peculiar system of roots and leaves, was a discovery of modern date. It is now generally sown with barley, or other spring grain of the culmiferous kind, and rarely by itself. The advantages proposed by this practice are three: 1st, the preparation given to the soil for the grain crop, which is exactly that best fitted for the clover: 2d, the protection given by the barley to the young clover against the combined effects of heat and dryness; and, 3d, the improved condition in which it leaves the soil for subsequent culture In this practice, however, a less quantity of barley must be sown than usual, because, without ventilation, the clover plants will perish. To this condition two others must be added, which are indispensable to a good crop: 1st, that your seed be good; and, 2d, that it be regularly and equally sown. The tests of good seed are, its comparative size and weight (the largest and heaviest being always the best), its plumpness, its yellow or purple colour, its glossy skin, and, lastly, its cleanness or separation from other seeds and from dirt.

The human hand was, no doubt, the first machine employed for sowing seeds. The difficulty,

---

* A seed of Holland clover, of the same volume with one of Normandy clover, weighs one seventh more. See Gilbert on Artificial Meadows.

however, of scattering them equally over every part of the field, soon attracted notice, and engaged mechanics in devising something which should better answer that purpose. China was the first to produce anything at all commensurate with this object ; and it was not till the seventeenth century that this, or some similar invention, was introduced into Europe by Lucateo, a Spaniard, who, meeting no encouragement at home, transmitted his real or pretended discovery to London. Here, as has been conjectured, it served as a model for the sowing-machines of Tull ; and from 1750 to 1770, the mania on this subject was at its height ; but from that period to the present it has been gradually subsiding, and the hand is now generally restored to its original functions.

The quantity of seed to be given to the acre should, in a great degree, depend on the soil ; if this be rich, ten or twelve pounds are sufficient ; and if poor, double that quantity will not be too much. The practice of mixing the seeds of timothy and rye grass, &c., with that of clover, is a bad one, because these grasses neither rise nor ripen at the same time. Another practice, equally bad, is that of sowing clover seed on winter grain before the earth has acquired a temperature favourable to vegetation, and when there cannot be a doubt but that two thirds of the seed will perish.

By the time your barley or other covering crop is harvested, your clover will be sufficiently established to live alone ; and, *if not pastured,** to brave the ensuing winter, and during the next summer to repay your labour by two abundant crops of grass or hay.

The period in the growth of clover at which it

---

* If the *crowns* of young clover roots be nibbled or otherwise wounded, the roots die. Sheep and horses (both of which bite closely) should, therefore, be particularly excluded from clover, unless intended for pasturage only.

is most profitably cut and used, presents a question much discussed and variously answered; because depending on extraneous and local circumstances (such as the state and proximity of markets, &c.), which cannot fail to vary the results in the hands of different persons, and even of the same person at different times and at different places. There are, however, some general remarks which belong to the case, and which ought not to be omitted in even this brief view of the subject.

1st. Clover cut *before* it flowers abounds in water, has in it but-little nutritive matter, and is even apt to produce indigestion in the cattle fed upon it.*

2d. The stems of clover cut *after* seeding are hard and woody, and no longer hold the leaf: and,

3d. All plants, when permitted to seed, exhaust the soil; and to this rule clover is not an exception.

From premises furnished by these facts, we would conclude that the short period between the flowering and seeding of clover is that in which its use would be most advantageous, whether regarded as a *forage* or as an *ameliorating* crop.

When *seed* is the principal object of culture, we cannot do better than adopt the practice in Holland, where the first crop is cut *before* it flowers, and the second is reserved for seed.

The largeness of the stems, the number of the leaves, and the aqueous quantity of both, render it a difficult business to make clover grass into hay; and the difficulty is not a little increased by the brittleness or disposition of the drying grass to fall into pieces during the process of handling. To meet this case, two supplementary means have been employed, which enable you to house or stack clover in a much greener or less dry state than would otherwise be safe. The one is to scatter over each

* This effect of clover (which we call *hoving*) is prevented in Alsace by watering the cattle before giving them clover, be- cause a certain quantity of water prevents *fermentation.*

cartload, while stowing away for keeping, two or three quarts of sea-salt : the other, to interpose between two layers of clover one of clean straw. By the first method, the whole mass is made acceptable to cattle; by the second, the quantum of nutritive forage is increased ; and by both methods the clover is effectually prevented from *heating.**

The next step in our system is to plough in the clover stubble as a preparation for the succeeding crop.

VI. *Of Wheat.*

This grain, so useful to man, because forming so large a portion of his subsistence, is happily found to adapt itself to a great variety of soils and climates. It grows vigorously in clay, in loam, in calcareous earth, and even in sand, when aided by manures, or in succession to pease, vetches, clover, &c. To the north it is found in the frozen regions of Siberia ; and in the south, under the burning sun of Africa, it yields, according to the declaration of Pliny, more than one hundred fold.†

In ancient Rome, its use, as a food for man, soon superseded that of barley and rye ; and in modern Europe it is denominated *corn*, by way of eminence.

Of this invaluable grain there are four species, distinctly marked and generally acknowledged, viz., many-headed wheat,‡ Polish wheat, spelts, and

* The more modern, and, we think, far better way of making clover hay, is to put it into small cocks as soon as it has become dried or wilted in the swaths ; and to leave it so for thirty or forty hours, when it will be found sufficiently dried, on being opened and spread to the sun an hour or two, to take to the barn or stack. In this way it makes the most and best fodder, and is cured with the least labour.—J. B.

† "Tritico nihil est fertilius : utpote cum e modio, si sit aptum solum, quale in Byzacio Africæ campo, centum quinquageni modii reddentur."—XVIII. L. Nat. Hist. Pliny. Nothing is more productive than wheat ; for a bushel of this grain, sown on a soil adapted to it, as that of the plain of Byzantium, in Africa, will yield a hundred and fifty fold.

‡ This is the *Triticum Compositum* of botanists, called wheat

8

common wheat. We shall speak only of the third and fourth species, because with the others we have little practical acquaintance ; and,

1st. Of *Spelts*. This species and its principal variety (Triticum Monoicum) is much cultivated in Germany and Switzerland. Deprived of its husk, the grain is smaller than that of common wheat, but yields a flour of finer quality, and better fitted for the purposes of pastry.[*] Two other circumstances recommend it ; it withstands the attack of insects, and will grow in poorer soil and with less preparatory labour than the fourth species.

2d. *Common wheat* has many varieties, some of which are bearded, and others bald ; some oval, and others round or square ; some yellow or red, and others white ; some soft, and others flinty ; accidents arising from culture and climate, and not, as we believe, the result of an organization uniformly and essentially different.

With regard to the culture of this plant, we shall confine ourselves to the following points : the preparation of the soil, the choice and preparation of the seed, and the time and different modes of sowing or planting it.

1st. Of the preparation of the soil.

Products of much value to man can only be obtained by corresponding degrees of labour. The sugar-cane, rice, and wheat, are more valuable than oats, buckwheat, or turnips, and require more labour and expense in their cultivation. Indeed, under the old system of fallows, the degree of both bestowed upon a wheat crop was enormous. Two years and five or six ploughings were sometimes given to this preparatory culture ; but, on the new plan of a rotation of crops, the necessity for this

of plenty, miraculous wheat, &c., yielding largely, but, on manufacture, giving much bran and bad flour.

[*] The bread of Frankfort, Nuremberg, &c., so much boasted in Germany, is made from spelts.

is in a great degree obviated, and two ploughings of a clover lay are in general amply sufficient. Still this takes for granted that these ploughings are well performed ; that no clods are to be seen ; and that the field presents an unbroken surface of mellow and finely-pulverized earth.

2. Of the choice and preparation of seed.

Seed should be taken from some fine crop of the *preceding year*,* which shall have ripened thorough-ly and been well preserved. This, after passing two or three times through the fanning mill, should be carefully washed in clean water, and again in water in which a quantity of fresh lime has been slackened ; or, if lime cannot be had, in which clean and recent wood ashes have been leached. This washing, as we have already suggested, should never be omitted : because, besides detecting the shrunk or shrivelled grains, and many seeds of other plants which will float on the surface of the water, it entirely removes the *dust* of *smut, rust,* &c., and thus prevents their propagation.† Our

* A great variety of experiments show that wheat preserves its germinating faculties under circumstances apparently very unfavourable, and that it may even be sown to advantage when several years old, after a slight degree of malting in the sheaf or the stack, and after having been subjected to a high degree of artificial heat. We mention this fact, however, not to invite to a selection of seed-grain of either of these descriptions, but to assure the farmer that, where better cannot be had, he may employ even such, without apprehending a total loss of his time and labour.

† *Smut, charbon,* and *rust* in grain, were, according to the old philosophy, attributed to storms, or some other particular state of the atmosphere ; but Messrs. Tillet, Tessier, B. Prevot, and Decandolle, have shown, that the two former of these diseases are produced by an intestinal parasite, of the uredo or mushroom family, the progress of which is much promoted by humidity and shade. Analogy favours the opinion, that *rust* owes its ori-gin to the same cause. The remedy for all is the same ; wash your seed-grain thoroughly in lime water, roll it in plaster of Paris, and sow it in the fall, before the cold and wet weather begins, or in the spring after it has ended.

next step in this process is to roll the seed in pul.
verized gypsum.

3d. Of the time of sowing wheat.

On this head there is a diversity both in practice
and opinion. Some prefer early, others late sowing : some sow in the full, others in the wane of
the moon, &c.

Theory is certainly on the side of early sowing ;
since i. gives time for the roots of the grain to establish themselves before winter ; and experience
proves that grain early sown throws up more lateral stems than that which is sown late.

Of lunar influences we know very little, excepting that they extend to the waves of the ocean ;
which probably first gave rise to the opinion held
by M. Toaldo and other philosophers, that the atmosphere, which is only another and more fluid
ocean, and which has much to do with the health
and diseases of animals and vegetables, is also subject to these influences. But the calculations of
M. de Place prove that the effect of lunar influence on the atmosphere does not make a difference
of one line and a half on the barometer, and that it
is wholly insufficient to account for those great
agitations of the atmosphere which have been supposed most to affect vegetation.

4th. Of the different modes of sowing wheat.

These are two, the one executed with the hand,
the other with a sowing machine, of which we have
already spoken. The latter has been advocated on
the ground of economy, employing less seed, and
distributing what it does employ more equally.
Nor will it be denied that, when wheat is very high
and labour very cheap, there may be a saving in the
use of this machine ; but in all other circumstances
the comparison is in favour of the other method, as
it requires less time and fewer labourers, and as the
waste and irregularity imputed to it are, in hands
practised and steady, reduced to little or nothing.

A third method of propagating wheat, viz., by transplanting the suckers at regular distances from the seed-bed into another prepared to receive them, has been practised on a small scale, and is found to yield abundantly; but it is so embar●●●ed with expense as to render it entirely unfit ●●●●eneral use.

Of the produce of wheat very different accounts have been given. To the extraordinary fertility of Byzantium, already mentioned, Pliny adds that in Leontium, in Sicily, its produce was one hundred for one; yet Cicero, who had been quæstor of that island, asserts that the produce of Sicily was but ten or twelve for one.* To conciliate these high and opposite authorities, M. Yvart has supposed that the product mentioned by Cicero was an average one of the whole island; and that that reported by Pliny was the result of one or more *transplanting experiments;* an opinion rendered probable from the fact that the parent stems and their offspring had been sent to Rome by the procurator of Augustus.

Some calculators have supposed, and on data not easily refuted, that the maximum produce of this grain over the whole face of the globe, and in a series of any ten given years, will not exceed six bushels reaped for one bushel sown.†

VII. *Of Pease.*

The pea is a native of the southern parts of Europe, and is found growing spontaneously in the western parts of our own continent. The family is a large one, containing several species; but of these the *field-pea* alone comes within the scope of our present purpose. Of this there are two varieties, denominated, from their colour, the gray and

---

* Orat. contra Verrem.

† The reader will remember that, on our plan, turnips follow wheat as they do rye, and without any difference in cultivation See article 3d of this chapter. To repeat what we have said there would be useless.

the green; both productive, and, when separated
from the skin that surrounds them, a food of excellent quality for man, wholesome, nutritive, and
pleasant; and for cattle, whether in a dry or green
state, much ▓▓▓ recommended. Sheep, cows, and
horses are ▓▓▓ cularly fond of them; and hogs are
more promptly and economically fattened on a mixture of pea and barley meal, in a state of acetous
fermentation, than with any other food.

The structure of the roots would indicate that
pease are an exhausting crop; and it is on this evidence that in Europe they are admitted only in
long, or six years' rotations; but if we examine the
leaves, in regard to both number and form, we shall
probably find reason to modify this opinion, and to
allow that, by stifling weeds, by checking evaporation, and eventually by their own fall, they ameliorate the soil, and render it more favourable to subsequent crops.

Following turnips in the rotation we are now dis-
cussing, the preparatory labour for a pea crop is not
great. One, or, at most, two ploughings, will be
sufficient. Sowing, as a general rule, ought to follow ploughing without loss of time; and care should
be taken that the seed be not laid too deeply. The
two methods, row and broadcast sowing, may be
indifferently pursued. By the former the seed is
economized, the product increased, and the soil better tilled; but not, as some have supposed, with
such decided advantages as to outweigh the saving
in time and labour, of the latter.

The length and feebleness of the stems of pease,
and the little tendrils they throw out for support,
indicate the advantage of mixing with them other
plants of more erect growth, which may prevent the
pease from falling and lodging. For this purpose
rye, oats, and beans have been selected, and with
great advantage.

This crop is employed either in a dry or in a

green state; between which every farmer will select according to circumstances. If the market for
pease be brisk and high, he will harvest, thresh, and
sell the grain; if, on the other hand, pease be low
and pork high, the moment the pods fill he will turn
in his hogs upon them, and with the following advantages : 1st, the hogs will feed and fatten themselves, without any additional interposition of his
labour; 2d, no part of their manure will be lost; 3d,
the remains of the crop, refused by the hogs, will
be given back to the soil; and, 4th, the rooting of
these animals, which in other cases is an injury,
will in this be a benefit.

VIII. *Of Indian Corn.*

This is a native of South America, and was introduced into Europe in the 16th century; where it
is known by the names of wheat of Turkey, Indian
wheat, Spanish wheat, &c.* Its productiveness and
other good qualities have brought it into general
use; for it is now found in every part of the globe
where its cultivation is not forbidden by the cold-
ness of the climate. With proper culture, it grows
well in a great variety of soils; but prefers old
and rich pasture-grounds, artificial meadows, warm
loams, and moist vegetable mould.

There are many varieties of this grain, denominated from its colour, number of rows, and different periods of ripening. The *white* and the *yellow*,
of eight and twelve rows, are the varieties generally preferred.

Corn, from its bulk, its prolific character, and system of roots, must necessarily be a great feeder,
and draw much of its supplies from the earth;
whence arises the rule that it ought not immediate-

---

* This is the *Zea* of the botanists. In what does this differ
from the *zea* or *semen* of the ancients? The favourite dish of
the Romans was *alica*; and "Alica fit e zea, quam semen ap-
pellavimus"—Alica is made of a grain called semen.—Plin. 18
L. Nat. Hist.

ly to follow or to precede any other cereal crop; and that it should not be found oftener than once in six years in the same field.

The seed should be taken from the finest ears of the last year's crop, and from those growing on stems which have had the largest number of ears. After steeping it twenty-four hours in a strong solution of nitre, it should be planted.*

There is some difference of practice, without any great difference of result, *in the modes of planting*. Furrows are sometimes made at the distance of three or four feet from each other, and in one direction only, and in these the seed is placed fourteen or sixteen inches apart. At other times the field is furrowed both ways, and the seed dropped and covered at the points of intersection; while, again, two rows of beans or potatoes, or mangel wurzel, are sometimes interposed between as many rows of corn. This last practice is most conformable to theory; but the other methods generally prevail, and pumpkins, beans, or turnips form the under crops.

Whatever method be adopted, the *time* of planting is that at which the earth first acquires the warmth necessary to vegetation, and which is sufficiently indicated by her spontaneous productions. If we plant earlier, the seed is apt to rot; if later, the ripening of the crop is hazarded.

No crop, while growing, requires more attention than corn, and none better repays the labour bestowed upon it. The objects of this are two: to extirpate weeds, and to keep the earth loose and open to the influences of the atmosphere. As soon, therefore, as weeds begin to show themselves, the surface of the field must be well harrowed. Plastering is the next operation, and may, at the dis-

---

* See in Judge Peters's Notices to Young Farmers, the effect of this solution on corn crops.

tance of a few days, be repeated with advantage. The weeds will now reappear, when the triangular harrow, accommodated to the width of the intervals, must be employed. This, drawn by a single horse, will do its work expeditiously and well. The plough called the cultivator, with a double mould-board, follows the harrow,* and is itself followed by the hand-hoe, which alone can perform well the last and great operation of *hilling*† the corn. The first effect of this is to enable the grain to form new joints near the surface of the earth, whence will issue lateral roots, fitted to receive an additional quantity of aliment necessary or proper for the plant.‡ Care must, however, be taken to flatten these little mounds of earth, so as to make them better recipients of water.

Corn is sometimes cultivated with a view only to the forage it may yield; in which case it is generally sown broadcast, at the rate of ten bushels to the acre, and cut green, while its saccharine qualities most abound. We are told by Bosc, that in the volcanic soil of Vicenteri, in Italy, corn managed in this way gives four crops in the year. As a dry forage, it is a great resource in warm climates, where natural meadows are rare, and artificial nearly unknown. In the eastern parts of Virginia, it furnishes the principal stock of horse fodder, and in our northern latitudes is a useful supplement to clover, timothy, and red-top hay.

The produce of corn is much affected by weath-

---

* The implement *now* termed cultivator, or horse-hoe, is of recent introduction among us. We have it of various patterns, and it is coming into extensive use in the culture of hoed or drilled crops, in place of the plough.—J. B.

† *Hilling* corn is becoming an exploded practice, as being rather prejudicial to the crop than otherwise.—J. B.

‡ Bonnet was the first to make this observation; but, if the reader wishes to see a full illustration of it, we refer him to the Memoir of M. Varennes de Fenillis, who has proved that the crop is increased 1 13th merely by hilling.

er.   If this be hot and dry, the leaves, stems, and ears are all diminutive; if wet, the leaves and stems are abundant, but the ears deficient and often diseased; if both wet and cold, no ears are produced; while, on the other hand, if it be moist and warm, more particularly when the grain is flowering, the crop will be excellent.   To produce this combination is not within the reach of human industry. All, therefore, that agricultural foresight can effect, is to interpose a few days between the planting of different parts of the crop, so as to multiply the chances of favourable weather.

IX. *Of Beans.*

Of these there are several species, which, to occupiers of *clay* soils, are of the utmost importance, because in them beans thrive best, while, at the same time, they greatly ameliorate and fit them for wheat and oat crops.   The species most recommended are the Heligoland,* or small horsebean of England, and the white bean.† The former is vigorous, hardy, and productive, and an excellent food for cattle; the latter is more delicate and nutritive, and much employed as a food for man.‡

If beans are made to commence.a course of crops, as they may very properly do, they ought to receive the dung of the year; which, as in the case of potatoes, should be spread over the surface of the field, and ploughed in without loss of time.   The moment the spring frosts are over, the planting should take place, in rows or in hills, as described in the last article for corn; and throughout the

* The Heligoland, and other beans of the *vicia* family, are not found to do well with us.   They grow and blossom, but do not fruit well.—J. B.

† This, as well as the China and other beans of the genus *Phareola*, are profitably grown on sandy as well as on clay soils. —J. B.

‡ Pythagoras forbade his disciples the use of beans.   Whence we may conclude that the Greeks cultivated only the horse bean, or bean of the marshes.

whole course of vegetation, the crop must be kept free from weeds : a condition, if well observed, that will secure an abundant produce.*

X. *Of Oats.*

Oats is among grains what the ass is among animals, very little respected, but very extensively employed. The *levis avena* of Ovid, and the *steriles dominantur avenæ* of Virgil, show the degrees, both of use and abuse, with which it was regarded by the Romans. In modern times, a great literary authority† describes it as food for Scotch *men* and English *horses*. It is probably this its state of degradation among poets and philosophers, that determined the botanists of Europe to give to America the honour of having produced it. Mr. Adanson found it growing spontaneously in Juan Fernandez ; whence the philosophers wisely concluded that it must be a native of Chili! But in this conclusion they appear to have equally forgotten the laws of nature and the decisions of history ; for the quotations with which we began this article show that oats were cultivated in Italy many centuries before the existence of America was known to any European, and few are ignorant that Chili is among the hottest and driest regions of the globe, and that oats perish in dry and hot climates.

Of the many different species or varieties of this grain, the *black* and the *white* are those which best deserve cultivation, because most hardy and productive. In the poorest soil, and with the smallest possible labour, they give something ; but because they do not give much, in circumstances under which other grains would give nothing, we infer that the grain itself is a poor one, and, at the same time, a great exhauster of the soil. We owe to Mr. Dranus a series of experiments and calcula-

---

* In a favourable season, under good management, the white bean gives thirty for one.

† Dr. Johnson.

tions which overturn this opinion, and demonstrate that " oats, in rotation, under proper culture and in good soil, are not less profitable than wheat or rye ; that after beans, cabbages, or potatoes, it yields great crops, and that it exhausts less than other grains which occupy the soil a greater length of time." As a protector of clover or other grass seeds, with some of which it should always be sown, it is second only to barley.

XI. *Of Cabbages.**

These have been long known among us as a garden vegetable, but are rarely met with in field culture ; a fact the more extraordinary, as in England they have been very extensively and profitably employed in that way for more than half a century.

The species most recommended are the early Salsbury and York, the great Scotch, the Drumhead, the Cavalier, and the green Savoy. Mr. Cobbett has remarked, with much good sense, that the species best for man are also best for cattle ; and that, on this ground, the last of those mentioned should form the principal part of our cabbage crop.

The seed of early cabbages, as the York and the Salsbury, should be sown in hotbeds about the middle of February ; and that of winter and fall cabbages in the open field about the 15th of May. The bed selected for the latter should be of good soil and well ventilated ; that is, exposed on all sides to the influences of the air, and without artificial shelter. When the plants rise, they should be sprinkled with unleached ashes or gypsum, and, if attacked by the fly, may be slightly and temporarily covered with branches of elder. If the weather be uncommonly dry, a little watering may be

* It is doubtful whether cabbages will ever constitute with us a field crop for feeding stock, since the introduction of ruta baga, beets, and carrots, which are found to be more certain and abundant crops here than the cabbage, and are more easily preserved for winter use.—J. B.

proper ; but much of this should be avoided, because plants, like animals, may become topers, and will then drink more than will be useful to them.

The transplanting of early cabbages should not be delayed beyond the 12th of May, nor that of the late kinds beyond the first of June.   An acre of ground will require about six thousand plants.

The preparation of the soil for this crop is exactly that described for potatoes, and which, therefore, need not be repeated here.   When the manuring, ploughing, and harrowing are finished, strike your furrows from east to west, four feet apart; place your plants in these, twenty inches from each other, and do not forget so to press the earth as to bring it in contact with every part of the roots.

The advantage of this crop will be best seen by contrasting it with another, hay for example.   If we get a ton of timothy per acre, we think we do well, and are satisfied; yet, if this acre had been well worked and manured, and planted in cabbages, it would, according to Mr. Young, have given you more than *thirty* times the weight of the hay.   Why not, then, prefer the cabbages to the hay ?   Our cattle, it may be said, will not like them so well.   Hear what the same author says on this head : " Young cattle go through the winter well on cabbages ; ewes and lambs thrive on them ; fatting oxen improve *faster* on *them* than on any *other food*, and never fall off, as they sometimes do on turnips ; and milch cows do better on cabbages, *six* to *one*, than on hay," &c.   But the difficulty of preserving them through the winter may be great.   Not half as great as that of preserving potatoes ; for a frost that will convert these into dirty water, will do cabbages no harm, and may even do them good.   Mr. Cobbett preserved them through a Long Island winter, and had them sound and fresh in the month of May, and by a method equally cheap and expeditious ; requiring only a plough, a few leaves, straw, or brush, and some shovelfuls of earth: "and here," says he, "*they were at all times ready; for* to this land I could have gone at any time, and have brought away (if the quantity had been large) a wagon-load in ten minutes."

XII. *Of Buckwheat.*

This excellent grain is a native of Asia, whence it was carried to Africa, and thence by the Moors to Europe. In France it yet retains the name of *sarrasin.*

. The species of it in cultivation are two, the common and the Tartarean (Polygonum Tartaricum of Linnæus.)* This last species is highly extolled by Professor Pallas and others. It ripens earlier, and produces more than the common species; but, on the other hand, it shells more easily, and has in it an unpleasant degree of bitterness.

Cattle, hogs, and poultry are particularly fond of this grain, and no food fattens them more promptly.

Being entirely destitute of *gluten* (the animo vegetable part of wheat), it is not convertible into bread, but, made into batter and baked into cakes, it forms a very tolerable substitute. Another great advantage of buckwheat is, that, with a small degree of labour, it thrives well in the poorest sand or gravel; and in clays which are only slightly moist, it gives a good crop, and never fails to leave them loose, friable, and clean. To the clay-land farmer this property is invaluable; and, to make the most of it, he should remember that this labour-saving grain ought to have more of attention and liberality than is generally given to it; for if, under the hard treatment and in the by-places where it is now cultivated, it yields so much and works these important effects on the soil, how greatly would its usefulness be increased, were it made to follow pease, beans, cabbages, or potatoes, in regular rotation and on a large scale.

* Called also *Indian wheat.*—J. B.

We have already spoken of it as a manure ; and we take this occasion to quote from a late editor of the Theatre d'Agriculture of O. Serres, the following passage : " We cannot too much recommend, after our old and constant practice, the employment of this precious plant as a manure. It is certainly the most economical and convenient the farmer can employ. A small quantity of seed, costing very little, sows a large surface and gives a great crop. When in flower, first roll and then plough it in. Its shade, while growing, destroys all weeds, and itself, when buried, is soon converted into terreau."*

The experiments of M. Vauquelin show that, of *one hundred* parts of buckwheat, *fifty* are carbonate and sulphate of potash, and carbonate of lime

CHAPTER X.

OF OTHER PLANTS USEFUL IN A ROTATION OF CROPS, AND ADAPTED TO OUR CLIMATE.

These may be brought under three classes ; those which yield a colouring matter, those which yield oil, and those whose bark is convertible into clothing. Of the first are madder, saffron, and woad ; of the second, poppy, colet, and palma Christi ; and of the third, flax and hemp.

I. *Of Madder.*

Madder is the *erythros* of the Greeks, and the *rubia* of the Latins, so called from its imparting a red colour to wool and leather. It is cultivated in the Levant, in France, in Flanders, and in England ; but nowhere more extensively or profitably than in

* Vegetable mould.

Holland. The province of Zealand is principally occupied with it, and the little island of Schowen alone gives annually one thousand tuns of the root.

The species generally cultivated are two, the *Azara* and *Izari;* names by which they are called in the Levant, whence the seed is generally imported to Europe, and preferred to that raised in more northern latitudes.

The soil most proper for this plant is a rich loam, and the manures fittest for it the sweepings of streets and gutters, and mud of ponds.* It is remarked in England that it succeeds better after a grain than after a grass crop. The preparatory labour should be performed in the fall, leaving a single ploughing only for the spring, which, like those that preceded it, should be as deep as possible. The planting should follow without delay. In the Levant they form beds, alternately, of unequal elevation; one high, the other low; on the latter the madder is planted,† and in the autumn of the second year the surface of the higher bed is scattered over that which is lower; and by a similar process the next year the lower bed is raised six inches higher than the other. By this management the earth retains sufficient humidity for the growing plants.

In transplanting madder, care must be taken to preserve the buttons which attach themselves to the roots, and that the roots themselves be ten inches apart in the rows, and their crowns not more than two inches below the surface.

The greatest duration of the plant is six years, but three is the permitted term; as, after that age, the roots lose in colour and soundness what they .

* Young's works.

† Madder requires more moisture in its first stage than is ordinarily furnished by rains and dews. Thence arose the method of raising the plants in a seed-bed, where they might be watered at will, and afterward transferred to the place where they were intended to grow.

gain in bulk. At three years a single root has been found to weigh between thirty and forty pounds; and, the larger the root, the less does it lose, in proportion, by depreciation.*

When the roots are taken up, they are suspended under cover for ten or twelve days to dry. During this time much of the water of vegetation is evaporated; the plant becomes soft, and is then subjected to the heat of an oven from which bread has been taken. After a second baking it comes out dry and brittle; and to disengage from it the earth, the small fibres, and the outer skin of the root, it is lightly threshed with a flail, after which it is fit for grinding.

Of Woad.

This plant, till 1756, was much employed, and furnished the finest blue colour; and, in the opinion of some dyers, is even now very profitably united with indigo, giving to the colour imparted by it more intensity as well as duration. The maturity of the *leaves*, which are the only useful part of the plant, is announced by their drooping, and by the yellow colour which they take. At this signal they must be stripped from their stems, housed, and left in mass till, freed from the water of vegetation, they begin to macerate by their own weight. They are then to be washed and reduced to a paste; after which a fermentation takes place, and the fecula shows itself and forms a black crust, which is not to be broken, because necessary to prevent evaporation. When the fermentation has subsided (which may be known by the diminished stench), the mass is pounded and formed into balls for use. The soil and preparation indicated in the last article for madder are most proper for woad.

Of Saffron.

This plant is cultivated only for the stigmata of the flowers, which give a yellow colour and are

---

* In large roots this loss is 6-7ths, in small ones 7-8ths.

employed in dyeing and in *gauche* painting. It succeeds best in a rich, friable, black earth, or in one
of a dark red or chocolate colour. Some writers
have remarked that the roots, which are bulbous,
grow to the greatest size in the former of these
soils, and that the flowers attain the highest perfection in the latter. The manure best adapted to it is
old and thorougly-rotted dung.

After being well ploughed, rolled, and harrowed,
the ground intended for this crop is trenched, and
the roots placed in the trenches nine or ten inches
apart. So soon as the flowers appear, which always precede the leaves, the soil about them must
be lightly hoed. When fully blown, and while wet
with dew, they are taken off carefully with the hand
and spread upon boards to dry. The stigmata are
then separated from the styles, after which they are
ready for market.

Of the Poppy.

The poppy is among the most important of the
oil-giving plants, as well for the value as for the
abundance of its produce. The oil is altogether
found in the seeds, and does not partake of any som-
niferous or other deleterious quality, as some persons have supposed. It is often mixed with olive
oil, and, so long as it is fresh, it is equally pleasant
and wholesome. It is much used in France, Holland, and Germany, in salads. Its only fault is,
that, if long kept, it becomes thick and viscous. The
plant is annual, and requires a good and well-laboured soil. The seeds should be taken from the ripest
and largest capsules of the preceding year; should
be sown early and thin, and in broadcast; because,
if thickly sown, the plants rot, and, if sown late,
they are injured by a too rapid vegetation. The
fall of the leaf, the dying of the stalk, and the brown
colour of the capsules, indicate the time for harvesting the crop. These last are carefully gathered
and dried, and the seed separated from them.

Of Cole.

Cole or rape is a variety of the cabbage, the seed of which yields an oil very useful to the arts, and renders the plant of great importance in agriculture. Its general management does not differ from that of any other variety of the kind. When the seed is ripe, it must be carefully gathered and separated from its chaff. The plantations of cole in Flanders, and particularly in the neighbourhood of Lisle, Hasbrook, and Douay, and on a part of the Escant, are immense. They generally follow a crop of well-dunged, well-laboured potatoes, and are followed by one of wheat.

Palma Christi, or the castor-oil plant, and the ricinus of botanists, has been cultivated in this state; but whether profitably or not we do not know. Its seed gives an oil fit for lamps, but principally employed as a medicine. The cultivation of this plant has been tried in the southern parts of France, but not on a large scale, as it was found to require much ground and to give few seeds, which ripen only in succession. In Carolina the stem attains the height of ten or twelve feet, and a diameter of four or five inches. As an ornamental shrub, the palma Christi is much to be recommended.

Of the Sunflower.

This plant is a native of Peru, and is cultivated in Europe principally for the seeds, which give a large proportion of oil, of much use for domestic purposes. It requires a good soil, well manured, and thoroughly worked and cleansed. The seeds should be sown one foot apart, and in rows two feet asunder. In France the stems are employed for fuel and peasticks, and the leaves for fodder.*

Of Flax.

Flax is of Asiatic origin, and, from its hardiness and usefulness, is generally diffused over the globe.

---

* See Crete de Paleuil on the Sunflower.

No plant undergoes a greater change in the hands of labour, and few, if any, better repays the labour bestowed upon it.* It is cultivated for two different objects : for the fibre which surrounds the stem, and which is convertible into cloth, and for the seeds, which yield an oil very important to the arts. These different purposes have been supposed to be best promoted by different kinds of seed and different kinds of culture. In England it is believed that the seed of this country gives a flax of greater length and of finer fibre ; and that the seed of Memel or Riga† produces a coarser plant and a greater quantity of seed. We doubt, however, the correctness of this distinction, and think ourselves supported by experience, as well as theory, in placing the difference less to the account of any peculiar quality of the seed, than to the greater or smaller quantity of it sown ; for we have invariably observed that, if flaxseed, wherever grown, be sown *thinly*, the stem is shorter, the fibre coarser, and the seed more abundant, and vice versa. This difference will necessarily be increased by different modes of culture. The row husbandry, admitting of more ventilation, will hasten more the maturity of the plant, and increase the quantity and quality of the seed ; whereas the broadcast method will, on the other hand, retard the maturity of the plant, lengthen the stem and the fibre that covers it, and, in the same proportion, diminish the quantity of seed.

Flax may be made to follow potatoes very advantageously ; and we have seen the practice of sowing it with a crop of that kind earnestly recommended.‡

The *time* for harvesting flax depends on the con-

---

* How wonderful the difference between the raw material and Brussels lace !

† The flaxseed of Riga is broad and flat, and of a darker colour than that of this country.

‡ See 2d vol. Varla's Husbandry.

siderations suggested above. If *seed* be the principal end of the crop, your harvesting ought not to begin till *this* is completely ripe; whereas, if the fibre be your main object, pull the flax two or three weeks earlier. Flax thus prematurely pulled is called *white flax*, and makes the finest thread. The exhausting quality of this plant is generally admitted, and has been long known. Pliny says of it, that it burns and degrades the soil in return for the nourishment it receives from it.*

Of Hemp.

The cultivation of this plant need not be attempted on soils which are not naturally or artificially very rich. They who possess the former will often find the culture of hemp useful in reducing the staple of the soil to that medium quality which is best fitted for the production of *grain*. In some parts of our own country hemp has been cultivated many years in succession, before this effect was produced; and in Italy, in the neighbourhood of Bologna, after centuries of cultivation, the rotation continues to be *wheat* and *hemp* alternately, and without fallows. So also in the environs of Termonde, near Brussels, the usual rotation is *hemp*, *flax*, and *wheat*.† It is, perhaps, to those favoured soils we ought to look for the best mode of cultivating this very useful and profitable plant. "During the first year," says M. Simmonde, in his Picture of Tuscan Agriculture, "the field intended for hemp is laid flat by the small Tuscan plough in the months of August and September. This is followed by the great plough, which reinstates the four-feet furrows, and throws up the intermediate earth into ridges. The manure is applied to these in the spring; after which the hemp-seed is sown and

* "Ut sentiamus, nolente id ferre natura, urit agrum deterioremque etiam terram facit." Nat. Hist., l. xix.

† Francis de Neauchateau's State of Husbandry in the senatoriat of Brussels.

the ground harrowed. This crop, like that of flax should be weeded when about four inches high."

Of Swallow-wort or Milkweed.

This is the *asclepias Syriaca* of the botanists, and not improperly called the cotton of northern latitudes. Its cortical fibre yields a fine, soft, and white thread, and the pods a silky material, usefully employed in waddings and in hat-making, &c. "There are few plants," says Sonnini, " the culture of which unites more advantages, or which is more worthy the attention of farmers. In Silesia it has made considerable progress; and experience shows that in a middling, or even a bad soil, it gives a product eight times more valuable than the finest crop of flax or hay. It requires a strong and moist soil, well laboured and manured, and may be propagated by seeds, by suckers, or by roots. The row husbandry is the most proper for it, and in the course of three years the intervals between the furrows will be completely filled up by new and multiplied shoots.

Of the plant called New-Zealand Flax.

This is the *formion tenax* of botanists; the leaves of which, by maceration in water, yield a fibre remarkable for beauty and strength. We owe to M. Labillardiere a series of experiments, the result of which shows that the strength of flax being 11, that of hemp is 16 1-3, and that of formion 23 5-11. In the hot countries, of which this plant is a native, it is found on the seashore, growing sometimes in wet or marshy soils, and sometimes in arid sands. M. Thouin has succeeded in naturalizing it in the north of France, which gives reason to believe that it may be made to succeed in this climate

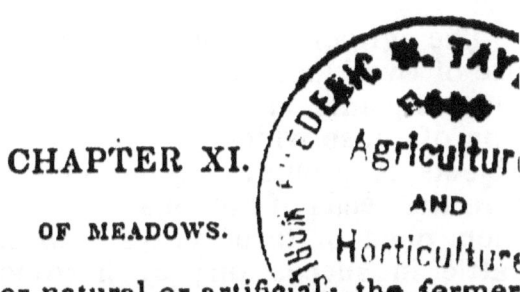

CHAPTER XI.

OF MEADOWS.

THESE are either natural or artificial; the former containing only plants of spontaneous growth, the latter those selected, sown, and cultivated by man. The better to keep this distinction in view, we shall speak of them separately; and,

I. *Of Natural Meadows.*

These have been classed by botanists according to their *elevation*; and have thence been denominated high, middling, and low. But as this principle fails altogether to indicate their agricultural character and properties,* a better one has been found in their relative moisture; whence they are denominated dry, or moist, or wet. The products of these have been carefully and skilfully analyzed in Germany, in Italy, in England, and in France;† and the result shows that wet meadows contain a smaller number of the different species of plants, but a greater number of those which are either useless or injurious; and, on the other hand, that *moist* meadows contain a greater number of the former, and a smaller number of the latter. The following simple table exhibits, at a glance, the present state of knowledge on this important part of our subject:

Whole number of Plants
in wet meadows, 30; useful 4, useless or bad 26.
Do. in dry meadows, 38; do. 8, do. 30.
Do. in moist meadows, 42; do. 17, ·do. 25.

* We often find bogs on the tops of mountains, and arid sands on the banks of rivers.
† See "Observations made by the Agricultural Society of Great Britain," and "Memoires sur l'Agriculture du Boutonnais," &c., &c., per M. Dumont de Coursit.

The agricultural labours suggested by these facts are of two kinds: the eradicating of useless or pernicious plants, and the continuance and multiplication of those which are good. The first of these objects is promoted by mowing the meadows before the seeds of noxious plants ripen, by pasturing them once in three years with sheep, horses, and cattle in succession; by harrowing them in the spring and fall; by weeding and hoeing them; and, lastly, by sufficiently draining those that are wet.

Many pernicious plants are annuals, and are killed by the first of these operations. A similar effect is produced by the second; the harrow, or scarificator, will best destroy mosses or other weeds whose roots are fibrous and superficial; the hand-hoe will extirpate such tap-rooted plants as resist the harrow and are refused by cattle; and draining will expel all worthless aquatics.

Of these remedies, the last may require some explanation. Meadows are wet from different causes; from obstructions, accidental or permanent, to the course of rivers; from occasional inundations; from high and uncommon tides; from neighbouring springs, issuing sometimes above and sometimes below the level of the grounds you wish to drain; and frequently from others rising up within the meadows themselves. In the first case, the remedy is obvious, and consists altogether in removing the obstructions; in the second and third, embankments, as in the Mississippi and Delaware, will exclude the flood; and in the fourth and fifth, the cure lies in creating a surface of lower level than that of the meadows to be drained, or in raising the water to a level above that of the meadows, and carrying it off by raceways or canals. The former of these methods is to be executed by ditching, or by digging through the subsoil into sand or gravel, whence the water will find a subterranean passage. The latter is effected by enclosing the springs within walls, and permitting them to rise to the level of their own source. It is evident, however, that if these be not higher than that of the meadow, the experiment will fail.*

The second object, viz., the multiplication and continuance of good plants, will be ensured by scattering in the fall or spring, or both, after the harrow or scarificator, the seeds of useful grasses,† particularly upon places rendered raw or bare by the harrow or the hoe; by covering the meadows in the fall with straw, dung, lime, or marl; and in the spring, with plaster of Paris or ashes; by folding or parking sheep or horned cattle during the summer, and while the ground is hard, on places requiring manure; by foddering on such places during the winter; and, lastly, by *irrigation*. This last and most efficient method of bettering the condition of meadows is sometimes characterized by the duration of its means, and sometimes by the mode of applying them. In the first case, it is called *temporary* or *permanent*, as the stream it employs may be the one or the other. In the second case, it is denominated *filtration* or *submersion*, according to the effect produced. If, for instance, the surface be only wetted by running water, it is called filtration; but if entirely covered with water, in a state of rest, it is called submersion. These different modes have some principles common to both, and some peculiar to each. The common principles are,

1st. Such command of water as will cover the largest surface with the least labour and expense.

2d. Muddy water (the effect of loosened soil and heavy rains) is most favourable to vegetation, be-

* See Anderson's Essays on Agriculture, vol. i., p. 119, &c.
† In selecting these grasses, care should be taken to employ those most resembling the spontaneous growth of the field, or, in other words, those which flower and seed at the same time with this spontaneous growth.

cause, besides giving the necessary moisture, it furnishes a considerable portion of alluvial matter.

3d. Water charged with sand or gravel, or containing iron or vitriol, or of a temperature very hot or very cold, is unfavourable to vegetation, and ought not to be employed, until, by standing in reservoirs, it deposites these injurious matters in the one case, and in the other acquires the temperature of the atmosphere.

4th. Clay and calcareous soils require less watering than others.

5th. Irrigation is of less importance in northern than in southern latitudes; and,

6th. In cold climates, or in situations of much elevation, irrigation is most usefully employed in the spring and autumn; and in hot climates and sandy soils in the summer.

The principles peculiar to the two modes may be collected from the following brief detail of the labours necessary to each. In irrigating by submersion, the first and great labour is to make a *dam* of such strength as shall resist the volume of water by which it may be pressed; of such height as will raise the water above the level of the ground you wish to overflow; and of such structure as will enable you to discharge the water it collects promptly and entirely. The signal for doing this is the rising of air-bubbles from the bottom of the pond, which never takes place until a decomposition of the plants below begins. In winter, this tendency to decomposition is corrected by cold; and the submersion may, of course, be continued for weeks and months, and the water permitted to freeze, not only without injury, but with great benefit to the plants, particularly if they have been closely pastured in the fall.

Filtration is a process requiring, in general, more labour and science than the other; because, besides a dam to raise a sufficient head of water, you must have your canal of derivation, your reservoir, your cuts or ditches, and, lastly, your fosse or pit of discharge, which, to be useful, must be well constructed and judiciously placed. The canal and reservoir will necessarily occupy the highest ground, and be proportioned to the quantity of water to be conducted and retained ; the cuts or ditches, supplied from the reservoir, will be parallel to each other, of nearly equal descent, but of diameters diminishing in proportion to their length, so as to give to the water the same swiftness it had when its volume was greatest. Stops or gates must be made in the cuts or ditches in such number as may be necessary so to pond the water as to make it overflow the lower sides of the ditches, and at such points as will, from the shape of the ground, diffuse it most generally. In this way, small streams, occasional showers, and dissolving snows may be turned to great account, and with this additional advantage, that they require no reservoirs, and little, if any, draining, and only cuts or ditches formed with a plough or a hoe.

A third kind, compounded of the two others, is sometimes seen in Europe, where the water, after being employed in irrigating the sides of hills, is brought upon flats for the purpose of inundation, or, more generally, for that of forming reservoirs, from which it may again be raised by machinery, such as the noria of the Moors, or the hydraulic ram of Montgolfier, &c.*

II. *Of Artificial Meadows.*

We have seen that natural meadows abound in plants either useless or pernicious ; and that it is among the principal labours of agriculture to eradi-

* Whoever may have occasion to study the two subjects (draining and irrigation), either separately or in connexion, cannot do better than consult the Hydraulic Architecture of Bellidor, the Hydraulics of Dubuat, M. de Ourche's General Treatise on Meadows, Defue on the Embankments of Holland, and Richardson's Agriculture.

cate these, and to substitute for them others of greater product or better quality. It was probably this process which first suggested the idea of *artificial meadows*, or those composed only of plants of our own choosing, and alternating with grain or root crops. And it cannot be doubted that, if the grasses selected be good in themselves, adapted to the soil, and carefully cultivated, we thus arrive at the highest possible degree of perfection of which this branch of the art is susceptible; because, besides having only *wholesome* and *nutritive* forage, we *double its quantity*, and, at the same time, put the soil in a state to give us a series of good subsequent crops.

France claims the credit of having been the first to discover the value, and to introduce the practice of this new system; and it may not be amiss to collect some of the reports of her writers on the agricultural changes wrought by it. "If," says Yvart, "meadows be the nerve of good husbandry, it is, above all, to artificial meadows we must apply this great truth. The state of those cantons which have adopted the new system is now as brilliant as it was before wretched and miserable. Alsace has put on a new face since the introduction of clover, and wheat crops have been increased more than one third. The village of Sebach, under the old system, bought annually 180,000 pounds of forage, and now sells 150,000. The canton of Virien, which gave formerly only rye and buckwheat (and poor crops of these), now gives abundant crops of fine wheat. This is altogether owing to clover and gypsum. The same remark applies to the department of Doubs. In the department of the Seine and Ouse, the four year rotation is adopted, of which clover is the basis, and more than doubles the produce for exportation. In Varenne, the soil of which is a poor sand, the same effect is produced by sainfoin instead of clover. In a canton of the department of Loiret, M. Sageret has doubled his income by the introduction and culture of lucerne." It would be mere waste of time to multiply quotations on this head. Few men of our own country who have had their eyes open for some years past, but must have seen the wonderful effects produced by plastered clover; and if there be any who resist these evidences, or are insensible to them, they must be far beyond the reach of instruction. We hasten, therefore, to another and important part of our subject, *the choice of grasses for artificial meadows.* Those most recommended by the experience of all countries are lucerne, sainfoin, and clover of the leguminous family; and timothy, oat-grass, ray-grass, and meadow fox-tail of the gramineal.* We shall say a few words of each, and, 1st. of *Lucerne.*—This plant is a native of Media, whence its Latin name Medica. It was well known and highly esteemed by the ancients, uniting in itself many valuable qualities, as early fitness for use, great productiveness and duration,† and juices the most nutritious and acceptable to cattle. In the south of Europe it still maintains this high reputation, and in our southern climates would entirely deserve it; but of its success *here* we have doubts, founded on the fact that all attempts made to introduce it, and coming within our own observation, have failed. Two conditions are, however, indispensable to its prosperity in any climate, and these are a *rich soil* and *careful cultivation.* In wet, or stony, or stiff ground, it does not thrive. Its long tap-root must plunge into the earth without obstruction, otherwise the plant suffers and dies prematurely. 2d. *Sainfoin.*—This

* Of the grasses here named, sainfoin is found not to succeed in the United States. We have not the chalky soil in which it thrives best, and our winters are considered too severe for it; and the ray or rye-grass is not well adapted to our hot summers. Neither seem to be congenial to our soil and climate.—J. B.

† " Tante dos est ejus ut eum uno situ *tricenis annis* duret medica."—Plin., Nat. Hist. Such are the valuable properties of lucerne, that it will flourish for thirty years on the same spot.

grows well in Europe as high as the 51st degree of
north latitude. A species of it is found growing
spontaneously in the Pays de Calais, which shows
itself earlier than the more common or Spanish spe·
cies. Its produce is less than that of lucerne ; but
the quality of its herbage, whether green or dry, is
better. Sheep are particularly fond of it. It affects
high, dry, naked, white, cretaceous soils ; amelio-
rates the condition of these, and holds them better
together than any other plant. The following extract may give both instruction and encouragement
to those who would cultivate this plant : " In Calabria, sainfoin is sown upon wheat or other stubble,
which is then burned, and the ashes made to furnish
a covering for the grass-seed. In the spring, without other care or culture, the field is found covered
thickly with sainfoin, and converted into a fine
meadow. This grass crop is cut and fed between
May and August, when the ground is ploughed for
grain, of which the crop is generally very abundant.
But the advantages of this husbandry do not end
here ; for, after the grain is harvested, the earth re-
sumes its covering of sainfoin, which, in this way,
is continued forty years and more, admitting every
second year a crop of fine wheat."* 3d. Like sainfoin and lucerne, *clover* is of the leguminous family,
and, though less productive than the others, has
one advantage that gives it a decided preference,
viz., its growing well in a great variety of soils. In
gravel, in loam, in alluvial and calcareous earths, it
does well ; and we have already seen that *in poor
and sandy soils it doubles the income* of those who
employ it, as well by increasing the quantity of forage, as by putting the ground into a state to yield
many and abundant future crops of grain. Still
there are soils, stiff, cold, and wet, in which it does
not succeed, and in which it ought to give place to

* Grimaldi on the agriculture of Calabria.

the gramineal family. 4th. *Timothy.*—This grass, in
Europe, is called herd-grass, cat's-tail, or phleum
pratense (the botanical name); but, as the plant is
of Yankee origin, we have chosen to retain the
Yankee denomination. Its reputation abroad was at
one time very high, and in moist grounds deserves to
be so at all times; but, being very tardy in showing
itself in the spring, it has in many places fallen into
disuse. 5th. *Ray* or *rye-grass*, to the good properties of timothy, superadds that precocity which timothy wants. "We have seen," says Gilbert, "in
the canton of Basle, rye-grass five feet high on the
first day of June;" and M. de Courset assures us
that he has obtained "three cuttings from it in one
year." Sheep are found to prefer it in the spring
to any other plant; and the shepherds of Spain have
a proverb which very energetically expresses its
nutritive qualities: "Bouccado van ventrado," a
mouthful is a bellyful. We particularly invite the
attention of farmers having clay, or other moist or
wet soils, to the cultivation of this and the two following species of grasses. 6th. *Oat-grass*, the Avena elatior of botanists, was first cultivated in 1754,
and, having been committed to a good soil, the results were highly favourable. It was accordingly
recommended as yielding abundance of forage, and
of a good quality: and that the first cutting might
take place as early as the last of March. Though
new and extended experiments have in some degree
diminished this reputation, still enough of it is left
to render this grass a favourite with every scientific
agriculturist. 7th. Of the *meadow fox-tail* there are
four species, but we shall speak only of the Alope-
curus pratensis, which, of all the grasses we have
mentioned, is the tallest, the most vigorous, and
the soonest fit for pasturage or the scythe. Its
hay appears to be of a better quality than that of
the gramineal grasses, because *equally* relished by
cows, horses, and sheep. It is only, however, in

soils neither too moist nor too dry that it attains the perfection of which it is susceptible.

What remains of this subject may be referred to the general principles of tillage, and the particular preparation necessary for clover crops, both of which may be found in the preceding chapters.

CHAPTER XII.

OF FARM CATTLE.

These consist of horses, mules, cows, oxen, sheep, and hogs. It is not the object of this chapter to discuss the relative value of animals of different kinds, nor to explain the principles on which an individual of either kind is preferred to another individual of the same kind, but merely to indicate the uses of each, and the modes most approved for giving extension and value to these uses. And,

I. *Of the Horse*.

Of this animal naturalists admit but one species, but many and widely different varieties, which are again subdivided under the denomination of races.* At the head of these, by common consent, stands the horse of Arabia, and after him the Persian, the Barb, the Andalusian, and the English. His flesh not entering, like that of the ox, into the general and ordinary subsistence of man,† he is valued only

---

* Bakewell and others have shown that you may multiply these races at will. By selecting two individuals of any given shape, size, and colour which you may prefer, you secure a progeny having all the qualities of their parents. This observation applies as well to horned cattle and hogs as to horses, and might be usefully taken as a rule of conduct in this country.

† Horseflesh is eaten by the Negroes of Africa, the Arabs, Tartars, and occasionally by the Chinese. Page 213, vol. 22d Buffon's Nat. Hist.

for the beauty of his form, the nobleness of his carriage, the rapidity of his march, and the strength, spirit, and patience with which he bears the heaviest burdens and the most ex:essive fatigues.

Of these powers some cut.ous and extraordinary instances are recorded. The couriers of Russia travel from Petersburgh to Tobolsk, a distance of 19° 26m., in twelve days. Their rate of travelling is, of course, about one hundred miles a day. What, in equestrian phrase, is called a great mover, will, without pressing, trot 640 yards in 80 seconds, and, if pressed, will go over the same distance in 50 seconds. In the first case, the rate of moving is 5 feet 3 inches per second, and in the other 8 feet 5 inches. The Roman horses, probably descendants from Barbs, ran at the rate of 27 feet the second of time; and the British horse Childers is said to have run at the rate of 45 feet 5 inches; and Stirling, another British horse, at the rate of 82 1-2 feet per second.* This may be regarded as the maximum of horse speed.

The ordinary load in France of a four-wheeled wagon, drawn by six horses on a pavement, is 10,000 pounds; that of a cart, drawn by four horses, 5500. With these loads they travel 10 leagues a day for six weeks together. A single horse has been known to draw 500 pounds at the rate of 140 yards in 112 seconds; and on the pavements of London a single horse has drawn 6000 pounds for a short distance, and 3000 for a considerable distance, and with facility. This appears to be the maximum of horse power in drawing.

* British Zoology for 1763-4. In Peru are two races of horses (originally Andalusian) well worth the attention of the rich amateurs of the United States. The names by which these races are known are the *Parameros* and the *Aqualillas.* See Ulloa's Voyage, tome i., page 370. In Chili also is a race which, for beauty, action, and hardiness, may be compared with the horse of Arabia, and with this advantage, that they are very cheap, while those of Arabia are very dear. See Molina's Nat. Hist. of Chili, page 505, et seq.

Under the pack or saddle, 300 pounds is the ordinary load for a horse ; but, according to M. Thiroux, a dragoon horse carries 340 pounds. This includes the weight of the rider and of his arms, accoutrements, and baggage. The well-known experiment of Marshal Saxe shows the maximum of horse power in this respect. He directed that a strong and vigorous horse, while in motion, should be loaded until he fell. The effect was not produced until the load amounted to 1200 weight.*

II. *Of the Mule.*

This is the well-known product of a jack and a mare, or of a horse and a jenny, the name given to a female ass. Their advantages over the horse are, that they are more patient of hunger and heat; less nice or delicate with regard to their food; sustain better, and for a longer time, fatigues of all kinds; carry heavier burdens; are more sure footed; less liable to sickness, and live to a much greater age. In Italy and Spain they are much employed in harness, and in the mountainous parts of those countries for the saddle. Their value and qualities, however, depend principally on the size of the jack : if he be large, active, and strong, his progeny will be proportionably valuable. Nothing, therefore, can be more ill-judged than employing small jacks.†

III. *Of the Cow and the Ox.*

It was long supposed that this animal was a native of Europe, and that the Auroch, found wild in the forests of Poland, was the type of the species. The researches into comparative anatomy of Cuvier have overthrown this theory, and men of science now substitute for it another, viz., that the cow is a native of Asia, and has thence been trans-

* See Fourcroy (of the corps of engineers) on the powers of the horse, quoted by the Nouveau Cours d'Agriculture.

† The asses of Arabia, Egypt, and the Barbary Coast are the best In Sicily is a race of inferior size, but of great power See Sonnini's Supplement to Buffon on this animal.

lated to other parts of the globe. Be this fact as
it may, her uses are so many, so various, and so
important, that we cannot hesitate to transfer from
the horse the distinction bestowed upon him by an
eloquent writer of the last century, and to pro-
nounce the cow " *the noblest conquest made by man.*"*
During two thirds of her life, which may be pro-
tracted to twelve years, she is annually producing
her species, and during the same period yielding an
abundant supply of that beverage so universally
known and so generally acceptable ; a beverage so
happily adapted, from its compound nature (part
animal and part vegetable), to all ages and conditions, to the young and to the old, to the poor and
to the rich, to the sick and to the sound ; and which,
in its concrete forms of butter and cheese, has, in
all civilized countries, become an article of the first
necessity. Nor is her value diminished by death ;
for, having been fatted and prepared for market, her
flesh forms our most savoury and substantial food ;
her tallow, in the form of candles, supplies the absence of natural light ; her skin, wrought into leather, furnishes shoes and other articles rendered necessary by habit or custom ; her horns are converted into combs and lanterns ; her blood is essential
to the refinement of our sugars ; chymistry draws
from her hoofs important uses ; her hair is made
to pad our collars and saddles, and, by entering into
the construction of our buildings, adds to their
beauty, comfort, and solidity. If in her progeny
(the ox) strength and speed be less combined than
in the horse, it will be also remembered that his
subsistence is cheaper, and his labour more continued and persevering ; that he is, besides, less liable
to accidents which diminish his value, and that he
may even become lame and blind without eventual
loss to his owner : for, when prepared for the sham-

---

* Buffon's Nat. Hist., vol. 22.

bles, like his parent, he gives us beef, tallow, &c., and those of a superior kind. How important, then, is it that this useful animal should be multiplied, and that pains should be taken to ameliorate the breed. In England and in Holland, wealth, enterprise, and philosophy have combined to exalt the character of domestic animals, and the effect has been to create many new, artificial, and more perfect races. These are examples we ought to follow, and these are the countries which can best enable us to do so.

It has, however, been found that, in temperatures either very hot or very cold, the bulk of the cow is diminished; and though it is by no means verified that animals secrete milk in proportion to their size, still, on other accounts, the largest cows may justly be considered the best. Treatment, or the quantity and quality of food, has a still more decided influence than climate on animal growth and development, and hence it is that, when the cows of England, Holland, or Switzerland are transferred to pastures less abundant or nutritive than those in which they have been reared, or are otherwise put on shorter allowance than that to which they have been accustomed, their qualities degenerate, and their progeny with them. The lesson that these facts inculcate cannot, we believe, be mistaken, and will not, we hope, be overlooked.

IV. *Of Sheep.*

Of the different races of sheep, we shall speak only of two, those of Spain and England; because in them are best united the two great objects for which this animal are reared, *wool* and *food.*

The sheep of Spain, generally known under the name of Merinoes, are composed of two classes, the *travelling* and the *stationary.* The former of these is again divided into two distinct races, called the *Leonese* and the *Sorian;* while the latter, composed of a number of degenerate breeds, are denominated

Charras. The Leonese and the Sorian winter in Estramadura, and are never parked or housed, excepting for fifteen days of each year, at the Esquilcos, or shearing houses, near Segovia. After this operation, their march to the mountains begins in two columns; the one to old Castile and the kingdom of Leon, the other to the province of Soria, and, subsequently, to Navarre or the Pyrenees. The preference of the Leonese to the Sorian is sufficiently established by the fact that the wool of the former sells for one fourth, and sometimes for one third more than that of the latter. But even in this pre-eminent race there is a marked difference between the different troops composing it; those of the late Prince of Peace, of Nigretta, of Montaco, of Peralez, of Fernando Nunez, and of l'Infantado, are particularly distinguished by the fineness, and what, in technical language, is called the *nerve* of their wool.*

The policy of Great Britain was early directed to the amelioration of sheep. It is, however, to Henry VIII. and to Elizabeth that the praise is particularly due of importing into England sheep of the finest Spanish races; of promulgating rules and regulations for their proper management; and, lastly, of commencing that prohibitory system, which has secured their continuance, and, what is of still greater importance, the *exclusive* fabrication of the wool they produce. It was not, however, in the power of laws entirely to abrogate, or even materially to alter, the effect of climate. That of England did not so much favour the production of *fine* as of *long* wool, and hence it is that the wool of that country is not so remarkable for the former as for the latter of these qualities. But in all cases, when our object is to unite the two great products of *wool* and *flesh*, it is to the English breeds we should look for the best

* The Saxon sheep of the Merino family were not known to us when this treatise was written.—J. B.

means of doing it. The flesh of the pure Merino is neither so abundant nor so well flavoured as that of the mixed races, and, when brought to the greatest perfection, the quantity of his wool is less. His carcass, when prepared for market, does not exceed 10 pounds a quarter, and the average weight of his fleece will not rise above four pounds; whereas the best English races give 25 pounds the quarter, and fleeces weighing 7 and 8 pounds each.

V. *Of the Hog.*

The wild boar is considered the type of this species, of which there are several varieties. The most distinguished of these are the Asiatic or Chinese hog, the European hog, with long, broad, and pendant ears, and the Solipede, or horse-hoofed hog of Sweden.* As this animal is principally useful as food, the improvers of the species have aimed only at forming a race which, with the least expense and in the shortest time, should acquire the greatest bulk and the highest degree of fatness. It is on this principle that the Chinese hog, which fats promptly and easily, but which attains only to a small size, is with great propriety mixed with the hog of Europe, which acquires a much greater bulk, but is proportionably slow and difficult of fattening. The result of this mixture has been many improved races, at the head of which stands the hog of Parma, and those known in England by the names of the *Bakewell* and *Byfield* breeds.†

The weight of the hog at eighteen months or two years of age (taking for granted a regular and sufficient nourishment), varies from two to four hundred pounds. Buffon mentions a hog killed in Eng-

* This is the *Sus angula indivisa* of Linnæus. Aristotle was the first to mention this species, and, after him, Pliny. Linnæus says, it is common in Upsal and other cantons of Sweden. Amenitat. Acad., tome v., page 450.

† The Berkshire has since come into notice, and has obtained a decided preference over other varieties.—J. B.

land which weighed 850 pounds. Sonnini, his commentator, mentions another, killed in France, which weighed 990 pounds; and Mr. Jefferson, a third, killed in Virginia, which reached the enormous weight of 1200 pounds.*

The value of the hog is increased by their natural fecundity, which much exceeds that of any other species of domestic animal. This subject was thought worthy the pen of Marshal Vauban, who left behind him a manuscript calculation of the offspring of a single sow. The paper was read in the Institute of France some years ago, was heard with great interest, and gave an enormous result, but not sufficiently recollected to be stated here.

As, from the constitution of the human mind, there have been skeptics on all subjects, little and great, so on this we find some doubting whether the hog did not, from his insatiable appetite, consume more during his life than the amount of his value at the time of his death. These doubts could not fail to engage calculating men in ascertaining this point. Their experiments show a profit of eight dollars on every hog reared and fed to the age of two years, by persons having no farms, and obliged to buy every article going to their nourishment. How much greater, then, the profits of those who have the means of subsisting them on grasses and roots, which cost only the labour of raising?

To these specific remarks upon different animals, we now proceed to add a few observations on the breeding of cattle, and a brief view of the general principles on which the fattening of such of them as enter into the subsistence of man more peculiarly depends. And,

1st. *Of the breeding of Cattle.*

It rarely happens that the breeders of cattle are the fatteners of them. The first of these employ-

---

* Notes on Virginia.

ments seems more particularly to belong to those who, other circumstances being favourable, are remote from markets ; the second to those who, from local situation or navigable streams, are convenient to markets. In the breeding business two conditions are indispensable to its success : 1st, that the *sires* of each species be well chosen, because their qualities and appearance have much more influence on the character of the offspring than those of the females ; and, 2d, that, during pregnancy, the females be abundantly fed, and otherwise subjected to no hard or injurious treatment.*

2d. *Of the fattening of Cattle.*

The objects in fattening cattle are two, the increase of tallow, which is an important article in domestic economy ; and the improvement of the fleshy or muscular parts ; the lean meat of fat animals being better flavoured and more nutritive than that of poor ones. The means of effecting this object are either living vegetables, or those which have been cut, dried, and stored for use. Under the first head are the whole family of the grasses, and under the second, grains, roots, pease, and beans. When we resort to the first, the only care necessary is, that the provision of plants be both abundant and nutritive. Upland pastures, where they unite these conditions, best fulfil this intention ; but the fat of cattle thus fed, though better distributed (the effect, as we believe, of exercise), is less in quantity, and of an inferior quality. The second mode, which is called *stall-feeding*, is more difficult and expensive, and requires great attention to the repose of the animal, to his cleanliness, and to the caprices of his appetite. In England, where this business is most practised and best understood, they envelop the head of

* The inhabitants of the Boullonois, in France, employ the mare instead of the horse for all agricultural purposes ; because, besides labouring the soil, they give yearly a foal, which they sell at eight months to the graziers at Normandy.

the fattening animal in several folds of woollen cloth
so as to deprive him, in a great degree, of the power of hearing, and altogether of that of seeing. The
doors of his stable are opened but once a day, to
change his litter, and his food and drink are given
through loopholes opening into his manger, which
are afterward immediately closed. With respect
to feeding, the first rule is to give little at a time
and often; because experience has shown that animals that eat much in a short time do not fatten so
well as those which eat less at a time, and more
slowly and frequently. The second rule is to begin
the course with cabbages and turnips; then to employ carrots and potatoes; and, lastly, Indian, oat,
or barley meal, the marsh bean, or the gray pea.
These aliments ought to be varied five or six times
a day, and oftener if convenient; and, instead of
always reducing them into flour, there is an advantage in sometimes boiling them. A little salt, given
daily, is very useful, and for drink clean water, but
neither frequently nor in great quantity. Warm
water, by its temperature, most favours digestion;
but, if long continued, will enfeeble the stomach. It
ought, therefore, to be employed only towards the
end of the term. The fattening is complete when
the· superficial inequalities of the animal, whether
muscular or bony, are filled up; when his body presents only a round and smooth surface; when he
becomes drowsy and inert, dislikes motion, and
is apparently insensible to everything about him.
These are the signals for death, and the sooner you
inflict it after their appearance the better; for,
should the feeding be farther urged, you run the
risk of inducing the disease called the *melting of the
grease*, or, in more scientific language, the reabsorp-
tion of it by the blood, which is always fatal.

They who are at all acquainted with the subject
on which we write, need hardly be told that there
are many circumstances independent of food, clean-

liness, and quiet, which influence the fattening of cattle. We shall mention them sepatately, and add a few words to each in explanation.

1st. *Constitution.*—If this be not sound and healthy, no care or expense will be sufficient to correct it. The animal will want appetite, or have too much of it, and what it eats will not better its condition.

2d. *Alteration.*—The flesh of unaltered males is hard, fibrous, and ill-flavoured, and that of females, not spayed, far inferior to the flesh of those which have undergone that operation. Where either are early and completely altered, the animals become more docile, less restless, and fat with great facility.

3d. *Temperature.*—Whoever makes the experiment will find that this consideration is very important. The cold of winter, the heat of summer, and the capricious character of the spring, are all adverse to the fattening of cattle, though perhaps not equally so. The autumn, on the other hand, long and temperate, is the true season for that business, not only from the greater abundance of food which is then to be found, but because the transpiration of the animal is then first checked, and immediately converted into tallow. And,

4th. *Age.*—Tallow is formed from the surplus nourishment given to animals beyond that necessary to their mere physical development; whence it follows, that those which have not attained their full growth are fatted with difficulty, and only by extraordinary means. Calves, for example, can only be fatted by great quantities of milk, to which must often be added eggs, barley, oat meal, or the flour of beans and pease; and with all this abundance and selection of food, they yield little interior fat or tallow. Whereas oxen, at six years of age, with correspondent treatment, give large quantities of that article. Old cattle are also, from loss of teeth, debility of stomach, or other internal disorganization, difficult to fatten. These facts sufficiently indicate what, on this head, ought to be our practice; *to fatten cattle as soon after they have attained their growth as possible.* Oxen generally attain their growth at five or six years, and sheep and hogs at two.

CHAPTER XIII.

OF THE DAIRY.

THE business of the dairy, besides its connexion with the subject of the last chapter, is too important in itself to be omitted in any professed treatise on Agriculture. We shall therefore consign what we have to say upon it to the present chapter. A few preliminary observations may be proper.

Milk is the well-known basis of all the operations of the dairy. Few things have more engaged the attention of chymists. Boyle, Boerhave, Hoffman, and Macquer, all the old school and many of the new,* have employed themselves in detecting its constituent parts; and in establishing their several proportions. In the first branch of the inquiry they have sufficiently succeeded, and we accordingly know that this very important fluid is principally composed of 'an oily matter, of curd, of an essential salt called sugar of milk, and of serum. But, in the other branch of the inquiry, so various have been the results of experiments made on the milk of different animals, and of the same animal at different times, that it continues to be the reproach of chymistry; and we have now before us the ac-

* Haller, Brisson, Deyeux, Parmentier, Fourcroy, &c., &c

knowledgment of M. Perthuys, of the French Institute, that "to determine these proportions with the necessary exactness is *impossible*." Fortunately, however, the pride of science is more affected by this failure than the interests of agriculture.

Milk is reducible to two species : that of ruminating animals, and that of animals which do not ruminate. Milk of the first description abounds in cream and in curd, that of the other in sugar and whey; and it is on this distinction that the milk of cows, sheep, and goats is principally employed for the purposes of the dairy, while that of mares and asses is, with similar propriety, yielded to the service of medicine.*

Observation has shown that this secretion is much influenced by circumstances of weather, of aliment, and of age. A stormy day lessens its quantity and alters its quality; bad or deficient food has a similar but greater effect, and the fact is well known that very young and very old cows give poor milk. Mild weather, on the other hand, promotes the secretion, and soft, nourishing aliments, easy of digestion and in sufficient quantity, make it redundant.

A fact established by the labours of Messrs. Deyeux and Parmentier, and long before known to the dairy maid, is, that the milk first drawn is serous; that that which succeeds is less so, and that what are commonly called *strippings* are nearly all cream.

Having premised these facts, we proceed to the business of butter-making, the theory of which is reducible to the following heads :

1st. Butter is found suspended in milk, in the form of a white and liquid oil. This suspension is the effect of the saccharine matter and the curd, which are among the component parts of milk.

* The medical uses of asses' milk have come down to us from Hippocrates and Galen. The milk of mares is only established in the pharmacopœia of Tartary, where, according to the reports made by travellers, it is food, physic, and brandy.

2d. In a state of repose and in a cool temperature, this oily matter separates itself, in a great degree, from the serum and curd, mounts to the surface, and there forms a pellicle of greater or less density.

3d. When in contact with atmospheric air, it draws from it a portion of oxygen, and thence acquires a yellow colour and a disposition to harden.

4th. Agitation and pressure are necessary to separate it from the serum and curd which may have mounted with it. And,

5th. To correct its tendency to decomposition, which first shows itself by a rancid smell and taste, it must be subjected to the action of heat, or a portion of the muriate of soda must be incorporated with it. From this theory of butter-making, it will be easy to deduce the rules necessary to practice.

1st. The formation of cream is, as we have seen, a process of nature which we best promote by giving to our dairies a northern exposition; by keeping them perfectly clean; because filth, besides other mischief, is predisposed to fermentation, and is, of course, productive of heat; and, lastly, by so forming our pans as to make them narrow at the bottom and wide at the top, to the end that they may offer to the atmosphere the largest possible surface.*

2d. The separation of the butter from the milk, with which it is still connected, is our own labour, and must be carefully and thoroughly performed. This is called churning, and ought to be only a moderate and continued agitation. If the movement be too slow or frequently interrupted, the effect intended is not produced; and if hurried and violent, the cream is too much heated, and yields a white and curdlike butter. When this operation is well performed, the butter is found adhering to the staff and flyers of the churn, is of an agreeable taste and colour, and of a certain degree of consistency.

* See, in Fourcroy's Chymistry, vol. ix., the effects of covering milk-pans.

3d. To increase this last, and more perfectly to discharge the milk from the butter, the latter is again subjected to frequent pressure and washing in cold water, which, readily uniting with the milk, carries it along with it.

4th. What now remains is to employ the means necessary to its preservation. These are of two kinds; a small portion of common salt, well dried and pulverized, may be wrought into the mass, and distributed as equally as possible; or the fresh mass, subjected to a demi-fusion, will throw up a frothy and feculent matter, which must be carefully taken off, and which, if neither evaporated nor skimmed in this way, nor absorbed by the salt in the other, would produce the rancidity of which we have already spoken. The butter of Prevalais, the finest in Europe, is prepared after this last mode. The secret was long and well kept, but was at length divulged by M. Tessier, about the year 1809.

Of cheese-making.

The *curd* of milk is known to be the basis of *cheese*, and the theory of making this may be brought under three heads.

1st. *Turning the milk*, or separating the curd from the other constituents of milk, by a chymical process, or by permitting it to separate spontaneously.

2d. *Expressing what remains of these from the curd* by mechanical means; and,

3d. *Seasoning the mass*, by the introduction of some matter of conservative quality, as muriate of soda, sage, balm, aromatic clover, &c., &c.

These principles may be much varied, and, under different managements, will produce cheeses of very different species, which may, however, be generalized as follows :

1st. Those in the fabrication of which the coagulation of the milk is spontaneous. This species retains a great degree of softness, is peculiarly liable to decomposition, and is therefore used in a shor* time after being made. Such is the cream cheese, and the cheeses of Viry, Mont Didier, and Mont d'Or.

2d. Those which have been deprived of their serosity by means only of compression. Such are the cheeses of Holland, of Cantal in France, &c. And,

3d. Those to which have been applied, not only the action of the press, but of fire. Such are the cheeses known by the name of Gruyere, Parmesan, and Cheshire.*

Of these different species it is our intention to speak only of the second and third, because these form the cheeses of commerce, and have most connexion with the public interest.

Turning the milk, which is the first step in the process, may be effected by many different substances, such as vegetable acids and astringents ; but the matter generally, if not universally employed, is either the second stomach of the calf or its contents, which are called *rennet.* A portion of either put into the milk, which must be left in a state of repose, will in a few hours produce the desired separation. The quantity of rennet employed is not, however, a matter of indifference. If too much be used, the curd will remain in parcels, without consistency, and altogether deprived of the cream of the milk. If, on the other hand, the quantity employed be too small, the separation of the curd from the serum will not be complete. The exact quantity necessary is an affair of experience, which only a number of trials on different portions of milk enables one to regulate and adjust. A cir-

---

* The *Schabzieger* (cheese made in Switzerland) is of a dif ferent kind. Instead of the curd, the Swiss employ the sedi ment of the serum, and macerate in it a few of the leaves, stems, or seeds of the trifolium oderatum, or blue clover. It is this which gives to the Schabzieger its peculiar and highly aromatic taste and smell.

cumstance of still greater importance, but of less difficulty, is that of determining the character of the rennet. If this emit any strong or disagreeable odour, it is bad, and should not be employed, as it will infallibly communicate to the curd its own offensive qualities.

As soon as the curd is separated, it must be broken into pieces, so that the serum, which is now collected into little cells, may have the means of escaping. By this operation the curd is reduced to a paste, which acquires coherency as fast as the fluid is separated from it. This paste is now put into moulds, and compressed until a farther portion of the moisture is expelled. When this effect is produced the curd is again divided, squeezed by the hand, replaced in the moulds, and subjected to heavy weights, which expel the last remaining drops of the whey. If the weather be warm, the cheeses will swell and cavities appear on their surfaces; an effect of the disengagement of air, which is the sign of interior fermentation, and the signal for removing the cheeses to the drying room, and beginning the application of salt to their surfaces and sides. This application must be continued daily, and the cheeses be turned as often, so that the salt be equally distributed throughout them. If they present a dry surface, they should be wetted with salted whey; and if a frothy appearance, they should be carefully wiped and the outer rind scraped with a blunt knife. They will soon acquire the necessary hardness and the proper colour.*

In these operations we have described the mode of making cheeses deprived of their serosity by *compression* only. What we have yet to say applies to those in the making of which *fire* is a necessary agent. The milk destined for these is

* The Italians employ saffron, and the English the bixa, to colour their cheeses. These are only expedients to make *new* cheese pass for *old* in the market.

placed in a boiler and on a moderate fire; the rennet is then applied, and the milk stirred without interruption. The moment the action of the rennet becomes apparent, the boiler is taken from the fire and the contents left undisturbed. A coagulation soon takes place, when a portion of the serum must be removed, and the remaining portion be left to boil the curd, which is seen floating in distinct parcels or lumps. The boiler must now be replaced on the fire, and the mass be continually stirred until the curd takes a degree of coherency. When this effect is produced the boiling is complete, and the curds, collected into masses, are taken from the serum and committed to moulds. The press is now employed and the salt applied, as in the preceding directions. During three weeks or a month, the moulds are gently and gradually tightened, and, so soon as a superabundant moisture appears on the surface of the cheese, the salting is discontinued.*

Various means have been used to improve the qualities of cheese, besides those employed in the process of fabrication. Though we give little credit to these devices, still, as others may have more faith than ourselves, it may not be improper to mention some of them. The most simple and most easily employed are, rubbing them with oil, with butter not salted, with the lees of wine, and sometimes enveloping them with linen dipped in vinegar, or in new hay moistened with warm water. Another, more compounded and not so easily obtained, has fallen within the scope of our reading. It is, given by M. Chazotte, inspector of mines to the Duke of Parma, who says of it "that cheeses the most dry and of the worst quality, if moistened daily for twenty or thirty days with a liquor composed of strong vinegar and alkalized nitre, and which entirely resembles the *foliated earth of tartar*, known

* This appearance shows that the absorption of salt is complete.

to chymists and physicians, will become excellent."
What on this head is suggested by our own experience is, that, if not made better, they are assuredly best preserved by dark apartments, neither very
dry nor very humid, and by shelves or tables frequently washed, and not containing in them any res-
inous matter.

Of the residuum or whey left after cheese-making.

This is not without its uses, and some of them important.   The medicinal virtues of whey have been
long acknowledged and much celebrated, and appear to be beyond even the reach of time, which
has neither abated their force nor diminished their
fame; for, when all other remedies fail, the modern
valetudinarian, like the ancient, is dismissed to
mountain air and whey diet.   The lives of literary
men furnish many striking instances of its nourishing as well as its medicinal properties.   Boerhave
persevered in the use of it, to the exclusion of other
food, for many months; and Ferguson for many
years.   Its effect in fattening hogs is universally
known.   This nutritive property exists in the mucus sugar with which it abounds; the extraction of
which has long employed the science and industry
of the Swiss cantons.*

* See Lichtenstein and Rocol on the sugar of milk.   The
maximum of its quantity 1-28th; the minimum 1-60th.   Scheele
has shown that this saccharine matter differs essentially from
the sugar of canes.   See Fourcroy's Chymistry, vol ix.

CHAPTER XIV.

OF ORCHARDS.

THESE are generally composed of apple, pear, peach, and cherry trees. The *apple* has been known from the most remote antiquity, and, from the names given to it, would appear to have been a native of many different countries.[*]

About the close of the 15th century, the varieties of this fruit in Europe were multiplied to the number of forty-six,[†] and it is not to be doubted but that four additional centuries have much increased this amount. While, however, the line was lengthening in this direction, it was shortening in another; for, according to the philosophy of the present day, vegetables, like animals, perish not only individually, but by whole races.[‡]

The uses of the apple are various. Besides those of the table, it yields the well-known liquor called cider, which is again convertible into brandy. We have, in our country, orchards which annually produce from five to eight hundred dollars. In the view of profit, therefore, fruit is an important object to the agriculturist.[§]

---

[*] The Syrian, Scanian, Pelusian, &c. About one hundred years before Christ, the Romans began to call them after particular men who had been instrumental in removing them; as the Appian, or Pomme D'Api of the French, after Claudius Appius.

[†] See Olivier de Serres.

[‡] See Davy's Elements.

[§] One of the most important uses of the apple in the present day, and to which it was not formerly applied, or but partially, is the feeding and fattening of pigs and other farm-stock. For this purpose alone, apple-orchards now constitute one of the most profitable objects of farm culture.—J. B.

The *pear* is less difficult with regard to soil than the apple tree. We have seen it grow well in light sand; and a part of Normandy, called Bocage, the soil of which is a stiff clay, is renowned for its pears, and for a liquor called *Perry*, made from their juices.*

Oliver de Serres counted *sixty-two* varieties of the pear; and, according to the treatise of M. Van Mons, published in 1808, the number then cultivated in Europe amounted to more than six hundred. Of these we shall name a few, in the order in which they ripen. The Muscat l'Allemand, in May; the St. John and the Bergamot of Holland, in June; the Petit Muscat and the Cuisse Madame, or Jargonelle, in July; the Salviat and the Bon Chretien d'Ete Musque, in August; the Beurre Gris, in September; the Bergamot Suisse and Messire Jean, in October; the Bon Chretien Turc and the fall Bergamot, in November; the Chasserais, the Beurre d'Hiver, the Merveille d'Hiver, the Vergouleuse, the St. Germain, and the Sarrussin, in December.‡

* When made without the addition of water, Perry is an excellent liquor, and keeps well in bottles.

† We offer this list as a direction to those who may wish to obtain the best succession of crops, and have therefore retained the names under which they are known abroad.

‡ The pears here named belong to the old catalogue; the quality of the new kinds, named by Van Mons, not then being known to us. The new varieties have since been introduced and fruited, and have added much to the value and variety of this fruit. We recommend the following, embracing mostly new varieties, as a better selection than the one named in the text. They should be added to old collections, and in new plantations may be advantageously introduced as substitutes for old, and, in many cases, degenerated varieties. Beginning with the early varieties, we recommend the Citron des Carmes, Jargonelle, Summer Rose, &c., ripening in July and August; the Belle et Bonne, Vergaleu, or White Doyenne, Flemish Beauty, Neill, &c., as ripening in September: the Autumn Bergamot, Aston Town, Capiaumont, Beurre d'Œil, Duchesse d'Angouleme, Maria Louise, &c., ripening in October; the Forello, Glout Morceau, Napoleon, Colmar, &c., ripening in November; the

The *cherry-tree* is said to have been first brought to Europe by Lucullus, from Asia Minor. A German amateur (the Baron de Truckless) has brought together, in his garden in Franconia, *sixty-five* species of it. Besides the raw fruit, the cherry is much employed in confitures, and gives also three liquors in much request, the Kirschenwasser of Germany, the Marrasquin of Venice, and a distilled but unfermented liquor of the Rhine, having nothing in it spirituous, and retaining only the watery and aromatic parts of the fruit. The cherry-tree dreads cold or wet soils, nor does it succeed well in those which are either hot or dry. Its outer skin differs in its organization from that of other trees; the fibres are longer and stronger, and sometimes so bind the woody part as to obstruct its growth. Hence the practice of making shallow and longitudinal cuts through the outer bark; a practice, however, which, like pruning, ought to be skilfully performed, otherwise the wound becomes gummy, chancrous, and incurable.*

The *peach-tree* is a native of Persia, where it grows without cultivation. Its varieties are very numerous, all of which are much influenced by climate and soil. In Europe it is only in the south of France, in Italy, and in Spain, where you find peaches that have reached the perfection of which this fruit is susceptible ; and in similar climates here we may, no doubt, have fruit equally good. Our own climate (that of New-York) does not appear to be favourable to its production. Our trees are often sickly, and our peaches generally sour and watery, and entirely destitute of that aroma· which forms the great excellence of this fruit. After these gen-

Nelis, Passe Colmar, Bezi Vait, Beurre d'Aremburgh, &c., ripening in December; the Easter Beurre, Beurre Rance, Chaumohtelle, &c., as late winter and spring pears; and the Cattilsc, Chaptal, Bezi d'Hui, as good baking or stewing pears.—J. B.

* Cut only the outer or circular bark.—J. B.

eral remarks, we proceed to what is more particularly the object of this chapter.

It has been said, and, we think, with much good sense, that "every farmer ought to raise his own trees," because, besides the risk, inconvenience, and expense of bringing our plants from abroad, we have, in pursuing that mode of supply, to encounter the tricks and blunders of nurserymen, and the ill consequences which follow a want of analogy between the soil in which the plants were raised and that to which they are to be transferred. The first step, therefore, towards obtaining a good orchard, is to create a good *nursery*. The situation most favourable for this is a piece of level ground, defended from cold and violent winds either by natural or artificial means, and which, in composition, is neither wet nor dry, and of only middling fertility. This condition of the soil is a circumstance of much importance, and ought to be rigorously observed, because the vessels of young trees growing in rich soils take a size proportioned to the quantity of sap they receive and circulate; and if their situation be changed for the worse, the quantity of the sap being necessarily diminished, the vessels become rigid and unhealthy, and unable to carry to the extremity of the branches the nourishment required by them. The ground, selected on these principles, must be securely fenced, thoroughly ploughed and harrowed, freed from stones and the roots of perennial plants, and then thrown up into three or four feet ridges, on which you will sow and cover your apple and pear seed, and plant your cherry and peach stones. It will now be useful to roll the beds for the purpose of bringing the soil and the seeds everywhere into contact; after which they may be covered with clean straw for the winter. In the spring your young apple and pear-trees will show themselves, and afterward your cherries and peaches. The treatment to all will be the same : they must be thinned to the distance of fifteen or twenty inches from each other, kept perfectly free from weeds, and, if the weather be hot and dry, occasionally watered. They require only a repetition of this process, with the addition of a little careful pruning, till they have attained the height of seven or eight feet, when they are fit for grafting.* It is generally known that by this operation we continue any given species of fruit; but a fact with which the public is less acquainted is, that if the graft be also grafted, the product is improved both in quantity and quality ; and, it is to be presumed, will continue to improve under every new and similar operation. Grafts, to be well chosen, should be taken from wood of the present year, from young and healthy races, and accommodated to the future use of the fruit. If, for instance, your object be cider-making, you will take your grafts from the crab or the redstreak ;† and if for barrelling, from the pippin, the Spitzenberg, the greening, or the Swaur. As we only speak of grafting incidentally, it will not be expected that we should go into a dissertation upon that art, nor to elucidate the many divisions and subdivisions which technical men have made of it.‡ It is enough for us to say, that, of all these different modes, the *scion* and the *slit* is the simplest and the

* Budding is generally preferred to grafting in nursery establishments, because it gives a longer season for propagating, is more expeditiously performed, more certain, especially with stone fruit, and may be performed upon stocks a year or two earlier than grafting. Budding should be performed when the stock is from the size of a pipestem to the size of the little finger.—J. B.

† The redstreak is no longer with us in a healthy condition ; it has degenerated. The Harrison, winesap, pippin, and crab, are our best cider fruits.—J. B.

‡ The two grand divisions are by *approach* and by *scion*. Their varieties and sub-varieties, nearly a hundred, are known by the names of ancients and moderns, as Varro, Virgil, Columella, Malherbes, Duhamel, Bosc, Michaux, &c., &c

best. When your grafts have acquired some inches in length, it may be well to rub off *all* the buds which have pushed *below* them on the stem, and perhaps a *few* of those which have appeared *above* them ;* and if the grafts themselves put out any lateral shoots, spare them till the succeeding year, when you are called to regraft such as have failed, and to furnish props to those which are feeble, or crooked, or ill-directed.

Planting is the next operation in the process ; but, as some preliminary measures, on which its success will much depend, are yet untouched, we will begin with these ; and,

1st. Of the soil chosen for your intended orchard. It is generally admitted that fruit-trees do well in a warm, friable, moist, and deep soil ; that they succeed but indifferently in one that is cold and stiff, and that they altogether fail in one either very dry or very wet; but a fact less known, though not less established, is, that the subsoil has a powerful influence on the health and prosperity of plants. If this be rock, or what is called hardpan, whatever be the surface, the tree and its fruit are much deteriorated ; nor will the remedy, sometimes resorted to, of cutting off the pivot or plunging-root, and leaving the tree to subsist by those which are merely lateral, be sufficient. It may palliate, but it does not cure.

2d. Next to soil, *exposition* is most important. In this climate northern and western expositions are bad ; because the tree has least time for vegetation, its juices are less concocted, and it is itself most

* Many grafts are annually lost by removing the upper buds, shoots, and limbs. It throws too much nourishment into the graft, which dies of repletion. Having omitted in the text to say anything of the different *stems* employed in grafting, we here remark, what all amateurs in fruit-trees ought to know, that scions, whether of apple or pear trees, grafted on *quince* stocks, give fairer fruit and much sooner than if grafted on apple or pear stocks ; but the trees are short-lived.

exposed to the action of high winds. These remarks will sufficiently indicate why eastern and southern expositions are favourable, and ought to be preferred. But the rule these facts suggest cannot be made absolute, since many persons occupy only the northern and western sides of hills. In these situations, therefore, the course most approved by theory and experience is, to plant only trees which are late in forming or maturing their fruit.

3d. The preparation of the soil is not to be neglected, and any summer crop in rows and well cultivated forms a good one. With these remarks we return to our general head of *planting*.

The *form* in which your trees stand is not matter of indifference. The *quincunx* is recommended as giving to them that position which is relatively best ; but the *caize* (straight lines intersecting each other), better admitting the movements of the plough, is generally preferred. Whichever of the two be adopted, the holes indicated in a former part of this section must be made accordingly, and ought to be six feet wide and as many long, and two feet deep. The advantages of these will abundantly repay the extra labour they require, as we find by M. Chalumeau's experiments on peach-trees, from which we make the following extract: "Four peach-trees, resembling each other, as to size and vigour of growth, as much as possible, were planted: No. 1 in a hole three feet square ; No. 2 in a hole two feet square ; and Nos. 3 and 4 in holes eighteen inches square. The soil and exposition similar. No. 1 has every year given the most abundant crops, and the relative sizes of the trees now are as follows: the stem of No. 1, 18 feet high and eight inches in circumference: that of No. 2, nine feet high and five and a half inches in circumference ; No. 3, six feet high, and three inches eight lines in circumference ; and No. 4, five and a half feet high, and three inches in circumference." Here is a difference between the largest and smallest of five inches in circumference and 12 1-2 feet in height; a most decisive proof of the advantages of trenching.*

When the holes are thus prepared, and at a distance not less than 30 feet from each other, and a portion of the soil, is mixed with marl, the mud of ponds, or bog-earth, returned to them, you may begin to take up your young trees from the nursery; and, in doing this, you must be careful not to wound or otherwise injure their roots or their bark; nor must they suffer any topping or pruning. Three hands are necessary to planting; one to place and range the trees, and the others to fill in the remaining part of the earth, mixed as above mentioned. It now only remains to fix short poles (technically called tutors) near them, to which they may be tied, and by means of which their true vertical position may be preserved.

The year after planting, and in the month of February,† when there is no circulation of sap, you will do well to begin to give to the heads of your young trees that form which you wish them ultimately to take. The more circular you make them, the better, always taking care to lop off those branches which do already, or may hereafter, cross others having a proper direction. This proper direction will be generally horizontal, but with a slight curve; an opinion requiring, perhaps, a little explanation. All straight branches produce what are usually termed gourmands, or gluttons, giving little if any fruit themselves, and exceedingly exhausting the tree. Curved branches, on the other hand, rarely produce gourmands; and, when the season is favourable, give much fruit. The observation of these facts, made

* The apple, pear, and cherry, occupying more room than the peach, require proportionate trenches.

† The last of June, after the tree has made its first growth, and is charged with elaborated sap, is recommended as the best time for performing this operation.—J. B.

long since, and probably growing out of the management of espaliers, first suggested the practice of bending straight branches by artificial means. The effect entirely justified the theory; these straight and barren branches, bent into nearly half a circle,* changed their character with their shape, and became very productive. But there is a time for this as for all other things, and, unless the experiment be began about the first of July and continued to September, it will fail, because it is only within that period that fruit buds are formed.†

As your trees advance in age, they will require *pruning*. Suckers must be removed, and dead and dying limbs taken off. For this purpose a hand-saw, a chissel, a mallet, and a gardener's knife, are the instruments to be used: all others must be proscribed, and particularly the axe, which, in the hands of folly and ignorance, has been so mischievous to fruit-trees. Wounds, if large, should always be covered from drying winds, from moisture, and even from air. In gummy trees, as the peach or the cherry, this precaution is indispensable, and the neglect of it a disgrace, since the best covering is that composed of cow-dung and clay; materials costing nothing, and always at hand.

On this subject we have but one other rule to give, and that is, to open the ground about the roots of your trees in the fall, to the influences of the air, rain, and frost. The last of these, besides promoting vegetation, destroys many insects in the chrysalis state, which, if left undisturbed, would in the spring be very injurious. Another part of the same rule is to cover with straw, in the spring, the ground you make bare in the fall; the object of which is to prevent evaporation by intercepting the rays of the

* More than half a circle will obstruct the circulation of sap and destroy the limb.

† The circulation of the sap is then slowest. See Art. Cour bure, Nouveau Cours d'Agriculture, vol. iv.

sun, and thus securing to the roots the moisture necessary to their welfare.

———

CHAPTER XV.

THE KITCHEN GARDEN.

THE first page of history informs us that, immediately after the creation, man was placed in a garden, "to dress and to keep it." Nor will the wisdom of this designation be doubted by those who duly consider the effects, moral and physical, of the occupation it enjoins. "Emollit mores, nec sinet esse feros," is an observation of great antiquity and acknowledged truth; to which might be added others of equal authority and importance, viz.: that it expands the mind, strengthens the body, tranquillizes the spirit,* and begets habits of order, diligence, temperance, economy, and observation.†

Thus recommended (apart from its pecuniary

———

* Lord Bacon calls it "the purest of human pleasures, the greatest refreshment to the spirits of man, without which buildings and palaces are but gross handiworks."

† Of those among the ancients who may be considered as authorities, Cicero is perhaps alone in regarding the retirement of rural life as tending rather to relax than to invigorate the mental faculties.—De Orat., i., 2. Pliny, on the other hand, remarks, "Experieris non Dianam magis montibus, quam Minervam inerrare." We need scarcely quote the well-known decisions of Horace and Virgil. "Scriptorum chorus omnis amat nemus, et fugit urbes." "Rura mihi et regni placeant," &c. The controversy, after all, is one of *words*; for besides that there may have been some peculiarity of mind in Cicero, calling for an uncommon kind or degree of stimulus, it must not be forgotten that his great and distinguishing talent could only receive development and exercise from the presence and agitations of a crowd.

profits), it will not be thought extraordinary that gardening, considered both as a science and an art should have engaged the attention of able and learned men, who, at different times and in various languages, have written upon it. To collect and methodize their remarks and experiments, to illustrate their different doctrines, and to adapt the whole to our own climate, soil, and social condition, form the leading objects of the present work.

Another important, though a secondary object, is to bring what is known and necessary on so copious a subject into the smallest compass, persuaded, as we are, that the highest service that can now be rendered to science is to shorten and illustrate its processes, and thus render attainable by many what otherwise would be known only to few.

Gardens are technically classed under five heads: the Kitchen Garden, the Fruit Garden, the Flower Garden, the Botanic Garden, and the Landscape, commonly, but improperly, called the English Garden. These have many principles in common, but some which are peculiar, and they consequently call for different kinds of culture, and different sorts and degrees of knowledge in the cultivator. We shall treat here only of the two first named; and begin with the Kitchen Garden.

This is the description of garden most important to man, because employed in the production of articles of the first necessity, and common to every class of society. Several conditions are, however, necessary to enable it to fulfil this intention. Such are, sufficient fences, a good soil, a favourable exposition, and abundant water. The *first*, to be sufficient, ought to have the property not only of excluding the depredations of man and beast, but that also of shutting out vermin, and even some of the tribes of larger insects. The *second* should be deep, rich, friable, and moist (not wet), because this description of soil is best adapted to the mass of garden vegetables, and not positively unfriendly to any. The *third* should have an inclination to the south and east, as this exposure will best secure that temperature both of the earth and of the air which is most favourable to vegetation; and of the *fourth* we need only remark, that it is emphatically called the life of plants.*

The size and shape of this species of garden are not indifferent, but admit no positive rules for their regulation, because depending on circumstances rarely alike in two cases; the nature of the ground, and the wants or ability of the occupier. On these heads, therefore, we only say that a parallelogram and a square are the forms most approved, because most susceptible of a cheap, and easy, and regular arrangement into beds; and that *two acres†* devoted to the culture of table vegetables will furnish an abundant supply for even a large family.

With these few preliminary remarks, we proceed to what is more peculiarly the object of this branch of our work, viz., an enumeration of the articles selected for garden culture, and the means best calculated for bringing them to that degree of perfection of which they may be respectively susceptible.

THE ARTICHOKE (*Cynara Scolymus*). The prototype of this race is a native of the south of Europe, and rarely to be found in northern climates, excepting in botanical collections; the varieties produced by culture are much preferable to the parent plant.‡

---

* Water impregnated with minerals is not merely useless, but injurious to vegetation. Such is often the water found in wells, and sometimes in rivulets. River and rain water may always be safely employed, as well from their constituent parts as from their temperature. Every garden should have a pond to receive and hold rain water.

† The author, doubtless, would include potatoes, and esculent garden vegetables of every kind in this estimate.

‡ Miller considers the globe artichoke, which he calls the Cynara Hortensis, as a distinct species from the Cynara Scolymus, and rests his opinion on the difference between the two

These varieties are numerous, and take their distinctive names from their colour : as the green, the red, the violet, and the white. The first of these (the green) is the best, as well on account of its larger size, as its better flavour and greater ability to resist cold and wet weather; the constant and most formidable enemy of the whole family.

This plant is propagated in two ways, by seed and by suckers; by the former when it is desired to obtain new races, and by the latter when we wish to continue old ones. The first method is occasionally practised by amateurs, and is that by which the plant may be soonest *naturalized*, and made to attain its highest perfection. The second is preferred by practical men seeking immediate profit, and risking as little as possible on experiments.*

If the first method be adopted, select sound and fresh seeds, and, in the month of February, sow them in pots filled with rich and mellow earth, and plunged in a hotbed. Each pot may receive three seeds. The young plants will soon show themselves, and, by watering and ventilating them at proper times and in a moderate degree, will be fit for transplanting in April. If the second method be preferred, after having carefully uncovered and cleaned the stems of the mother plants, take from them, with the hand, as many sprouts or suckers as may be wanted, remembering that those nearest the heart are the best ; and taking care also to crop the sprouts close to the stem, and always below what gardeners call the *nut*, and without chafing or otherwise injuring the fibres which surround this, and which are destined to become the roots of the future artichoke.

Such are the two modes of obtaining plants, to

in relation to bulk and to shape. The later, and, we think, the better opinion is, that this difference is the effect only of culture.

* The average loss of plants from the seed-bed is one half, that from suckers only one tenth.—Cours d'Ag.

which we now add the subsequent management common to both.

In hot and dry climates, the soil best adapted to the artichoke is that which is most retentive of moistnre, and vice versa. In our own particular climate, which may be regarded as a medium between the two extremes, a soil neither very wet nor very dry is to be preferred. A portion of this, of such extent as the required number of plants may render necessary, which has been previously and thoroughly worked and manured, should be raked smooth, and so scored, both lengthwise and across, as to form a number of beds or squares of *three feet* —in the centre of each of which a hole is to be dibbled and an artichoke placed—remembering, however, before you do so (if the plants are seedlings), to pinch off the tap or pivot root,* and to leave as much of the native soil as the lateral roots will hold together, and (whether seedlings or suckers) to press with your hand or your dibbler the earth into close contact with the buried part of the plant, leaving only the heart uncovered. When this is done, sow rows of lettuce seed in the intervals between the artichokes; which, besides giving an additional and useful article to your crop, will best protect from the ravages of the grub that which is your primary object; for many observations concur in showing that, where the grub has the power of

---

* The facts on which this theory rests are two. 1st. That it is the peculiar office of the pivot to give sustenance to the stem and leaves, and of the lateral roots to supply the suckers and heads, which are the things we want. Now if the pivot be removed, the lateral roots acquire an increased vigour, and the head is made better in proportion. " M. Feburier, of Rennes, planted two rows of artichokes, the one with pivot roots, the other deprived of them. The former threw out leaves so long and numerous, that it became necessary to thin them; but their fruit was neither abundant nor fine, while the latter grew well, and gave fruit much better and earlier than the other."—Cou s d'Agri., art. Artichoke.

choosing, it never fails to prefer the lettuce to the artichoke.

The processes of watering and hoeing are next in order of time, and are either multiplied, or decreased, or discontinued, according to circumstances. The rules which regulate these labours are two : if the weather be dry, and you wish to hasten the maturity of the fruit, you must hoe often and water every other day. If, on the contrary, the weather be wet, and you have other beds to draw from for the supply of the current year, hoe seldom and do not water at all ; and by this management you may either quicken or retard the progress of the plant.

To have large artichokes, you must leave only one sprout to a stem ; and in this case, the taking off the surplus suckers should not be delayed beyond the first week in July. If, on the other hand, you disregard the size of the fruit, you may leave the plant to regulate its own products as to number. The maturity of the fruit is indicated by the opening of the scales, and we must be careful to take it before the flower begins to show itself ; and in doing this, to cut it close to the ground, leaving no stump to impoverish the root. It is a practice not uncommon to dig and loosen the earth around the roots in the fall of the year, and in dry and warm winter climates the practice is not a bad one ; but in ours, where frosts are severe and snows frequent, it would be highly injudicious, as earth recently dug absorbs and retains moisture more, and, consequently, freezes sooner and deeper, than that which has not been worked for some months preceding ; a remark which, by-the-way, calls us to the consideration of the best means of preserving the outstanding plants during the winter.

Various means have been employed for this purpose. That which is most commonly used is, after stripping off the dead or decaying leaves, and trimming down the sound ones to three or four inches to open trenches around the plant, and to draw up about it the earth furnished by these.   This is again covered with long dung or stable litter, so as entirely to exclude rain, and snow, and frost.   But, in making these provisions against cold and wet weather, we must not forget that it is possible to be careful over-much; for if the mounds of earth and litter be large and close, we expose our plants to suffocation from want of air; to exhaustion from a continued vegetation, and to scorching from the fermentation of the covering matter, which, if the weather be wet and but occasionally warm, seldom fails to occur.

To obviate these difficulties, it has been proposed that the mounds be *gradually* formed; that the first covering be merely a wrapping of long dung, and that the additions made to it be conformed to the weather, leaving openings in all cases on its southern side for the purposes of ventilation, and in no case permitting the covering to exceed two feet in thickness.*   But even this mode of treatment is not free from objection; for, first, the direct application of the dung to the plant will always alter its flavour, and very much degrade it; and again, the capriciousness of the weather does not generally give either warning of its changes, or time to accommodate ourselves to them: they often take place in the night, and often (whether in the night or in the day) under circumstances which prevent us from giving to the plant the additional covering it may require.   Two other methods, therefore, not dissimilar in themselves, have been suggested; the one, to employ hollow cylinders of earthenware, covered with a tile or piece of slate, and of capacity sufficient to embrace the plant; the other, to form caps of straw (such as are used for lodging bees), and having a moveable top of the same ma-

* This suggestion is M. Thouin's; the writer of the excellent article on the artichoke, to be found in the Encyclopédie Methodique.

terial.* To the last method we see no room for objection: in application it is easy, requiring no skill and little labour, while the material and workmanship are both cheap and durable, and their property of excluding rain, snow, and frost, not to be doubted.

Every gardener who understands his trade will take care to set apart a few of the finest heads of his own crop for seed; but as the stock is upright, and the head so formed as to receive and hold water, it often happens that the seeds rot. To prevent this, the stems of the plants so set apart should be tied to stakes driven into the ground near them, and gradually bent, so as to give to the heads that degree of declination that will be sufficient to carry off the water that may fall upon them.

When well managed, the artichoke will give fruit four or five years in succession; but, to avoid accidents, new plantations should be made every year.

In some parts of Europe, as in France and Italy, the taste for this vegetable is excessive, and much beyond what it merits on the score either of nutritiousness or flavour. Of this partiality the gardeners avail themselves, and by employing the varieties which ripen soonest and latest, contrive to keep the plant in the market (in its natural state) seven or eight months of the twelve; and means are then employed to prolong its use, by converting it into a comfit. In this country the taste for it is neither common nor great; and as the culture is expensive and not always successful, we have doubts whether, to gardeners who cultivate for the market, it is deserving of much attention.

ASPARAGUS (*Maratimus Officinalis*). Of this plant there are ten species, one of which only is an object of garden culture, and to this botanists have given the name prefixed to this article.

* The earthen cylinders have been proposed by M. Bosc, of the French Institute, and the straw caps by M. Feburier, of Rennes.

Vegetables which have been long cultivated have in general many varieties; but to this law the asparagus appears to be an exception, having, as we believe, but *two*, and these differing from each other only in volume. They are found growing spontaneously in high northern latitudes, near the mouths of great rivers, where the soil is annually covered with a new coat of alluvial matter. The natural life of an individual plant does not exceed five years; but, left undisturbed in its native bed, it rises in the spring, ripens its seeds in the summer, and in autumn sheds them on the soft and rich surface which the spring floods have prepared for them: and in this way continues to propagate the race from one century to another.

These facts could not have been either long observed or much considered, without suggesting the kind of treatment which would be most proper for the plant when transferred to an artificial bed; yet the modes indicated for this purpose have been very different, and, like other things of even less consequence, have given rise to much and warm discussion. Of these disputed points the principal are, whether sowing or planting gives the most profit; whether plants of one, of two, or of three years are to be preferred; whether the seedbed should be as rich, or less so than the plantation; and, lastly, whether this (the plantation) should be formed on the surface of the earth in its natural state, or on an excavation filled up with new and better materials.

The first of these questions appears to us to turn principally on convenience. If we can postpone the use of the plant for a year or two, sowing is to be preferred; because the crop it gives (other things being equal), though later in coming, is more abundant, of better quality, and of longer duration; but if our supply must be prompt, planting is best, for by this mode we no doubt soonest obtain the fruit

The same or similar considerations influence the second question; but there are others which affect, and which may be thought sufficient to decide it. Roots of three years will not only give fruit sooner than those of one or of two years, but their fibres being harder and roots more numerous, are better able to sustain the violence inseparable from transplantation, and the other accidents (such as heating and chafing) which often accompany it, particularly if the roots be brought from a distance.

With regard to the third question we would only remark, that the translation of seedlings from the nursery to the plantation always forms a crisis in their health and character, during which they are best supported by giving to them an increased stimulus or nutrition. But if the seedbed be as rich as that of the plantation, the transferred plant has no support of this kind; and hence it is that, though it may not perish, it will not thrive.

The last question may be considered as one altogether of means or ability in the cultivator; and as among our readers there may be both poor and rich, we will give a sketch of both methods, the saving plan, and that which, though more expensive, is decidedly better.

First Method.—Manure the square (allotted for asparagus) largely, in the fall of the year, with well-rotted dung. Trench it to the depth of twenty or thirty inches, and leave it in a rough state during the winter. As early as possible in the spring, cover it with two or three inches of manure, and dig it to the depth of ten or twelve inches, taking care to mix the earth and the dung intimately together. The square being now dug and manured, level and smooth its surface, divide it into beds of four feet, drill these lengthwise with the spade or the hoe, and in the drills (which may be a foot apart) sow your seeds sparsely, or plant your roots, as the case may be, at the distance from each other (in the rows) of fourteen inches. If you sow, cover the seed with an inch of good soil; and if you plant, cover the roots to the depth of three inches with a similar soil. No other crop should be sown in these beds, and weeds should be carefully taken out by the hand from time to time. On the approach of winter, mow off the young asparagus, and cover the bed with stable litter. In the spring, rake off this covering, and keep the beds clean and loose during the summer. Continue the same process till the third year, when you may begin (but sparingly) to cut the plants for table use. Formed and managed in this way, and manured every third year afterward, an asparagus-bed will last ten or twelve years.*

Second Method.—In the summer or autumn preceding your sowing or planting, divide the square intended for asparagus into four feet beds, marking the angles by stakes, and leaving alleys between the beds of 1 1-2 or 2 feet. Excavate the beds to the depth of twenty-six inches, and if you find the bottom cold, and clayey, and retentive of moisture, sink it half a foot deeper. Lay on this six inches of coarse gravel, or stones, or both, and on these place a layer of equal depth of tanner's bark or chips, brushwood, weeds, horns, hoofs, or any other slowly-decomposing matter, vegetable or·animal. Over this spread another layer, composed of cow and horse dung mixed, to the depth of twelve inches, and on the top of all replace the surface soil you have thrown out, adding to it as much well-rotted dung as will entirely fill up the excavation. In this way you proceed to form the remaining beds; and, when all are finished, level and rake them, and remove the poor soil′thrown out in trenching. As early in the spring as the temperature of the weather and the state of the ground will permit, dig the beds

* American Gardener.

ten or twelve inches deep, and work into them as much well-rotted dung as will bring them to the level of the alleys (for they will have sunk considerably); after which, rake and smooth them, and trace out with the spade or the hoe four small trenches on each, not more than one inch deep; and in these sow fresh, and large, and well-ripened seed, and so sparsely, that, when the plants rise, they will not be found nearer together (in the rows) than fourteen inches. Draw an inch of mould over the seeds, and then ro'l or tread the rows, so as to press the seed and the earth everywhere into contact.

If, on the other hand, you prefer planting, select roots of one, of two, or of three years, remembering that "the *white* are only to be employed, and that those of a violet or livid colour are always hollow and unproductive."* In putting these down, your trenches must be deep enough to receive the roots and a covering of three inches. The crowns of these roots must be placed upright, and the *pattes* [or fingers], as they are sometimes called, spread and directed downward; for on their taking this direction (to the food provided for them) the prosperity of the plantation will principally depend. It now only remains to cover them, and that should be done with three inches of good fresh mould. In winter the plants may be left to themselves, as many experiments show that, in beds constructed in the way and of the materials we have described, they are never injured by frost; and farther, that, if the surfaces of such beds be entirely exposed to its

* Duchesne, Prof. Nat. History, Versailles. Another remark of this author is, that the *male* plants are much more profitable than the *female*, and that, therefore, whether we sow or plant, the number of seeds in the one case, and of roots in the other, should be double the number usually employed ; and that, at the time of flowering, when the sexes can be readily discriminated, the females should be destroyed.

action, the crop will be less liable to the attacks of insects the ensuing spring.

In the month of March or April (during the whole existence of the plant) the beds must be carefully forked and dressed, and kept clear of weeds.*· Occasional waterings are necessary till the third or fourth year, when the plants will be sufficiently established to do without them; but it is at this epoch, and in some degree as a substitute for watering, that you must cover your beds with three inches of additional earth.

With regard to the cutting of asparagus, it may not be unnecessary to remark, that this should not be done till the third year, and then but sparingly and late in the season; and that it should be discontinued the moment you find the buds dwindling in size and diminishing in number.

It will be readily perceived, that the modes of cultivation we have indicated are those only which furnish the article in its natural season; but as winter asparagus, like winter roses, takes an increased value from its rarity, it remains to say something of the method technically called *forcing*. The first step in this process is to procure a supply of three-year old plants (for none else are fit for the purpose), and the next to have a hotbed of proper temperature ready to receive them. You now trench its surface lengthwise, and by drawing the earth to the side of each trench, you form ridges, against which you set the roots, at the distance of two inches apart, the buds upright, and the fingers spread as directed in method second. They are then to be covered

* It has been lately asserted, and with sufficient confidence, that a pickle of salt and water, of the ordinary strength for preserving meat, may be very usefully applied to asparagus beds in the spring. The effects ascribed to it are its stimulating power upon the crop, and its tendency to destroy the seeds of weeds and of insects lying near the surface. Experiments on this subject should be multiplied, and with pickles differing in strength and quantity.

with mould, and the glasses to be replaced on the frames, and, when the buds begin to show themselves, they must have a second and similar covering.

The ventilation first of the bed, and subsequently of the plants, has distinct rules, requiring the strictest observance. With regard to the former, the general direction is, to give to the bed as much air as possible, without permitting the earth to be either frozen or chilled; with regard to the latter, so soon as the buds show themselves through the second covering of mould, ventilate every day, and throughout the day if the weather be good; but during the night, whatever may be the state of the weather, keep your glasses down, and constantly covered with straw matting.

Though we have thus far taken for granted that the temperature of the hotbed is a proper one, still, as accidents sometimes occur in that respect, and of a character and with effects directly opposite to each other, it may not be amiss to remark that, for ten days after the roots are put down, the degree of heat in the bed must be carefully watched, lest it be too great; and, if found to be so, holes must be immediately bored, with a stake of two or three inches diameter, into the fermenting mass from without, and other similar holes into the earth directly below the roots; and when, by these means, the heat is sufficiently moderated, the holes are to be carefully stopped. On the other hand, should the heat be found insufficient or to decline too rapidly, a moment must not be lost in giving a new lining of fresh and hot dung to the sides of the bed. The common method of ascertaining the degree of heat in these cases, is to run down a sharp-pointed stick between the roots, and, if it become suddenly and greatly heated, or heated in a small degree, or not at all, the conclusion is drawn accordingly. For ourselves, we have found the finger a very safe ther

13

mometer, and having this advantage over any other, that it is sure to be always at hand.

In four weeks the plants will be fit for use, and, if well managed, will give buds for three weeks to come. But it may be useful to notice, that the mode of taking these differs from that used for plants raised in the natural way. If you employ a knife, you cannot fail to destroy many young plants (on account of the closeness with which they stand to each other); but the mode by which you do least mischief is to thrust your finger down along side of the bud, and break it off at the root.

We shall close this article with the description of a method practised in France, which will probably be new to most of our readers, and which, we think, may be usefully employed as part of the hot-bed method just described. We quote from the N. Cours d'Agriculture, art. Asperge. "M. Sequen, of Baz-Sur-le-Seine, introduces the bud, the day it shows itself, into the neck of a broken or cracked bottle, through which it alternately mounts and descends until it completely fills the whole cavity. One of these plants is sufficient for a dish, weighs 14 oz., and is as tender and well flavoured as the buds taken in the ordinary way. The neck of the inverted bottle is pressed into the earth as far as it will go, and other means employed to keep it upright; a condition necessary to the success of the experiment."

The BEAN (*Faba*), a genus of plants according to Tournefort and Jessieu, and a species [of Vicia] according to Linnæus and other botanists. Olivier found it growing spontaneously in Persia, and considers it a native of that, or of some neighbouring part of Asia.

The ancients had many ridiculous prejudices in relation to this vegetable. In Egypt, to look at it was an act of uncleanness. In Greece, Pythagoras forbade its use; and at Rome, the Flamen Di alis was not permitted to name it. This proscription is differently accounted for by different writers. Clemens Alexandrinus ascribes it to a supposed property in the bean to create barrenness in animals; and Theophrastus superadds a similar property in relation to vegetables; while Cicero accounts for it by alleging that it "disturbed the mind, and obscured the faculty of divination by dreams." It has, however, surmounted all these prejudices, and has long been in general use, either in a green or dry state, in every part of the world.

Of the species we have mentioned, the horsebean is supposed to be the type, and has many varieties, known in different places by different names, as the Julian, the Mazagan, the Toker, the Sandwich, the Spanish, the green Genoa, and the Windsor. Of the Kidney bean (the Phaseolus Vulgaris), the varieties are still more multiplied, as they alter. when planted near each other, by reciprocal fecundation. La Buriays, in his La Quintanie, enumerates sixty, and M. Bosc says that, in the garden of M. Gavoty de Resthe, he had seen four hundred.*

But, however multiplied the races, the character and habits of the plants continue to be nearly the same. They all affect a strong, substantial, moist soil, well dug and abundantly manured; and the enemies they most dread are late and frosty springs, and early and hot summers. These circumstances cannot fail to attract the attention of the cultivator, and the more so as they involve a practical contradiction; for as the one invites to late planting, so the other would appear to forbid it. The only remedy, in this case, is to regulate our labours, not by the almanac, but by the temperature of the weather and the earth, which will never deceive us. When these begin to favour vegetation, and not before, dig and manure your ground thoroughly, and

* N. Cours d'Agriculture, art. Feve.

(after smoothing the surface and forming the drills) begin by planting the Toker, broad Spanish, and Windsor, and subsequently the Mazagan, early Lisbon, long pod, white blossom, and green Genoa, the former four inches apart in the rows, and the latter half that distance. The effect of this management will be to secure a succession of fruit, according to the different degrees of precocity in the plants ; and to make the varieties which bear cold the best the *first*, and those which are least injured by heat the *last* in the series.

The kidney-bean, being more sensible of cold and wet weather than the preceding species, must be planted later. Its varieties are divided into two races; the climbing and the dwarf (scandens et thumilis), the former requiring poles to support them, the other requiring no support. Of the first of these races, the most approved are, the Prague, the Prudhome, the altogether-yellow, and the red ; and of the second, the Dutch, the Laon, the yellow, and the Swiss.* After the preparatory labour indicated above, the climbers should be planted in groups (four or five together), with a pole, well fixed in the earth, for them to mount upon ; while the dwarfs should be placed in rows, at the distance of two or three inches from each other, and carefully covered. Squares of these (the dwarfs) may be planted from April till August, according to the taste and convenience of the cultivator. ·

The last species we shall mention and the latest to be sown, is the *Lima bean*, which ought not to be hazarded before the frosts are completely over, and then committed only to a rich, warm, and well-laboured soil. It is usually and best cultivated (like all other climbers) in what gardeners call *hills*, composed of rich mould, and separated six feet from

---

* A new variety of climbers, called the Horticultural bean, has lately come into notice, much admired for its rich flavour and prolific properties.—J. B. ·

each other. Four or five beans, and two or three stout poles nine or ten feet in length, are sufficient for each hill. When the beans begin to run they should be trained to mount the poles, for it is only by doing so that they will receive that degree of air and of sunshine which is necessary to the production of their fruit.*

Our remarks thus far have been confined, or nearly so, to the sowing of the bean. Those which follow apply to its management after that work is over, and are common to the labours necessary or useful to the whole family. When the plant has attained the length of three or four inches, the earth about its roots should be loosened with the hoe, and a fresh portion of it drawn up to the stem. The rule for subsequent labours is to hoe again when the flowers begin to show themselves, and a third time about a month after the second hoeing; but the better practice is to take as our guide, in this respect, not the condition of the plant, but that of the soil and of the weather; and, whenever the latter is dry and hot, or the former hard, or baked, or infested with weeds, repeat the hoeing; remembering that it is not easy to commit any excess in this way; and, in general, that the oftener the work is repeated (unless the weather be wet), the finer and more abundant will be the crop.

When the bean is sufficiently in blossom (which is taken for granted as soon as the lower or first formed pods begin to swell), it is a practice not uncommon to pinch off the tops of the vines; the object of which is to prevent the plant from having more pods than it can bring to perfection, and to render better those which are left, by giving to them a nutriment which would have otherwise gone to

* The Carolina bean is but a variety of the Lima, and is therefore to be managed in the same way, with the exception that, being less in volume, four feet t 'tween the hills give sufficient room for it.

the support of a useless portion of stem. But of this practice, and of the theory on which it is founded, we may be permitted to doubt, because it does not appear to follow that, when the growth of a plant is checked or suspended in one direction, it will not exert itself in another as injuriously to the crop as any increased length of stem would have done. Every day's experience shows that, if we pollard an apple-tree, we indeed stop its growth upward, but that, instead of sending its surplus juices to the support and enlargement of the fruit (as this practice supposes), it hastens to throw out lateral stems or suckers, which give no fruit whatever. Our creed therefore is, that in the vegetable economy, certain juices go to the production of stem, and certain others, more elaborated and of a different quality, to that of flowers and fruits; and that, whether desirable or not, the art of giving to either a destination different from what nature intended, is yet to be discovered.

The bean, of every species or variety, is exempt, as we believe, from the depredations of insects; but, left for seed or winter use, it often suffers from very dry or very wet weather; the one diminishing the bulk, and hardening and shrivelling the skin; the other rotting the bean, and, when it does least mischief, altering its flavour. For the former, frequent watering may be a cure, but for the latter there is perhaps no remedy.

In the neighbourhood of cities, the dwarf varieties are often cultivated in hotbeds, but the product is always of a very inferior kind; for, of the whole catalogue of table vegetables, none is more apt to take a disagreeable flavour from hot and fermented dung (which is the basis of these beds) than the bean. Of this process, therefore, we only say, that it differs in nothing from that already described for forcing asparagus.*

* N. C. d'Agriculture, art. Feve.

The BEET (*Beta*) is of the family of the Cheno-podees, and contains five species, two of which, the Beta Cycla and Beta Hortensis, are objects of garden culture. The former is what the English call the Maratime beet, and the French the Poirée. Some botanists have regarded this as the type of the genus, while others consider it a product of cultivation. Its varieties are two, the tall and the Dutch which are used for the same purposes; the leaves as salad, or as an ingredient in soups, either alone or mixed with sorrel ; and the roots as food for cattle, and particularly for hogs.

Of the second species there are five varieties, which take their names from their colour or size : the yellow, the white, the large red, the small red, and the white with red veins. It is to this last variety that M. Commeril has given the whimsical name of *Scarcity*, though its products per acre is greater than that of any other garden vegetable.*

Like all other garden plants, the beet is nutritive in proportion to the saccharine matter it contains. Of the varieties we have named, the yellow has the most, and the white veined with red the least of this matter. Yet the experiments of M. Deyeux prove that colour has less to do with this production than culture. "Two beds," says he, "of similar soil, and laboured alike, were sown with beet-seed of the same variety. One of these was highly manured with well-rotted dung, the other had no manure of any kind applied to it. The beets grown in the former were large, but, on analysis, yielded no saccharine matter, while those grown on the latter gave the ordinary quantity of sugar."

Margraff† was the first to extract from the beet

---

* See Arthur Young on the product of the beet, and a memoir of M. d'Aughbigny, in the 16th volume of the Transactions of the Agricultural Society of the Seine.

† About a century ago.

a marketable sugar, or what is called the sugar of commerce. Achard followed in the same track, and with a success that led him to believe that it might be afforded at the low price of five or six sous the pound; but later experiments, more carefully and scientifically made, under the direction of the French Institute, demonstrate that this product can never come into competition with sugar made from the cane.*† The saccharine mucus in which it abounds, and the disposition it has to vinous fermentation, has, however, long since suggested another employment of it, that of making brandy, and hence it is, that in countries in which the vine does not prosper (as in the north of Germany), great quantities of it are distilled into an ardent spirit.

The cultivation of the beet, whatever be its species or variety, is the same. Having prepared (by a thorough digging) a square of loose, rich, and deep soil‡ (which has been well manured the preceding fall), divide it into beds of four feet width; score

---

* It may not be amiss to mention here the process for making sugar from the beet, ascribed to Professor Gottling, and detailed in the 16th volume of the *Bibliotheque Brittanique.* "To disengage the saccharine matter from the mucus, which prevents it from crystallizing, cut the roots into long slices, and as thin as possible, and dry them on tiles in a stove. When thoroughly dry, put them for some hours in a small quantity of cold water. The sugar will pass from the beet to the water before the slices are softened, and may be again separated from it (the water) by evaporation and crystallization. If we attempt to dry the beet in the open air, many of them will rot; and if you put them in an oven, you run the risk of baking them. The residuum which this process leaves is useful for cattle, poultry, &c."

† This prediction has not been verified; for in France beet sugar *has* come into serious competition with that made from cane, in consequence of the manufacturing process being greatly improved and simplified, and the whole of the saccharine matter being now extracted from the roots.—J. B.

‡ Yet Mr. Cobbett recommends sowing beet seed in the fall, like parsnips, and says the frost cannot injure them!

these lengthwise about an inch and a half deep, and one foot asunder; drop the seeds* into these rows thinly, and draw over them a light covering of the surface soil, trodden down with the foot.

As the beet is easily affected by frost, the planting of the main crop should be delayed till the middle of May. A month after, or so soon as the plants have put out three or four leaves, thin the rows so as to leave the young beets at the distance of twelve or fourteen inches apart; and if there be chasms in the rows, as will sometimes happen from bad seed or unskilful sowing, fill these up with the surplus plants. The intervals between the rows should at the same time be thoroughly cleaned from weeds, and the oftener this operation is performed and the ground stirred during the whole course of vegetation in the plant, the larger will be the product and the better its quality. In dry weather, and during the infancy of the plant, watering is indispensable.

Some writers have proposed raising the beet in seedbeds and transplanting it; but experience forbids this practice, as the fact is well established that, other things being equal, the transplanted beet is never so fine as that which has been left undisturbed; a remark, by-the-way, which applies generally, perhaps universally, to tap-rooted plants.

As soon as vegetation is over, which always occurs after the first hard frost, take up the plants, expose them a day or two to the air to evaporate

---

* The same author attributes the *forking* of beets, not to stones or clods, as is generally done, but to working and manuring the ground around their roots, which, according to his theory, attracts one side of the root to the right and the other to the left, and never stops till it gives the plant two legs to stand upon instead of one. How happens it, then, that in deep, rich, .oose soils, whatever be the labour, there is no forking, and that in stony or cloddy ground, though little worked, there is so much of it? This subject will be found fully discussed in the N. C. d'Agriculture, art. Beterave.

their surplus moisture, and then house them carefully. This is best done by putting them in layers in a dry cellar, and interposing between them a slight covering of sand.

A few of the largest and finest roots should be kept for seed. Twenty of them, set out in the spring and occasionally laboured, will give nearly a bushel of seed.

THE CABBAGE (*Brasica*) is a genus of plants containing several species, of which the cabbage, properly so called, and two or three others, are objects of garden culture. It is only of the first (to which botanists have given the name of Brasica Oleracea) and its varieties that we mean to speak at present, and of these there are more than fifty;* some of which differ so entirely from others as to have puzzled the savans in finding for them any common character.† To extenuate, if not to extinguish, this reproach to science, M. Duchesne has ingeniously divided them into six races, distinguished by the parts which severally render them objects of cultivation, viz. :

The Oleracea, cultivated for the seed, which gives an oil ;

The Viridis, for its open and upright long and broad leaves ;

The Capitata, for its leaves, in a round or flat and compact form, called a head ;

* When Brussonnet was at the head of the great national garden at Altfort, in France, he had collected more than fifty of these varieties.

† "Le chou, dont les varietes sont si nombreuses (j'en ai vu cultiver simultanement plus de cinquante) et si differentes les unes des autres, qu'il est impossible de leur assigner un charac tere commun, est une plante annuelle originaire des bords de la mer."—PARMENTIER.

The cabbage, of which the varieties are so numerous (I have seen more than fifty different kinds cultivated together), and so unlike each other that it is impossible to ascribe to them a com mon character, is an annual plant, originally growing on the borders of the sea.

The Coliflora, for its branches, buds, and flowers
The Rapa-Brasica, for its root; and
The Napus-Brasica, for its stem.

With the first and last of these varieties we have nothing to do, as they belong exclusively to field culture. We begin, therefore, with

The *Green*, of which there are many sub-varieties, called by different names, as borecole, Jerusalem kale, Scotch kale, Brussels sprouts, Cavalier, &c., &c., some of which are red and others green, some curled and others smooth, but agreeing in two circumstances: the open erect leaf, and a power of resisting frost much beyond that of any other variety of the family. It is this last circumstance that particularly recommends it; for a frost that would be destructive of head cabbage will make kale better. This fact determines its use in garden culture, which is always for winter and spring greens.

Head cabbage, like the preceding, is subdivided into races, distinguished from each other by the smoothness or curl of the leaf, and by the colour of the flower. Of the smooth-leafed and yellow-flowered race, the most approved varieties are the early dwarf, the early York, the early Bonneuil, the white Alsace, the red cabbage, and the Strasburg or Quintal.* Of the curled sort, the early Milan, the Milan taper, the golden, and the green dwarf Savoy, are the best.

The Cauliflower.—The organization of this race differs considerably from those we have mentioned. In *them* the juices are principally determined to the leaves, whereas in *this* they are directed to the peduncles, producing a mass of branches and buds equally tender and delicate. Of this race there are

---

* In the cultivation of the cabbage (and in this they appear to have been very successful), the Romans particularly aimed at giving to the plant great size. "Caule in tantum saginato, ut pauperie mensa non capiat," says Pliny. "The cabbage of such size that the dish would not hold it."

two varieties : the cauliflower proper and the broccoli, each of which has its sub-varieties. Those
of the former are the *hard* (called also the English
cauliflower) and the *tender*. The first, being occasionally very productive, would be exclusively cultivated, did it succeed equally well at all times and
in all places ; but its capriciousness makes the cultivation of the second sort proper, because, though
this may sometimes give little, it will always give
something. The sub-varieties of the broccoli are
two, the *common* and the *Maltese*,* distinguishable
only by the number, the bulk, and the colour of the
flowers.†

Turnip Cabbage.—Like the preceding, this has its
peculiarities ; for, after attaining its ordinary height,
the leaf falls, and the stem swells to a circumference of many inches, enclosing a succulent, nutritious, and agreeable matter, for the sake of which
the plant is cultivated.‡

Races so different in appearance and in the laws
which govern them, may be supposed to require
different kinds and degrees of culture : but what of
this is common to all forms not only the larger, but
by much the most essential part of the treatment.
We shall, therefore, speak first of this, and then of
the less important particulars in which their management may differ.

Every variety of cabbage grows best in a strong,
rich, substantial soil, inclining rather to clay than
to sand ; but will grow in any soil if it be thoroughly
worked and abundantly manured with well-rotted
dung. As soon, therefore, as the ground designed
for the crop has been thus prepared, and offers signs
of spontaneous vegetation, the planting of early cab-

* Now generally denominated " Kohl-rabbi," or " turnip-rooted cabbage."—J. B

† The common terms now given to the broccoli by gardeners
are the White and Red Cape.—J. B.

‡ Some of the bulbs get to be *twenty-three inches* in circumference, and weigh *twelve pounds*."—M'Mahon, page 317

bages should begin. But without plants this cannot be done, and these are only to be had from a hotbed prepared in January or February (as for asparagus), and sown with the seeds of cauliflowers, of broccoli, and of the early sorts of the head cabbage.* When the plants are two or three inches high, they should be removed to another hotbed of lower temperature and larger surface, where they should remain until transferred to the open air, and to the bed where they are permanently to stand. The time for doing this (as already indicated) is when the earth, by its spontaneous productions, discovers the warmth necessary for vegetation. To do it earlier would be to risk your plants, and not to do it now would be to fail in your intention of having early cabbages. The time of this last transplanting is also that for forming seedbeds in the open air for your winter supply.† As in the former case, the plants, when two or three inches high, must be removed to beds prepared for them, and thence, between the 1st and 20th of June, be transferred to their permanent beds. No vegetable bears transplanting better than the cabbage. The advantages resulting from it are shorter and stouter stems and larger heads, which rarely burst or run to seed.‡

The act of planting should be performed carefully. Holes of sufficient depth and width should be dibbled, for the smaller sorts of cabbages at the distance of two feet and a half, and for the larger sorts of three feet every way. In these the plants should be placed up to their lower leaves,§ and the

* M'Mahon advises sowing the seeds of the early sorts in September, in the open air, transplanting them to hotbeds in November, and pricking them out in the spring.

† We have found that from the 25th to the 28th May is early enough to sow winter cabbages and broccoli. If sown earlier, they mature too early, and many of the heads of the cabbage break open before winter, and the broccoli runs to seed and waste unless there be a market at hand.—J. B.

‡ See Millar, Beriays, M'Mahon, &c., &c.

§ The turnip cabbage is an exception to this rule. The earth must only be brought to the bulb.

earth brought closely about the roots, which is best done by pushing down the dibbler at a small angle with the plant, and then bringing it up to it with a jerk. This leaves no chambering (as gardeners call it), no vacancy between the plant and the soil.

The state of the weather when these operations are performed is not a matter of indifference, and has been a subject of controversy; some recommending dry weather, others wet. As in many other disputed cases, the truth lies between them; that is, moist weather, which is neither dry nor wet, and is precisely that which is best for putting out cabbages, or any other vegetable. We ought not, however, to wait long for even this most favourable state of the atmosphere, since, with a little labour, we have the means of making up for its absence. If the weather be dry, water green and head cabbage plants *once a day;* and cauliflower, broccoli, and turnip cabbage plants *twice a day,* till they have taken root. Without a good deal of water, the last is apt to become stringy and even ligneous; and in Spain and Italy, where cauliflowers and broccoli are finest, they are generally planted in trenches, on the very margin of little rivulets, natural or artificial.

The three last-mentioned varieties require more of manure and labour, as well as of water, than the others; and in this circumstance consists the principal difference of treatment in the cultivation of them. The most successful method with the cauliflower race is to place them in trenches two feet and a half from each other, and on layers of equal parts of earth and cow-dung thoroughly mixed together. Whenever weeds encroach upon these, let them be well hoed; and, whenever hoed, let fresh earth be brought up to the plants. For head cabbage, hoeing and earthing *once a month* is the ordinary rule.*

* Once or twice a week is preferable.—J. B.

The modes of preserving these varieties through the winter are also somewhat different. The open-leaved sorts may be left where they have grown,* and used as wanted. Head cabbage may be set in cellars, or buried in holes or trenches in the garden, and covered with straw and earth; cauliflowers must be housed in cellars or barns, and hung up by their roots; and broccoli, which does not bear this treatment, may be left in the garden,† and managed in the way last suggested for head cabbage. The *stalks* of the more common species are worth preserving; and, when set out in the spring, give sprouts,‡ which furnish an excellent and well-timed article for the table.

A few of the best plants of each variety should be kept for seed; and, in setting them out, care must be taken to keep them as far apart as possible.

THE CARROT (*Daucus*).—This genus comprehends several species, the principal of which is the Daucus Carota. Of this there are three varieties, the white, the orange or yellow, and the red: having perhaps different qualities in different soils and climates, as we find the white preferred in Italy, the yellow in France, and the red in England. Abbé Rozier says of the white variety, that " it is less injured by humidity than the others;" which, as is justly remarked by the compilers of the Cours d'Agriculture, would be a good reason why it should be preferred in England, or in some of the northern or western provinces of France, but a very bad one

---

* Even the open-leaved sorts are better to be buried in trenches. A hard winter will utterly destroy them in the open ground. —J. B.

† In France, the winter management of the broccoli is exactly that of the artichoke. See Parmentier and the Phytologie Universelle of Jolyclerc.

‡ It has been suggested that cabbage sprouts, taken off like suckers from artichokes, and planted, will give good heads, and sooner than they can otherwise be obtained; but of this we have ourselves no experience.

why a preference should be given to it in Italy, where the climate is remarkably dry. Many writers speak of a fourth variety, the round or turnip-rooted carrot of Holland; but M. Thouin considers this form of root as a mere imperfection in the plant, arising from a stiff subsoil, which prevents its penetrating into the earth.

The carrot, like the beet, contains much saccharine matter, but of a quality less valuable, as it cannot be made to crystallize. An extract may, however, be taken from it, which forms no bad substitute for honey.

The culture of the carrot does not differ at all from that of the beet. The seeds (from their long and hairy covering) are apt to catch and hold fast to each other; and should therefore be well rubbed with sand, and separated before they are sown. If the plants come up too closely, thin them, leaving twelve or fourteen inches between them. They will be the finer, not only from the increased space to grow in, but from the greater room which such space affords for the hoe or the hook.* They are taken up at the same period as beets, and, like them, are preserved through the winter in cellars or root-houses made for the purpose.

A few of the roots put out in the spring, when the frosts are over, will give abundance of seed.

CELERY (*Apium Graveolens*).—Of this there are two species, the branching and the turnip-rooted. Some botanists have conjectured that the latter (which is sometimes called Celeriac) was only a variety of the former; but Millar points out distinct characteristics, and asserts that, in the course of many years

---

* M. Trolli advises, for the last weeding, the employment of a hook of two teeth, 15 or 16 inches long. He says that, weeded by this instrument, the carrots are remarkably improved. As soon as the tops are fully out, no farther weeding is necessary, as *these* will suffocate everything growing under them, and preserve by their shade the necessary humidity in the soil.

cultivation, these have never disappeared. The roots of the one are short and thick, and, in the process of vegetation, throw up tall and erect branches; while those of the other have the shape, and, in favourable situations, the size of a turnip. The leaves of this last species are shorter than those of the other, and its top, instead of rising upright, spreads horizontally. The essential property, which renders the plant an object of cultivation, is its *flavour*, which is alike in both species, and existing in all their parts, roots, branches, leaves, and seeds. Of each species there are several varieties, taking their names from colour and organization; as the red, the solid, the hollow, &c., modifications, as we believe, entirely of culture.

Celery is said to be a native of the marshes of Italy; a fact which sufficiently indicates the warmth and moisture necessary for its proper treatment here. Sown in the spring and in the open air, the seeds, like those of all the other parsleys, will be slow in germinating; whence it follows that, to have early plants, we must resort to the aid of artificial heat. A hotbed, such as that mentioned under the head of asparagus, will supply a whole neighbourhood; but one of cheaper form may be found in a couple of flower-pots of the larger size, filled with good soil, and kept in a room moderately warmed during cold weather. If the apartment has a window of southern or eastern aspect, the pots should be placed before it, so as to give them light and air as well as heat. With the aid of water a little warmed, the seeds sown in the pots will show themselves in a fortnight; and in four weeks more will be fit to set out in the garden. The success of the experiment thus far will, however, greatly depend on the sowing; for, if this has been done with a heavy hand, your plants will come up tall, and feeble, and diseased; whereas, if sparsely sown, they will rise strong, healthy, and verdant, and will bear the

subsequent transplanting with little, if any, injury.
As soon as the frosts are over, this last operation
begins; and to meet it, a trench or trenches, according to the quantity of the article required, must be
cut from east to west, remembering to throw the
displaced earth on your right hand, and in such way
as to form an additional protection against the north
wind.   On the bottom of the trench must be placed
a layer of well-rotted dung, wood ashes, and garden-
mould, thoroughly incorporated, and on the surface
of this set your plants (trimmed down to about six
inches in length), at the distance of six or eight
inches from each other.   Care must be taken to fix
the roots, and to keep the young branches closely
together, the better to prevent any portions of earth
from lodging between them; after which, they must
be watered frequently and abundantly.*   The next
business is to *earth* them.   Some of the French
horticulturists direct this to be done at a single operation, and not till after the plant has acquired its
full size; but the more approved method is to do it
gradually and at different times.   The objects to be
obtained by this operation are two: 1st, to alter the
colour of the plant from green to white; and, 2d, to
render it more tender, sweet, and succulent, by
shutting out light and heat, and preventing dryness,
which give it an acrid taste, and render its fibres
tough and hard, and even woody.

* In planting out celery, as well as cabbages and other plants,
we have successfully adopted Cobbett's plan of transplanting in
fair warm days, and, if the ground be dry, it is not the worse.
The plants are carefully taken up, well grouted, that is, their
roots dipped in mud of the consistence of porridge, planted in
the after part of the day, and watered at evening. By the grout
they become saturated with moisture, and, placed in a warm
soil, they in a few hours send forth their radicles, revive and
grow. By transplanting in this manner we have seldom found
it necessary to water a second time; and the plants rarely fail
to obtain an early and good growth, without ever being covered
to protect them from the sun. We prefer transplanting this way
in a clear hot day, to doing it in a wet and cool one.—J. B.

The Abbé Rozier has suggested that the whole labour, delay, and risk which unavoidably attend transplanting, might be saved by preparing trenches as above described, and sowing the seeds in them directly; but though obviously the best method in climates of the south, which admit sowing in February, it is by no means clear that it would be equally fitted for ours, where culture in the open air does not begin till April. Coming, however, from so high an authority, the plan may be worthy of an experiment; and, if even successful in giving a crop for winter use, it would no doubt tend to simplify and abridge our labours.

We need scarcely remark, that it is of the culture of the *branching* or *upright* celery that we have been thus far speaking, as the turnip-rooted sort requires neither trenching nor earthing. Both species are preserved through the winter in the same way, either by covering the plants where they grow with boards and stable litter, or by setting the roots in sand, in the corner of a dark and moderately warm roothouse or cellar. Plants which have been kept in the former way are the fittest for giving *seed*, and should be preferred for that purpose. When this (the seed) is ripe, it separates easily from the chaff, and should then be rubbed out by the hand, put in paper bags, and hung up in a dry and ventilated room for future use.

Succory (*Cichorium*).—But two species of this plant are cultivated in gardens, the Intybus and the Endivia; the one for medicinal purposes, and the other for the uses of the kitchen. Of the last, which alone falls within the scope of our work, there are several varieties, the best of which are the *endive*, properly so called, the *Celestine*, and the *always-white*. The first of these is the most prolific, and the second the most tender and fittest for salads.

In stiff clays and poor sands succory is a feeble plant; in dry soils it becomes tough and disagreeably bitter; and in ground manured with fermenting dung, or too abundantly, its flavour is both altered and degraded. The soil most favourable to it is a light, and fresh, and moist loam, thoroughly dug, moderately manured, and copiously watered. This last circumstance is not only essential to its germination and development, but is the best remedy against the disposition, always shown by the plant in hot weather, to run into seed. An auxiliary means to secure this end is to tie up the heads so as to give them the form of a cone, which, by-the-way, is the method also employed for *bleaching* the plant. This is done by two tyings (one near the roots of the leaves, the other near the tops or points), and which should be made in succession, and at the distance of a few days from each other.

The seeds of this plant are generally and best sown in small beds. When the plants attain the height of three inches, transfer them to the place where they are to 'stand, and set them in rows at the distance of ten or twelve inches apart. Keep them free from weeds, water them frequently, and, when full grown, tie up the heads, or cover them with earthen pots reversed. The first and the last crops (those of spring and autumn) are best, but, with proper care, good ones may be had at midsummer; in this case, however, your plantation must have a northern exposition. After tying, keep the heads erect, for such as lean are apt to burst.

The green curled endive is the best for fall planting, being the hardiest of all the different races. The winter management of this plant does not differ from that of celery.

CORN (*Zea*).—This is a native of America, was cultivated from time immemorial by the aborigines, and was introduced into Europe about three centuries ago. After a cultivation so long continued and so general, the great number of varieties it now presents cannot be thought extraordinary. These are distinguished from each other by the colour or the size of the grain, the number of rows on the cob, the length of time they respectively take in ripening, and the degree of hardness acquired by them. Some are white and others black, some yellow and others brown, red, or violet, &c. Some have cobs twelve inches long, studded with twelve rows of large grains, while others have only six rows on a cob three inches long, and covered with grains even smaller than peppercorns. Some are five months in ripening, while others ripen in forty days; and, again, some are hard and even flinty, while others are soft and succulent, and cannot be long preserved but by means of artificial heat. It so happens that, of this great variety, the sorts least valuable in commerce are those most sought after in garden culture, viz., the small, from its ripening soon, and the soft, from its greater tenderness and sweetness. It is, therefore, of these last varieties only that we shall speak.

Observation has shown that, in raising Indian corn, something is gained, 1st, by taking your seed from plants which have each ripened two or more ears; 2d, by rejecting the grains growing on either extremity of the ears, and employing only the central grains; and, 3d, by steeping these in a solution of nitre for twenty-four hours before sowing. With regard to this operation (sowing), one of two modes may be adopted; either score your ground (which ye take for granted has been well dug and manured) at the distance of three feet and a half both ways, and plant at the points of intersection (three grains at each), or score only one way (east and west), at the distance of four feet, and plant in the rows single grains eight or ten inches from each other. Hoe every ten days after the corn shows itself till it begins to set, and at each hoeing draw up a little earth round the roots of the plants; this is what is called hilling, and is a necessary part of the treatment. Pulverized gypsum, applied in small quantities to the hills at the first and second hoeings, is found to be useful. The same remark may be made of wood ashes, used in the same way, but in larger quantity. To supply seeds for the next year, cut off the tops of a few of the best plants the moment the ears fill.* The effect of this is to let in the air and sun on the ears, and, at the same time, to concentrate in these the remaining juices of the plant.

THE WATER CRESS.—There are two plants of this name, belonging to different genera ; the Cardamine, of the Cruciform, and the Hortensis, of the Passerage genus ; the first includes two useful species : the water cress, and the cress of the meadows ; the other has several varieties, as the golden, the cress of Brazil, that of India, that of Mexico, that of Para, all better than the parent plant, and between which there appears to be but little choice. The qualities and uses of both kinds are the same ; their taste is hot and piquant, and they are principally employed in the composition of salads. Lasteyrie tells us that in Germany great pains are taken to propagate the water cress, and gives the following account of their mode of doing it : " The water (says he) most favourable for its production is that in which it grows naturally, and which in winter preserves heat enough to prevent it from freezing. The situation on which to form a cress plantation ought to have a little slope or inclination ; because water, in a state of repose, alters the flavour of the plant. Having chosen the place, it is formed into heights and hollows alternately ; the latter are destined for the cresses, and the former for the culture of other plants. The size of the hollows is made to depend on the quantity of water you can bring into them, and the de-

* Decidedly a bad practice. Cut up the whole stock, or leave the whole to mature the seed. Either mode is better than topping.—J. B.

mand for the article to be raised. If the soil of the hollows is not sufficiently rich, better earth must be brought to amend it; and, if the bottom be marshy, you throw over it some inches of sand. Your next step is to cover it with water for some hours, after which you drain and sow, or plant. At the end of a few days you let in the water and drain as before, and continue these processes until the cresses appear, if sown, or until they have taken root, if planted. The quantity of water let in is always to be regulated by the growth of the plant; for, though it cannot live but in water, it will not bear to be long covered with it. Planting is always surer than sowing, and is therefore preferred. The time for this is either March or August. The distance between the plants should not be less than ten or fifteen inches. Moving the earth about their roots with the hoe, from time to time, is useful; but for the rest (having once taken root), no farther care is necessary. A cress plantation is in full bearing the second year, and lasts a long time. When it begins to fail, it may be renewed by taking off a foot of the surface soil of the old beds, and replacing it with good and fresh earth. In winter the beds are covered more deeply with water, which protects the plant against the frost."

The same writer informs us how they manage their cress plantations near Paris. "Having there (he says) no running water, they cultivate it in the neighbourhood of wells, and water it every day. The cress vegetates promptly, but becomes acrid in its taste. They accordingly prefer sowing to planting, because, if cut when only six inches high, and treated in all respects as an annual, it has least of this pungency."

THE GARDEN CRESS requires a moist and well-laboured soil, and, if possible, a cool and shady situation. The north side of a wall or fence is its true place in a garden, and, if frequently and abundantly watered, it will there arrive at all the perfection of which it is susceptible.

CUCUMBER (*Cucumis*).—This genus of plants includes many species, varying in foliage, and in the size and shape of their fruit. The more common and useful of these are the bouquet, or cluster cucumber, and the white, which are best fitted for frames; the *yellow* and the parrot, which are most robust, productive, and best flavoured, and the *green*, which, being nearest the wild state, is the fittest for pickling. In our climate, this plant is raised in every description of soil, and with a small degree of labour. The ground being dug and smoothed, line it into squares of six feet. In the centre of each dig a hole about fourteen inches deep; fill this with well-rotted dung, and sow on it five or six cucumber seeds;* cover these with mould, and, when they are grown to have a rough leaf, select two for each hill, and draw out the remainder. You have now to choose between three methods of treating the plant, each of which has many and warm advocates. 1st. Permitting it to regulate itself with regard to the production and the length of the stem; 2d. The pinching system, which, by shortening the stem, compels it to push lateral branches; and, 3d. The plan of Rozier, which, by burying the runner at short distances, avoids the hazard of pinching or cutting, and, at the same time, obtains new roots from the buried joints. Of the three methods, the last has, in our opinion, the preference; but, as others may come to a different conclusion, we will point out the time, the mode, and the effect of shortening the stem. Soon after the plant acquires a second rough leaf, you will discover about the foot of it a bud which, if left to itself, would become a runner. This must be pinched off, taking care, howev-

---

* Twenty is a better number. Plants can be more readily diminished than increased, and seeds cost little or nothing.—J. B.

er, not to wound the joint from which it proceeds. The effect of this pinching will be the production of side shoots, which in their turn must also be pinched off, leaving only two eyes on each, destined to become future *runners*, and so to be conducted that they will not shade or crowd each other.

The sowing, of which we have here spoken, cannot be safely made in our climate till the 10th of May. For the fall and pickling crops, you must sow the first or second week of July. The treatment of these is in all respects like that prescribed for the first crop in the open air, excepting that the pinching part of it is altogether omitted, as at this season the vigorous vegetation (which this operation is intended to correct) is much diminished.

It now remains to say a few words with regard to *early* cucumbers. To obtain these we must have recourse to artificial heat; and with the less reluctance, as, of all plants, the cucumber is that with which it best agrees. To this end, therefore, scoop out as many large turnips as you propose to have *hills*; fill these with good garden mould; sow in each three or four seeds, and plunge them into a hotbed (as described in the article Asparagus). When the runners show themselves, spare them, or pinch them, or bury them, as you may think best, and on the 10th of May transfer them to the beds where they are to stand. The advantage of the scooped turnip as a seedbed over pots or vases, will now appear, for, instead of the ordinary difficulty of separating the mass of earth and the plant from the pot which contained them, and without injury to either, we reinter both pot and plant, and even find in the one an additional nutriment for the other. The subsequent treatment does not differ at all from that of plants sown and cultivated in the open air.

A debate has long existed on the preference to be given to *old* or to *new* seeds, and which. like many others, appears to be interminable. The Abbé Ro-

15

zier and his followers think that the most vigorous
plants, of all species and kinds, are the best; and
accordingly prefer new seeds, because more likely
to produce such than old ones: while, on the other
hand, their opponents maintain that plants may have
too much vigour as well as too little; and that,
whenever an excess of vigour exists, according to
all vegetable analogy, it shows itself in the production of stems and leaves, and not in that of flowers
and fruits; whence they conclude that old cucumber seeds (like those of all the rest of the cucurbi-
taceæ family) are better than new, because *less vigorous*. The best practical use to be made of this
controversy is to sow *old* seeds in the *spring*, when
vegetation is most powerful, and *new* ones in *July*,
when it begins to abate.

GARLIC (*Allium*).—A genus of plants found growing spontaneously in very different and even opposite climates. Jollyclerc says it grows without
care in Sicily and in the south of France, and the
continuator of Cook's Journal informs us that it was
found in the open fields and forests of Kamschatka.
Its species are many. Lamarck mentions thirty-
nine, and Wildenow fifty-eight, the principal of
which are the onion, the leek, the eschalot, and the
cive.

The onion is the Allium Cepa of the botanists, and,
like other plants which have been long subjected to
cultivation, has many varieties, distinguished by
colour, size, and taste, and one of them by organization (the Canadense), which carries its fruit on its
head in the place of flowers. Of these varieties
the red is the largest, but most acrid; the pale red
and the yellow are less in size than the red, and
somewhat milder; but the white (of Spain and
Florence), though the smallest, are the mildest, the
soonest fit for use, and the best for keeping. They
are eaten like apples, and without any wry faces.
On analysis, they are found to possess less of those

elements (oil and sulphur) which give to the common onion its peculiar taste and smell. Light and frequent waterings have the effect of diminishing this odour.*

A rich moist sand is the soil most favourable to the onion; and "when to this," says Bosc, "we can add a long and hot summer, their development is prodigious. I have seen them a foot in diameter, and have heard of others which were larger. But it is to the south of France, to Sicily, to the isles of Greece, and particularly to Egypt, where we must go to see the onion in its most improved state." In clay or stony soils, or pure sand, the onion does not prosper; it becomes small and acrid, and experience shows that fermenting or half-rotted dung is by no means favourable to it.

It is propagated either by the seed or by the bulbs.† In the first case you sow in shallow drills, twelve or fourteen inches apart, cover with mould, and when the plants come up, thin them, so that they may stand three or four inches from each other. The sooner this is done in the spring after the earth has acquired a temperature favourable to vegetation, the better will be your crop. It only remains to keep the earth loose and clean about the roots, and, if the vegetation be too vigorous, to break down the tops, so as to determine the juices to the bulbs. In the other case you employ the small and half-grown onion of the preceding fall instead of seed. In this consists all the difference of the two modes. The *Canadense* variety is, we believe, always managed in this way.

To preserve onions, of whatever variety, through the winter, they are best formed into ropes (tied to each other), and kept in a dry and moderately warm

---

* Cours d'Agriculture.

† The Tartars propagate them by cutting. They slit the bulb downward, and leave to each cutting a portion of the fibrous roots. Cours d'Agriculture.

cellar. A few of the largest of these are set out in
the spring for seed; and, when this is perfectly ripe,
the stems are cut and the seed left in the capsules
for use; as experience shows that, preserved in
this way, it retains its germinating power much
longer than if threshed immediately after ripening.

The *leek* is the Allium Porrum of the botanists,
and a native of the southern parts of Europe. In
Spain it has become one of the scourges of agriculture, as the fields are literally infested with it. In
no country is this plant eaten alone, excepting perhaps in Spain, and the more southern provinces of
France; but in many countries it is employed in
the composition of soups. The culture of it resembles entirely that of the onion, excepting only that
it requires more water. Of its many varieties we
have seen only the *long* and the *short*. The former
is the milder of the two; the latter the more bulbous, acrid, and hardy.

The *eschalot* (Allium Ascalonicum) is said to be a
native of Palestine. Of this there are three sub-
varieties, two of which are generally found in gardens, the large and the small. The bottoms of
these, when the plant is ripe, is composed of several bulbs of different sizes, under a common covering, the larger of which are taken for culinary
uses, and the smaller kept for planting. The culture of these bulbs does not differ from that of the
common, or of the Canadense varieties of the onion.

The *cive* (Cepula) is a small plant much used in
soups and salads. Of this there are three sub-
varieties, the Cepula Minor, Cepula Britannica, and
Cepula Major. The bulbs of all grow in clusters,
and the plant is usually propagated by separating
these into small tufts (half a dozen of the roots together) every third or fourth year, and setting them
out in borders or in beds eight or ten inches apart.
The leaves only are used, and, to have these tender,
they must be cut often. In the fall and on the ap-

proach of frost, clip them close to the ground, and cover the roots with dung or stable litter. They require little if any other care, and will last many years.

LETTUCE (*Lactuca*).—Of the native country of this plant we are not sufficiently assured. Lamarck thinks that the Quercina of Linnæus (a product of an island in the Baltic) is the type of the genus, while Rozier regards the Scareola of the same author as entitled to that distinction. Of the known species there are twenty-one;* the most remarkable of which are the *Capitata*, the *Romana*, and the *Spinosa*. The first and second are found in all kitchen gardens, while the third is rather a medicinal than a culinary plant, and principally useful for its narcotic powers, which are said to be little inferior to those of opium. The varieties of the Capitata and Romana have, by long culture, been multiplied to the number of one hundred and twenty, and are separated by lines so nearly imperceptible and so difficult to characterize, that botanists have found it convenient to arrange them into series, the principal of which are, 1st, the Head Lettuce; 2d, the Curled Lettuce; and, 3d, the Lettuce with open, straight, and erect leaves. These are again subdivided by gardeners, according to the season most favourable to the plants respectively, as spring, summer, fall, or winter lettuce; and as this view of them is likely to be best known and most useful, we shall employ it in what we have to say on the subject.

The varieties known by the names of the brown Dutch, Capuchin green, and grand admiral (being the most hardy), are those which should be sown in the fall, to remain in the ground through the winter, and vegetate early in the spring. If the soil be

---

* Brisseau Mirbel. One of these species is American (Lactuca Elongata of Dr. Muhlenberg).

clayey, the beds should be thoroughly manured and dug in the month of October, and thrown up into four-feet ridges, well trenched, and with an inclination on one of their sides or corners to carry off superfluous moisture. The seed should now be sown and covered with a short-toothed rake, and subsequently, as the frost approaches, with a light layer of stable litter. This should be removed in the spring, and the surfaces of the beds loosened with an iron-toothed rake. The first vegetation that shows itself will be that of the lettuce, and, if too thickly sown, the surplus plants should be taken up, and set out in rows for head-salad. In warm and sandy soils the treatment is the same, with the exception that the trenching and ridging will be unnecessary : but, in every kind of soil, the precocity of the crop will be best assured by a temporary wall of straw or cornstalks, held together by a few stakes and wattles, and so placed as to protect the beds from north and northwest winds.

The varieties most approved for spring culture are the white, the green, the spotted coss, the Silesia, the Great Mogul, and the India ; for summer use, the white Dutch, the imperial, the Aleppo, and the green Egyptian ;* and for that of autumn, as already stated, the white coss, the brown Dutch, the grand admiral, and the New-Zealand. We need scarcely remark, that the straight-leafed sort is best cultivated in broadcast, and does not require transplanting, but that the curled and head lettuce cannot succeed without it. In summer culture this may be especially necessary, as the lettuce, like the cabbage, has at this season a strong propensity to run

* Millar says that the white coss obtained the preference over all other branches of the family till the introduction of the green Egyptian. This is probably the variety mentioned by Oliver and Brugiere as forming the delight of the Egyptians, and which among them is eaten by all ranks at all hours. See Memoire sur l'Egypte.

to seed, which can only be effectually checked by transplanting. The plants should stand at the dis tance of ten or twelve inches apart in the rows. The curled sort, when the heads begin to spread, should be tied up, and will then blanch finely; but it must also be noticed that the effect of this compres- sion is to hasten the progress of vegetation, and, of course, to precipitate the seeding.

All the varieties of the three series will grow well in hotbeds, but the Romana species is preferred for this culture, 1st, because it bears squeezing or crowding the best, and, 2d, because, by throwing up erect leaves, it occupies less room under the frames than either of the other sorts.

THE MELON (*Cucumis Melo*).—This is one of the many useful and delicious presents furnished by Asia to the rest of the world. There are but two species; the melon with a rough or embroidered coat, and that with a thin and smooth skin. The first is called the musk, from its peculiar flavour, and the other, from its thin and abundant juices, the watermelon. Of each of these species there are many varieties, differing in shape and size, and in the colour of the rind and of the flesh. The most approved of the muskmelon species are the cante- lope, the citron, the nutmeg, and the Persian; and of the watermelon, the Carolina, the Maltese, the Candia, and the Chatè or Egyptian.*

Both species and all the varieties succeed best in a hot climate and sandy soil, and in these their culture is easy and alike, and their product abun- dant; nor is it to be complained of here, where our

* Prosper Alpin says that he has seen watermelons so large in Egypt, that three or four formed the ordinary load of a cam- el. Of this species there are seven known varieties, according to Brisseau Mirbel. The Chate is one of these, and the Egyp- tian mode of using it is to make a hole in the side, through which, by means of a stick, they reduce the pulp to a liquid. This is then poured into a cup and drank.

summers are frequently long, and hot, an l dry. To succeed in raising them for market, the *Honfleur* method, as described by M. Calvel, may be employed. Select a spot well defended against the north wind, and open to the sun throughout the day. If such is not to be found in your garden, create a temporary and artificial shelter producing the same effect. At the end of March, form holes two feet in diameter, and distant from each other seven feet and a half; fill these with horse-dung and litter, or a mixture of mould, dung, and sand. At the end of twenty days, cover the holes which have been thus filled with hand glasses. When the heat rises to 36 of Reaumur, sow the seeds four inches apart; and when the plants have acquired two or three leaves, pinch off the end of the branch or runner.* This will produce lateral branches, which must again be pinched off so soon as they respectively attain the length of ten inches. When the plant has outgrown the glass, the latter becomes useless and may be removed; but, should the weather be wet or chilly, substitute coverings of clean straw for that of the glasses, until the young plant becomes strong enough to bear the open air. Two or three melons only are left to each vine, and under each of these is placed a slate, without which the upper and under sides will not ripen together. Two months are required to mature them. The people of Honfleur attribute their success in melon-raising to the *sea vapour* which surrounds them, and to the *saline parti-*

---

* There is much controversy among gardeners and savants on this point; nor are the *pinchers* entirely united in opinion how far this practice should be carried. Some content themselves with taking off the cotyledons when the plant has acquired three or four leaves, while others take off the principal branches at the first eye above the fruit, and suppress all the secondary branches, male flowers, and tendrils. "These operations," says M Bosc, "are founded in bad reasoning. A cutting which suppresses two thirds of the plant at once cannot fail to disorganize what remains."

cles contained in it; an advantage to be anywhere commanded by dissolving a little salt in the water employed to moisten them.

If we want melons at a period earlier than this method will give them, we must employ a higher degree and longer continuance of artificial heat; in a word, we must resort to *hotbeds;* and in these the point most important, and, at the same time, the most difficult of attainment, is to secure a certain degree of heat, and no more, throughout the whole process. To lessen the difficulty in this case, gardeners who understand their trade make choice of those varieties which have the thinnest skins and the least bulk; as experience proves that, other things being equal, they require less heat* than those of thicker rinds and greater size, and are, of course, less subject to some of the accidents to which this species of culture is exposed. In choosing the seeds, those of the last year are only to be used, because they are of quicker vegetation than old ones, and, accordingly, best fulfil the intention of the hotbed which is to give *early* fruit. Another practice conducive to the safety of the plants is to sow the seed in small pots, and then to plunge them · into a hotbed. If the heat be deficient, they are, in this case, made no worse than they would have been if sown directly in the bed; and if it be excessive, it is only necessary to raise the pots, without in the smallest degree disturbing the plant. These things being premised, it only remains to show what ought to be the subsequent management after the seed has been sown and the pots placed under the frames. One of the most important points now to be observed is sufficiently to ventilate the

---

* No one is ignorant that surfaces augment as the squares, and that solids follow the proportion of cubes. If, for instance, the surface of the melon be four, the quantity of its matter will be eight; and if the surface of another melon be nine, its matter will be equal to twenty-seven.

bed, as well before as after the plants show themselves. This should be done at midday and in sunshine, and as often as a necessity for it shall be indicated by an accumulation of steam under the
glasses. At night these (the glasses) should be care
fully covered with matting. These two prelimina-
ries (ventilation in the day and covering at night)
being carefully observed, your plants will soon show
themselves in a vigorous and healthy state, and
may be kept in that condition by a continuation of
the same means, and by moderately moistening the
earth when it shall appear to have become too dry.
The water employed should be of the temperature
of the air under the frames; and, to secure this, it is
well to keep a supply of it in a pot placed in a corner of the hotbed. In about a month, the plants
thus raised will be fit for transferring to a second
and larger hotbed, constructed like the preceding,*
with the exception that the mass of dung must now
be greater, and that, after earthing, the bed should
not be less than three and a half or four feet in
depth. The plants, with the earth in which they
grow, are now to be taken from the pots; an operation in which practice only will make us expert, and
which consists in placing the neck of the plant between the first and second finger of the left hand,
reversing the pot, and gently striking its sides until
the earth be disengaged. The discharged mass is
then placed in a hole previously prepared in the
square, where it is intended the plant shall ripen and
produce. The male flowers should not be disturbed. When they have fulfilled the intentions of nature, they will fall of themselves; and if the branches
be vigorous and long, stretch them carefully over a
level surface, and bury every fourth or fifth joint.
This is best done by means of a wooden crotchet.
The objects of pinching or shortening the stem are

* See article Asparagus for the formation of hotbeds.

thus completely fulfilled, without any of the risk
which attends that operation, and with advantages
peculiar to this method; since, wherever the plant
is buried, new roots are formed for the better nutrition of the stem and the fruit. Melons should be
permitted to acquire a bulk not less than one inch
in diameter before you venture on reducing their
number, and no reduction of the leaves should be
made at any time; for from the size, number, and
thickness of these; and the smallness and little extension of the roots, it is evident that this plant derives more of its nutriment from the atmosphere
than from the earth. If the weather be dry, multiply the hoeings, but water sparingly, as many experiments show that water alters the juices of the
fruit, and that, though it may augment its quantity,
it never fails to degrade its quality. The ripeness
of the muskmelon is known by its colour and its
odour, and by the drying of the stem where it at
taches itself to the fruit.* The watermelon furnishes neither of these signs, but affords another
peculiar to itself, a *hollow sound* on being struck on
the rind, the result of an actual hollowness, beginning and increasing with its maturity. The seeds
of both species are best preserved by drying in the
shade, and in a portion of their own juice.

EGG PLANT.—MELONGENA (*Solanum Melongena of
Lin.*).—Of this plant the principal varieties are the
long purple and the long yellow, each of which
has a sub-variety which is round. Like other plants
of tropical origin, it requires a dry soil and warm
weather, and with these advantages grows vigorously and bears abundantly. To have early plants,
sow the seeds in a hotbed towards the end of March,
and, as soon as the frosts are over, transfer the young
plants to the open ground and a southern exposure.

* When fit to pick, the stem will separate from the fruit by a
gentle pressure of the thumb. It will be in best eating condition the following day.—J. B.

Keep them clean, and water them (if the weather be dry) often, but lightly. To have a succession of this fruit throughout the summer, you must occasionally renew the sowings. A few of the largest plants should be left for seed, and when the fruit begins to rot is the time for taking it. Cut off the plant and dry it in the shade, for seed immediately removed from the pulp is rarely good.

The family connexions of this plant (the Solanums) have made some persons question its salubrity, but, as we think, without reason. If in certain cases it prove indigestible, of what fruit may not the same be said, particularly if eaten to excess? The general impunity with which our southern neighbours use it, even habitually and largely, is in itself a sufficient guarantee of the safety with which it may be, occasionally and temperately, employed here.

MUSTARD (*Sinapis*).—Two species of the mustard are objects of garden culture : the black, which is cultivated for the seed, and the white, which is a good substitute for spinach, and which is sometimes used with pepper-grass as an ingredient in salads.* Both species grow well in a great diversity of soils, and with a small portion of labour; but the richer the soil and the greater the care, the more vigorous will be the plants.

If the seed of the first species be our object, we should remember that, as the pods do not either form or ripen but in succession, we must not delay our harvest until all have been matured ; as in this case we should lose the seed soonest ripe (which is always the best), for the sake of preserving that which is later and worse. The best rule, therefore, is to pull up or cut off the crop as soon as the stems

---

* In Spain, and throughout the south of Europe, the seed of the white species is preferred for the fabrication of mustard ; because giving a whiter and milder flour than the seed of the black.

become yellow, and carry it into the barn, where it may remain, covered with straw, for a month. At the end of this time it will be fit to thresh; and this should be done on cloths, and not with flails, since these would bruise and break the seed; but with bunches of rods. Passed two or three times through a fanning mill, it will be fit for use; and the sooner it is used after cleaning, the better mustard it will make.*

The MUSHROOM (*Agaricus of Lin.*, *Fungus of Tour.*). —The latter of these botanists numbers not fewer than seventy-five plants of this genus, differing from each other in colour, in smell, and in the size, form, and number of their heads or chapeaux; and Withering, if we do not mistake, makes them to amount to more than two hundred. To describe, or even to name them, would be an unprofitable task, and entirely beside the object of the present work; as of the whole number, the Agaricus Campestris, or Fungus Sativus Equinus, is the only species admitted into garden culture.

This plant is propagated from the seeds only: which are threads or fibres of a white colour, found in old pasture grounds, in masses of rotten horsedung, sometimes under stable floors, and frequently in the remains of old hotbeds. They are also always to be met with on the growing plant, sometimes on the upper, at others on the under surface, and oftener in the interior. Their extreme smallness makes them difficult to detect; but, by placing the plant on ice, and enclosing it for a day or two, they may be readily discovered, and will be found to be *semeniform*, and in this respect differing from the seeds of all other vegetables, and even raising a doubt whether the mushroom does not partake more of the animal than of the vegetable character. Nor is this fact the only one that warrants

* Its duration seems to be limited to two years; older than this, it is rarely good.—Bosc.

the suggestion; s nce, on analysis, it is found that the product of the mushroom is almost altogether animal; whence it is that those botanists, who are tenacious of what is called the *natural* order, make it the first vegetable link in the chain, as zoologists make the polypus the last in the animal series.

Another suggestion, of more practical importance, is that, whether animal or vegetable, the mushroom is often poisonous; either from some quality inherent in itself, or from some adventitious matter (such as the larvæ of insects) being imbibed and held by its spongy surface. On this head there has been no want either of inquiry or of admonition. Naturalists, in succession, from Pliny to Parmentier, have investigated the subject, and come to nearly the same conclusion, viz., "that many species of the mushrooms are active poisons,* and that the best are dangerous, as well from the total want of any general rule for distinguishing between the good and the bad,† as from the tendency of all to produce indigestion."‡ In despite, however, of these sage discoveries and councils, the mushroom continues to be eaten, and even to be a favourite; for, not contented with the abundance of the article provided by nature at a particular season, means are employed to have it at *all seasons*, and it is of this culture we have now to speak.

Prepare a bed early in October, either in a corner of the hothouse, if you have one, or of a dry and warm cellar. The width of the bed at the bottom should not be less than four feet, and its length pro-

---

* Geoffroi, Paulet, and others.

† "It has been said that the mushroom which it is safe to eat is distinguished from the bad by a membrane which surrounds the footstalk. This sign is, however, the less sure, as this membrane is found to belong to a species the most danger ous." Phytalogie Universelle, vol. ii., p. 161.

‡ Parmentier on Poisonous Mushrooms. Strong vinegar and emetics are the surest remedies against the effects of these.

portioned to the quantity of spawn provided. Its sides should rise perpendicularly one foot, and should afterward decrease to the centre, forming four sloping surfaces. We need hardly say that the materials of the bed at this stage of the business must be horse-dung, well forked and pressed together, to prevent its settling unequally. It should then be covered with long straw, as well to exclude frost as to keep in the volatile parts of the mass, which would otherwise escape. After ten days the temperature of the bed will be sufficiently moderated, when the straw is to be removed, and a covering of good mould, to the depth of an inch, laid over the dung. On this the seed or spawn of the mushroom is to be placed in rows, six inches apart, occupying all the sloping parts of the bed, which is again to be covered with a second inch of fresh mould and a coat of straw. If your bed has been well constructed your mushrooms will be fit for use at the end of five or six weeks, and will continue to be productive for several months. Should you, however, in the course of the winter, find its productiveness diminished, take off nearly all the original covering, and replace it with eight or ten inches of fresh dung and a coat of clean straw. This, by creating a new heat, will revive the action of the spawn, and give a long succession of mushrooms.

The flavour of this vegetable is highest in the button state; when the heads attain to the diameter of an inch, they are still good, and most profitable in the market; but, when fully developed, they are not worth picking.

PARSLEY (*Apium Petrosilinum*).—A native of Sardinia, according to Jollyclerc, and, according to Bosc, an article without which the cook could not exercise his trade.* There are three or four varie-

* " Oter le persil d'entre les mains d'un quisiiiier c'est presque le metra dans l'impossibilite d'exercer son art."
Take away the parsley from the cook, and you make it impossible for him to practise his art.

cties, the fine, the curled, the variegated, and the large-rooted. Of these the curled is the most delicate, but most apt to degenerate. The large-rooted is the hardiest, least liable to change, most abundant in foliage, and quicker in renewing itself. These circumstances give it the preference.

Parsley will grow in almost any soil, but prefers that which is light, and fresh, and rich. It is best sown in the spring in a well-laboured bed, manured with old and thoroughly rotted dung, and in rows sufficiently far apart to admit the hoe and the weeder. The cultivator must not be out of patience at the slowness with which it shows itself. It seldom appears before forty days, and not always at the end of that term. Hoeing and watering are, however, all it requires after it does appear. The leaves are cropped in the fall, and hung up in bundles for winter use. If the soil in which the plants grow be stiff and moist, the roots ought to be covered in the fall, otherwise there is a risk of their being thrown out by the frost.

PARSNIP (*Pastinaca*).—Of this there are five species, but one of which (Pastinaca Sativa) is admitted into the garden. This has two varieties, the round or turnip parsnip, and the Siam, neither of which is much known.

Like other tap-rooted plants, the pastinaca thrives best in a rich, deep, friable soil, growing in the drills where it was originally sown, and undisturbed by transplanting. The rows should be twelve or fourteen inches apart, and four of these in a bed, and the plants themselves should not stand nearer together than eight inches.

The first crop may be sown in March, as no degree of cold injures either the seed or the plant; but the seedtime of the main or winter crop need not begin till the first of June, as enough of the season will then be left to mature it, and as the hardest frosts but make it better. It is evidently a plant of northern origin, contains much sugar, is very nutritious, and merits more both of cultivation and use than it has received.

The PEA (*Pisum*) is a native of the south of Europe, of which, according to Linnæus, there are four species, and according to Millar six, while other botanists recognise only two (the field and the garden), and some even contend that the latter of these is merely a variety of the former, produced by cultivation. What these naturalists better agree in is the arrangement of the whole family into two classes, those having coriaceous pods (tough and parchment like), and those having pods tender and edible, like the pea itself. These are again subdivided into dwarfs and climbers, and, for more practical use, into early and late pease. Of the former, in their order of ripening, the most approved sorts are, the early frame, early Charlton, and golden Hotspur, and of the latter, in the same order, the large marrowfat, the white Rounsevil, the Spanish Marotto, and large imperial.* The dwarfs are generally employed in hotbed culture, which, however, succeeds badly, and is neither worth attending to or describing, and the less so as early crops may be more certainly had by sowing in the fall in sheltered situations, and covering in the winter with a layer of leaves, and another of long stable litter loosely applied, to keep the leaves in their places. After the earth acquires a temperature favourable to vegetation, your pea-sowings should be made once a fortnight to keep up a regu-

* The dwarf sugar, the dwarf Spanish, and Leadman's dwarf, may be usefully interposed between these. These dwarf varieties are all excellent, the last, perhaps, more prolific than any other of the family. In France the varieties of early and late pease are different, or, at least, called by different names from those we have mentioned. The series of both sorts there are, the Michaux of Holland, the baron, the Blois, the cluster, and the forty days, which are early; and the nonpareil, the Laurens, the Swiss, the Eul Noir, and the Calmart, which are late

lar and successive supply. A loose and warm soil is most favourable to this vegetable, which, by-the-way, is neither improved in quality nor quantity by stable manure. The soil of Clichy, and of Point de jour des Çolombe, &c., &c., in the neighbourhood of Paris, is a pure sand, principally devoted to pea-crops, and yielding these most abundantly, without the application of dung, new or old. What, however, is essential in their treatment is, frequent hoeing, and occasional watering if the weather be dry, and seasonable propping for the tall sorts, which ought to be completed by the time the plants get to be three or four inches high. All the varieties of this last description of the pea require double the room given to dwarfs. The rows in which they stand should not, therefore, be less than four feet apart, and they should grow in these six inches from each other, and their covering should not exceed two inches, nor be less than one, according to the nature and condition of the soil in which they are sown. We need scarcely remark that the different varieties should be cultivated apart.

Like other vegetables, the pea is susceptible of considerable improvement, by the simple means of marking the finest plants of each variety, and keeping them for seed. Wilson's frame and the Knight pea have been formed in this way, and afford sufficient proof of the *wonders* produced by a very small degree of observation and care.

The general relish for the pea has induced the employment of means to have them on the table the year round. The methods in use for this purpose are two. According to one of them, the pea is subjected to the action of boiling water for two or three minutes, when it is withdrawn, cooled in fresh spring water, dried in the shade, and, lastly, hung up in paper bags in a dry and well-aired closet. The other process is later and perhaps better; in this the pease are put into bottles, which are afterward hermetically sealed, and subjected to the action of boiling water for fifteen minutes. In both cases the pease require boiling a second time in the ordinary way to make them fit for the table; and, when preserved according to the first method, a great deal of boiling; Bosc says twenty-four hours. All the varieties are not found to be equally fit for this process; the Michaux of Holland and the Calmart are those exclusively employed in France.

PEPPER, RED (*Capsicum*).—This is the Annual Pepper of the botanists, of which there are two species, the Grossum and the Frutescens, the latter of which we have only seen in hothouses.

Like other natives of southern climates, the capsicum requires a warm soil, and, if sown early, a good deal of dung and a favourable exposition. The seeds may be placed in rows three feet apart, or in hills at the like distance from each other. In dry weather the plants require watering, and, in all kinds of weather, weeding and hoeing. The seeds are best preserved by running a string through the pods and hanging them up in a dry garret.

THE POTATO (*Solanum Tuberosum*).—Of the sixty varieties of this vegetable, two are particularly recommended for garden culture; the one from its precocity (ripening in forty days), and the other from its excellence. This last is most generally known by the name of the *yam* potato, and is so called from its great resemblance (in taste) to the vegetable of that name.

The hardiness of this plant enables it to grow in any soil and under very negligent culture; but the soil most propitious to it is a rich loam, and the more hoeing and hilling it gets before it flowers, the better will be your crop. In gardens it is best placed in rows three feet apart. Gypsum applied to the leaves of the growing plant will be found useful.

The POTATO (sweet) is a species of convolvulus,

originally from Asia, making great part of the food of tropical latitudes, and occasionally cultivated as far north as Long Island. Of its many varieties three only are known to us, and these take their denominations from their colour. The red is the earliest, the yellow the sweetest, and the white the largest. In the sandy and humid parts of South Carolina, all these races attain to a considerable size. On Long Island they are small and (what is more to be regretted) very inferior in the nutritive and agreeable qualities which distinguish the fruit when growing under more favourable circumstances.*

This plant is easily cultivated, and, whether it gives us fruit or not, its beauty is such as will well repay us for the trouble of raising it. Score the square intended for it (which should have been previously well dug and manured) both ways, and at the distance of four feet each way, and place and cover the seeds at the angles of intersection. When the plants rise, keep them clear of weeds, and, as in hilling corn, draw up the earth well about the roots.

The PUMPKIN is a species of the Cucurbita. Among its varieties are the Maltese, the Barbary, the Iroquois, and the white, which is the winter pumpkin.† The culture of all is the same. They are less nice than cucumbers and melons with regard to soil, and will grow in any dry and well-laboured earth. The best time for sowing them is between the 15th and 25th of May.

The RADISH (*Raphanus Sativus*).—Of this there are

---

* Parmentier analyzed the sweet potatoe in 1780. The result was sugar, amidon, and an extractive matter; but he well remarks that " these principles vary with the age and variety of the plant, and with the soil and climate in which it grows."

† Many new varieties have been recently introduced, and among the best is the Valparaiso, known under different names. —J. B.

two species, distinguished only by the shape of their roots; that of the one being long, and that of the other round. The principal varieties of the former are the early, the salmon, the red, and the large, which last has no characteristic colour. Those of the latter species are also distinguished by their different colour and size; some are large, others small; some are white, others black; some are ash-coloured, and others are pink and purple. All require a similar soil (loose and rich) and a careful, seasonable, and cleanly cultivation. The sowings of the radish, like those of spinach and lettuce, must be frequent. "Sow every fourteen days" is the. common rule, and it seems to be a good one, and founded on the known disposition of the plant to run promptly to seed.

The RADISH [horse] (*Cochlearia Armoriacia*).—This plant is one of six species having the common English name of spleenwort or scurvy-grass. It is generally propagated by cuttings or offsets taken from the crown of the parent plant, and having each a bud, and set in a trench ten inches deep and four or five inches apart. The cuttings are then covered with mould, and the surfaces of the trenches kept clean and loose. The plants will soon take root, and, after doing so, will fear no rivals.

RAMPION (*Campanula*).—Two or more species of this plant are cultivated for purposes merely of decoration; as the pyramidal, the peach-leaf, the mirror of Venus, &c.; but that which alone interests us is the Hortensis, and which, from its abundant mucilage, is regarded as both nutritive and refreshing, and an excellent ingredient in salads. The seed is remarkably small, and should be sown thin in the month of June. It requires little, if any, covering and germinates best in a loose, moist soil, and shady situation.

ROSEMARY (*Rosmarinus Officinalis*).—The leaves of this plant abound in aroma, and are employed in soups and sauces. It is, besides, the basis of the celebrated liqueur called La Reine de Hongrie, and is yet more famous for giving to the honey of Narbonne its acknowledged superiority. The tops of the branches furnish an essential oil, which, according to the experiments of Proust, contain much camphire. It is propagated by cuttings and suckers. " Planted in the month of March six inches apart, and inserted two thirds of their lengths in the ground, they will take root freely, and by the month of September be fit for transplanting wherever they are destined to remain."*

Rue (*Ruta Graveolens*).—This plant is a native of mountainous and arid regions, and, so far as we have any acquaintance with it, exclusively medicinal; but, having obtained a place in the kitchen garden, it is not for us to reject it. As with other aromatics, a light, and warm, and dry soil is that which agrees best with it. It is propagated from cuttings and offsets planted in March or April, and kept clear of weeds throughout the summer. Its beauty is much increased by lopping the branches close to the earth every fourth year.

Rhubarb (*Rheum*).—Most of the known species of this plant are of Asiatic origin, but the two which alone enter into the food of man (the Rhaponticum and Undulatum) are natives of Thrace and Russia.† The stalks, which are the parts used for culinary

---

* M'Mahon.
† Several new varieties, if not new species, of this plant, adapted to culinary uses, have recently been introduced. Among those most worthy of culture is the giant, the leaf stems of which grow upon rich soils to the size of six and seven inches in circumference, and give a leaf a yard in diameter. Those who are fond of pies and tarts cannot obtain a more convenient article for these than the rhubarb, from March to September; for, placed in a tub with earth in autumn, and set in a cellar or basement kitchen, and merely watered, the roots will send forth an abundance of stalks, which may be used early in March.— J. B.

purposes, grow to the length of twenty-four inches, and acquire the thickness of a man's thumb. Stripped of their outer covering, they yield a substance slightly acid,* which is much admired, and employed as an ingredient in the composition of puddings and tarts. Cobbett supposes that a hundred wagonloads of these stalks are annually sold in the markets of London, at a shilling sterling per bunch.†

The rhubarb is propagated sometimes from seeds, and oftener from offsets from old roots.‡ It requires a soil dry, and rich, and well-laboured. Two years are necessary to render it fit for use, but, once established, it will last a century.

SAGE (*Salvia Officinalis*).—This is one of the hundred and more species of Salvia enumerated by botanists. It has many varieties, the most important of which are, the large-leaved, the curled,§ the three-coloured, and the variegated. They are all propagated alike, by seeds, by suckers, and by portions of old roots, and grow well in any soil not positively wet. Till three or four years old, they have a healthy and agreeable appearance, forming full and regular tufts; but after this period they lose the central branches, and even become ragged and broken on their edges. The treatment already suggested for rue might be useful for sage. Under it the roots would probably renew their vigour, and throw out new and healthy shoots; but of this theory we have no experience.

SALSIFY (*Tragopogon*).—This is a native of the southern mountains of Europe, has been long cul-

---

* The stalks, like the roots, yield, on analysis, sulphur and lime.

† American Gardener.

‡ The best mode is to propagate from seeds which ripen in July. If then sown, the plants may be put out three feet apart the next spring, and will give a good crop the second summer after transplanting.—J. B.

§ This is made a distinct species by Wildenow, under the name of Salvia Tomentosa.

tivated, and has several varieties, of which it is unnecessary to speak.   Deep and humid soils are most
favourable to its production.   After the preliminary
labours of digging and smoothing, the square intended for it should be formed into four-feet beds,
and the seeds be sown and covered in rows eight
or ten inches apart.   This should be done as soon
as the frosts are over in the spring, for the earlier
the sowing the finer will be the crop.   Two hoeings, and frequent watering during dry and hot
weather, are indispensable.   It is only in the autumn that the plants attain to their full size.   In
mild climates they winter where they grow, like
parsnips; but in cold regions they must be taken
up and preserved in roothouses or cellars, under
coverings of sand or litter.   Plants intended to give
seed should be left to winter in the ground where
they have grown, and be there protected by leaves,
straw, &c.

SALSIFY BLACK (*Scorzonera Hispanica*) affects the
same kind of soil, and requires the same kind of
culture and management as the preceding kind, and
is of the same family.

SAVORY (*Satureja*).—Of this plant Millar describes
nine species, but two of which come within our
views, and which are denominated from two of the
seasons, winter and summer.   The former is a perennial plant, and is propagated from seeds or slips;
the latter is an annual, and is propagated from seeds
only.   For either process, sowing or planting, April
is the time.   Neither sort is nice with regard to
soil; and it is said of one of them (the winter species) that it grows best in barren sands and bleak
situations.

SEAKALE*.(*Crambe Maratima*) is a native of the
seashore, growing vigorously in sands occasionally

* We have found by experience that *good* seakale, like Frank-
lin's whistle, costs more than it is worth.   We have given up
its culture.—J. B.

inundated by salt water. When the head of the plant first shows itself, it is white, and tender, and well-flavoured, and not inferior to asparagus; but, after reaching the light and the air, it soon becomes green and bitter, and quite unfit for the table. The natural condition of the plant would appear to indicate the best mode of cultivating it, and that the bed destined for it should be pure sand, moistened by a solution of salt in water; but we have on this head the assurance of practical gardeners, that, in a well-manured and thoroughly dug loam, the seakale does even better than in its natural bed.* This plant is propagated by cuttings and by seeds, and most surely by the former; but the quality of the product is inferior to that given by the other mode.† In case of *planting,* your beds must be so prepared as to receive each two rows of the slips, which are to stand fourteen inches apart (in an upright position), with their crowns not more than one inch under the surface. In five or six weeks they may show themselves above ground, and during the second year, if kept free from weeds and occasionally watered, will be fit for use. If *sowing* be preferred, after labouring the ground thoroughly, form a number of hills as for Indian corn, and sow in each six or eight seeds. Should they all vegetate, they may be reduced to two, which you will manage in the way prescribed for the cuttings. In November, whether your bed has been filled with plants or with seedlings, be careful to cover them with a thick coat of well-rotted dung; and so soon in the ensuing spring or summer as you find them pushing through this covering, put over each a garden-pot inverted, having first stopped the bottom-holes.‡ The signal for cutting is when the plants have risen about three inches above the surface.

* M'Mahon. † Idem. Millar.
‡ The object in doing this is to exclude the light, for under its influence the plant becomes green and bitter

THE SKIRRET (*Sium Sisarum of Tournefort*).—This is called by Millar the Water Parsnip, and is found growing spontaneously in many parts of England, in moist or wet grounds. There are six species, but one of which is cultivated in the garden. The root, which is the only edible part of the plant, is long and fibrous, wholesome and nutritious; but to some palates it is disagreeably sweet. It is propagated indifferently from seeds or from cuttings, though Millar prefers the latter, as furnishing roots of greater size and better quality. April is the month most proper for either operation, sowing or planting. In both modes the culture is in drills, taking care that the plants be not nearer than four or five inches to each other. The soil in which it succeeds best is a loose, moist loam; and the culture and subsequent management do not differ from those already described for parsnips.

SORREL (*Rumex Acetosa of Linnæus*).—Of this plant there are four species, distinguished by the shape and size of their leaves, as the pointed, the obtuse, the round, the large, the small, &c. All soils not positively dry or wet are adapted to this vegetable; nor do they require more than a light dressing. It is propagated as well by cuttings as by seeds. In the former case the slips are put down in the fall, and in the latter the seeds are sown in the spring. In gathering it, many gardeners cut off an entire tuft close to the ground; but a better method, because more favourable to reproduction, is to crop the outer leaves first, always leaving the central ones to be last taken.* We need scarcely mention that, besides culinary uses, sorrel furnishes an acid salt, much employed in taking out stains from linen, and that the roots yield a beautiful red water, known in medicine as a sudorific.†

---

* This is the practice of the gardeners of Paris.
† Bosc.

SPINACH (*Spinachia*).—Of this there are but two known species, the Fera and the Oleracea ; the one a native of Siberia,* the other of Persia.†‡ It is the latter only that is known in garden culture, and of it there are four varieties, distinguished by the shape of their seeds, and the greater or less abundance and size of their leaves, as follows : Spinach with sharp-pointed seeds and small leaves : spinach with round seeds and small leaves ; spinach with pointed seeds and large leaves ; and spinach with round seeds and large leaves, commonly called spinach of Holland. The first of these varieties is recommended by its hardiness ; as it stands the winter better than either of the others, and is, of course, to be preferred for fall sowing. The third gives most foliage, and is fittest for spring culture. The fourth unites, in a great degree, the advantages of the first and third, bearing the winter well, and producing an abundance of foliage. If, therefore, we cultivate but one of these varieties, this is the one which we ought to prefer. The soil most proper for spinach is a moist, rich loam, well dug and well manured. The seed should be sown in drills six inches apart, and lightly covered. For fall sowing the middle of October is a good time ; and for the spring crop the seed should be sown the moment you are able to get it into the earth. To the former a light covering of straw, during the winter, will be useful. According to the opinion of the French physicians, this plant is not only food, but physic ; and is hence emphatically called " Le balai de l'estomac"—the broom of the stomach—sweeping and deterging every hole and corner of that organ, without giving pain, or in' any degree inter-

* Phyt. Univer., art. Epinard. † Olivier.
‡ The New-Zealand spinach has been recently introduced. It is an excellent pot-herb ; but, being natural to a warmer climate, it does not come forward till warm weather, and until other garden productions are in abundance.—J. B.

rupting the ordinary avocations of the persons using
it. It may be useful to remark, that, to have the
full benefit of this nutritious and curative vegetable,
the spring and summer sowings should be made
every month, and that those of the latter should
have a shaded or northern exposition, as otherwise
they will run rapidly to seed.

THE SQUASH is a species of the cucurbita, and
seems to be the link that connects the melon with
the pumpkin. According to Millar, this species is
very inconstant in its appearance, rarely preserving
the same form three years in succession, sometimes
taking that of a shrub, and at other times that of a
vine. Our own experience does not warrant this
reproach.* The Bush and the Bell varieties appear
to us to be sufficiently distinct, nor have we noticed
any proneness in them to exchange characters.
With regard to soil and culture, those which are
fittest for the pumpkin are also most propitious to
the squash.

THYME (*Thymus*) is of a species embracing not
less than twenty varieties, but one of which (the
common or cultivated) comes within the plan of
our work. This is generally found in gardens,
sometimes in tufts, and sometimes in rows; but,
however placed, always growing best in poor, light,
and warm soils. In those which are cold, stiff, or
moist, it does not thrive; its branches become ragged, its leaves few, its flowers faded, and their peculiar aroma is less strong. When cultivated under
circumstances more propitious, it requires a change
of place every fourth or fifth year. All the parts of
this plant, but particularly the calix of its flower,
yields an essential oil, yellow and odorous, and

---

* The pumpkin and the squash seem to be first cousins, and
consequently will intermix, and produce an infirm progeny.
They should be kept apart. The vegetable marrow is a new
and superior variety; good both in its green and matured state
whether for summer or winter use.—J. B.

highly charged with camphire. In the kitchen it is used as an ingredient in sauces and stuffings, and in what are technically called *forced meats*. The plant may be propagated either by seed or by suckers, and requires only to be kept free from weeds or grasses.

TOMATOES (*Solanum Lycopersicum*).—This plant is of the same family with the potato, and, like it, is a native of Southern America. It has several species, two of which fall under our notice as garden vege tables, and are distinguished from each other only by a difference of size.* The smaller of these is held to be the parent plant, and has the advantage of ripening sooner than the other, and better resisting cold weather. To have an early crop, sow the seed in a warm and dry soil, and sheltered situation, in October,† and cover the bed with straw or stable litter during the winter. For summer and fall use sow again in May, and water freely. If the soil and situation be favourable, and the culture proper, the product will be great. Bosc says, " J'ai vu de ces pieds qui couvraient une toise de terrain, et qui fournissoient plusieurs centaines de fruits."‡ The distance between the plants should not be less than two feet.

JERUSALEM ARTICHOKE (*Helianthus Tuberosus*) is a native of the mountains of Chili, and a species of sunflower, having roots somewhat resembling potatoes in bulk and shape, and more nearly approaching the artichoke in taste. Its nutritive principles are less abundant than those of the potato, carrot, &c. On analysis it yields neither sugar nor amidon, and is not susceptible either of the panary or the

---

* The varieties are now numerous, and differ in size and colour.—J. B.

† They may as well be sown in a hotbed in April. The plants will attain sufficient size to be planted in the open ground as soon as the season will permit.—J. B.

‡ I have seen as many of these plants as covered a space of two yards square, producing several hundred heads of fruit.

vinous fermentation. It is, however, recommended by its hardiness (fearing neither cold, nor heat, nor drought) and by the cheapness of its culture; for, if once committed to the earth, it calls for no additional care; continuing itself, and spreading and flourishing in the midst of rivals and enemies. It is this last property which renders it so precious to the agriculturist as a permanent hog-pasture; and the more so, as it will accommodate itself to any description of soil, though that most congenial to it is a deep, moist, or marshy loam. Like the potato, it is propagated by cuttings.

The Turnip (*Rapa*).—This plant is of the cabbage family. But, unlike its relations, it requires a loose, warm, and dry soil, either sandy or calcareous; and as a manure, wood ashes rather than dung. There are many varieties, four of which are common to garden and field culture, viz., the Dutch, whose vegetation is most rapid, and, of course, fittest for early crops; and the Swedish, the green, and the purple top, which do not succeed unless sown late, and which, on this account as well as on account of their greater solidity and less evaporation, are the most suitable for winter use. Turnip seed is generally sown broadcast; but the experiments of Lord Townsend have clearly established the preference of the row or drill method, as well for a greater economy of time and labour, as for a better and more abundant product. The time of sowing, as already indicated, will depend on the variety selected. If the Dutch, sow early; if the ruta baga, sow about the 1st of June;* and if the green or purple top, do not sow till the last week of July or first week of August. After sufficiently covering the seed, press it down with a heavy roller; the object of which is not merely to bring the earth and the seed into contact, but to protect the rising crop against the fly, as many experiments concur in proving that these in-

* The 15th or 20th is preferable.—J. B.

sects are much multiplied by leaving the surface of
the earth loose and pervious, and much diminished
by rendering it close and compact.

The only variety of this plant made better, or,
rather, not made worse by transplanting, is the ruta
baga. A few feet square will give a sufficient number of plants. Draw and set these about a foot from
each other, on ridges three feet apart. Keep the
plants free from weeds during the whole course of
their vegetation, and you will rarely fail to have an
abundant crop.

CHAPTER XVI.

THE FRUIT GARDEN.

NEXT to bread corn and culinary esculents, tne
products of this description of garden holds the
highest place on the scale of table .economy. As
articles of food and drink, ripe fruits and their prepared juices are equally wholesome and pleasant;
and in many complaints are auxiliary to medicine,
while in others they serve as substitutes for it.
Every portion of ground, therefore, set apart for
the purposes of horticulture, should contain a few
fruit-bearing trees and shrubs of the more common
and useful kinds (as apples, cherries, peaches,
&c.), to be placed in the borders of its northern and
western sides, where they will least interfere with
other products, and even be useful in defending
these from high and cold winds. But in all cases
where the occupant has room for an exclusive fruit
garden, this ought to be preferred, as possessing
many advantages over the mixed kind, and particularly *that* of giving to trees and shrubs the soil, exposition, culture, and arrangement best fitted for
their several kinds and species. To the end, how-

ever, that either plan may be pursued according to the taste or convenience of the cultivator, we shall take up the list of fruit-giving plants under the common and technical division of *kernel* and *stone* fruits, *berries* and *nuts;* and, under separate heads, indicate the soil, exposure, &c., &c., most proper for each.

The APPLE-TREE (*Malus*).*—Of the many fruit-trees in cultivation, this may be deemed the most important; not only from the great abundance, diversified character, and numerous uses of its products, but from the small degree of care and labour required in its culture, and the uncommon facility with which it adapts itself to a great diversity of soils, climates, and situations. One of its varieties (the crab) is a native of our own forests; but the cultivated sorts among us have all been derived from Europe, as those of Europe were originally derived from Asia Minor.

No general catalogue of the varieties of the apple-tree has ever, so far as our reading extends, been given to the public, nor is it probable, from their great and increasing multiplication, that any successful attempt could now be made at their enumeration and description. In the time of Pliny twenty different sorts were known at Rome, whence they gradually spread themselves over the other parts of Europe. It was not till 1572, according to Stow, that they appeared in England. In 1629, Parkinson enumerated *fifty* varieties growing there; in 1650, Hartlib counted *two hundred;* and in 1822, London offered a list of *two hundred and forty approved sorts* then selling at the London nurseries.†‡

* Linnæus places it in the family of *pears,* and thence denominates it Pyrus malus; but Millar and others regard it as a distinct genus.

† Encyclopædia of Gardening.

‡ The varieties in the London Horticultural Garden alone exceed fourteen hundred, and this collection comprises but a part.—J. B.

In choosing between so many varieties, old and young, though disappointment would perhaps be impossible, still selection might not be easy; and in this view it may not be amiss to furnish the reader with a short list, in a tabular form, of those sorts which stand highest in horticultural estimation, for the hardness and productiveness of the tree, the excellence of the fruit, and the variety of uses to which this may be applied.* (See *next page.*)

It was perhaps a comparison between modern and ancient lists which first suggested the idea that " the varieties of the apple-tree have but a limited duration, and that they disappear by whole races." The Moil, the Redstreak, the Musts and the Golden Pippin, the Stire and the Fox Whelp, according to the observations of Knight,† are rapidly declining; and some recent facts warrant us in the belief that our own Spitzenberg is fast hastening to its end.

Before the discovery of this law of nature, little, if any, attention was given to the propagation of the apple-tree by modes other than those which perpetuate a favourite race; and hence it was that scions, buds, layers, and cuttings, were long and exclusively employed. But this practice is now considerably qualified, and many horticulturists and amateurs are engaged in producing new varieties from the *seeds*, and from a *commixture of the farinas* of sorts whose merits are already established.‡ Of

---

* Such has been the improvement in the apple, that not more than one half of these varieties would now be ranked in the first class of fruit.—J. B.

† Treatise on Apple and Pear Trees, p. 15.

‡ The credit of this discovery is due to Mr. Knight, the distinguished president of the Horticultural Society of London. On this point, however, there are skeptics, and of considerable name. Williamson and Speechley consider the deterioration of the apple-tree as accidental, not uniform; as the temporary effect of weather, not that of a settled law of nature; and, therefore, that " genial summers will restore to old trees their ordinary health and duration."—Hort. Trans., vol. iii., p. 291; and Hints, p. 188

NAMES.	Quality as Bearer.	Character of the tree and fruit.	USES.
Golden Pippin, } Old varieties.	Good.	Supposed to be de-[clining.	Fruit fine. } For the dessert, or the kitchen.
Newtown do. } Old varieties.	Do.	Hardy.	Do.
Fall do.	Great.	Do.	Do.
Elton, } New varieties.	Do.	Do.	Do.
New Scarlet, } New varieties.	Do.	Do.	Do.
Padley,	Middling.	Do.	Do. } the press, or the kitchen.
Spitzenberg, } Old varieties.	Do.	Do.	Do.
Swaa¯, } Old varieties.	Good.	Feeble.	Excellent. } Do.
White Calville, } Old varieties.	Good.	Hardy.	Do.
Red do. } Old varieties.	Great.	Do.	Fine.
Autumn do. } Old varieties.	Do.	Do.	Do.
Kentish Russet, } Old variety.	Good.	Do.	Do.
Beauty of Wilts, } New.	Great.	Hardy.	Do.
French Crab, } Old variety.	Do.	Do.	Do.
Hollow eyed	Do.	Do.	Do. } Principally culinary.
Cornwall Pearmain, } Old varieties.	Do.	Do.	Do.
Keswick Codling, } Old.	Very great.	Do.	Do.
Dutch do. } Old.	Great.	Do.	Do.
Alexander, } New variety.	Middling.	Do. the largest of the genus, [weighing 19 oz.]	Fine.
Rennet Frank, } Old varieties.	Good.	Do.	Do. } For the dessert or the kitchen.
Rennet of L. Island, } Old varieties.	Do.	Do.	Do.
Grey Rennet,	Do.	Do.	Do.
Golden Rennett.*	Do.	Do.	Do.

* As most of the above apples are unknown in our common nurseries, at least by the names here given to them, I take the liberty of appending, from Coxe's Treatise on Fruit Trees, a selection which he recommends to the admirers of fine fruit. I give them in the order in which they ripen.

hese different methods of propagation, the first we
shall describe is that

By seeds, which has two objects; the supply of
stems, on which to ingraft or inoculate old and favourite races; and the production of varieties which
shall be entirely new. In the first of these cases,
sound and thriving stocks are necessary; and these
are only to be had from the seeds of apples grown
on healthy and vigorous trees.* In the other case,
it is not enough that the parent plant be sound and
thriving; it should possess those properties also
which the cultivator is most desirous of giving to
his orchard: such as bearing abundantly, giving its
fruit early in the season, or of a fine flavour, or colour, or size, &c., &c. The observance of these
rules is indispensable to the success of all experiments made of this method; and is so because the
rules themselves are founded on an immutable law
of nature, *that vegetables, like animals, transmit their
properties, good or bad, to their offspring*.

The culture of the seeds, whether intended for
stems or for fruit, will be the same for the first
year. Sow them in autumn, in beds of light mellow earth of middling quality; cover them an inch
thick with garden mould; and, at the end of the

Table Apples.—Junating, Prince's Harvest, Bough, Summer
Queen, Early Pearmain, Summer Rose, Codling, Maiden's
Blush, Hagloe Crab, Catiline, Romanite or Rambo, *Fall Pippin*,
Doctor Apple, Wine, Late Pearmain, Burlington, Greening,
Bellflower, Newark Pippin, Pennock, Michael Henry, *Spitzen-
bergh, Newtown Pippin*, Priestley, Lady Apple, Carthouse,
Tewksbury, Winter Blush.

Cider Apples.—Hewes's Crab, Grayhouse, Winesap, Harrison,
Styre, Roane's White Crab, Gloucester White, Redstreak,
Campfield, American Pippin, *Golden Rennet*, Hagloe Crab,
Cooper's Russeting, Ruckman's Pearmain.

There are propagated in our nurseries several new varieties,
obtained from seeds, worthy of cultivation.—*Editor.*

* The usual method of employing the pumice from a cider-
mill is very slovenly, and necessarily rejects all discrimination
between good and bad, sound and unsound stems.

year, thin the plants to the distance of a foot from each other.   Such of them as are intended for grafting or budding may remain in the nursery till these operations have been performed : but those cultivated with a view to new races should be transplanted, and in rows ten feet apart every way.*   Left to themselves, they may be slow in producing fruit ; a circumstance which has engaged artists in a search after means which should bestow upon them an artificial precocity.   These divide themselves into two classes :. such as operate exclusively on the soil, and such as apply directly to the plant.   If the young tree abound in leaves, branches, and suckers, with a bark green, smooth, and shining, the remedy will consist in removing from its roots a portion of the original earth, and substituting for it a soil containing less vegetable food ; such as sand, gravel, or schist, &c.   If, on the other hand, the tree be small and weak, having little foliage and few branches, and a bark rough, dry, and spotted, there is reason to suspect that its want of fertility is occasioned by a want of nourishment, and we must hasten, by reversing the management just laid down, to give it an additional supply of food.   As belonging to the second class of means, we may enumerate partial decortication, piercing, wiring, grafting, pegging, cutting a portion of the roots, &c., but all depending on the same principle, "the obstruction, in a greater or less degree, of the descending sap."   Of these, the first (which has got the name of *ringing*) is the most ancient and best recommended.   The Romans were well acquainted with it,† and Du Hamel revived its use in France about the year 1733,‡ whence it extended itself to Holland and Germany.§   The

* Encyclopædia of Gardening.
† Virgil and Columella.
‡ Memoires de L'Academie des Sciences, 1788.
§ Works of Dederich and Diel. Darwin's Phytologia describes and explains it, yet it was considered as a new discovery

practice, however, never became general; probably from discovering that the intended effect was not always produced, and that, in other respects, the tree was injured by the process. Still, as some of our readers may wish to make the experiment for themselves, we subjoin the following directions: "Cut out with a knife a ring of the outer and inner bark. If the tree be large, the excision should be made in the branches; but if small, in the stock. In apple or other trees bearing kernel fruit, the wound should not be larger than will fill up in two, or, at most, three years; and in peach or other stone-bearing fruit, in one year."[*] The time for doing this is early in the spring, and before the sap begins to circulate, as the rationale of the practice takes for granted that, " by preventing the descent of *this* below the ring, you accumulate a force above it, which shows itself in the production of fruit buds."

Another means of effecting this object is mentioned by Williams (the discoverer of it), and consists altogether in leaving the plant to throw out lateral shoots, with little, if any restraint. By pursuing this method, " the leaves soon take that peculiar conformation which is necessary to the production of blossom buds; and seedling apples give fruit in four, five, and six years, instead of eight, ten, and even fifteen, as is the case by the usual method of planting close and pruning to naked stems."[†]

2. *Of propagation by Cuttings.*—Every variety of the apple-tree may be propagated by this method, and will give the finest fruit in the smallest compass for many years.[‡§] But it does not follow that

by the London Horticultural Society as late as 1817! (See a paper from Dr. Nohden in the Transactions of that year.) And, what is hardly less extraordinary, Hemphill, a German clergyman, claims the discovery as his own in 1815!

[*] Hort. Trans., vol. i., p. 108. See a paper on Ringing, by Williams.

[†] Idem., p. 333.　　　　　　　　[‡] Loudon's Encyclopædia.

[§] So far as our experiments indicate Loudon is wrong. Cut

all the varieties adapt themselves equally well to it. Cuttings of the pippin, of the rennet, of the pearmain, and of some other tribes, do not succeed with the same facility as those of the codlin races; and between these there is some difference. The varieties known by the name of the White, the Keswic, the Burknot, and the Carlisle, are best fitted for it, as they produce roots sooner and in greater abundance than the others.

Whatever variety we employ, care must be taken in selecting the cuttings. Shoots growing on top branches are not so good as side shoots; and, other things being equal, the nearer these can be got to the ground, the better they are, having in them more of the living principle. Another rule is to choose those having an oblique or horizontal direction, rather than such as grow perpendicularly. A cutting of eight or ten inches will be sufficiently long; but, as the power of putting forth roots is found to reside principally in the *joints*, and as these are formed of woods of different ages, we must remember to give to the cuttings a portion of both: and hence the rule, "to leave to one of six or eight inches of the wood of the present year, an inch or half an inch of that of the last year."

The time for planting is that of the full flow of the juices, as it is then that, being most strongly determined downward, they will soonest form that callus or ring which is destined to become the basis of the future roots. Nor is the manner of planting them a matter of indifference. When your holes are ready, put into the bottom of each some hard substance (pieces of crockery are the best), and so set your plants that they shall rest on these, and not on the earth;* after which, fill up what is left of

tings cannot be depended on for propagating the apple by any mode which has been tried in our climate.—*J. B*

* "The Orange and Ceretonia, &c., if inserted in a mere mass of earth, will hardly, if at all, throw out roots; while, if

the holes, and press the ground closely about the plants. They must now be covered with hand-glasses, shaded in hot weather, and watered and ventilated occasionally and moderately. In August the glasses may be dispensed with, and in October the cuttings should be transplanted to the nursery.

3. *Of propagation by Layers.*—This mode was probably suggested by observing the habits peculiar to some trees and shrubs (as the laurel and the currant), of pointing their branches to the earth; where, finding an habitual moisture, they strike root, and become distinct plants. In imitating this natural process, the artist notches the lower side of the branch he employs, buries it in the earth three or four inches deep, and keeps it down by a wooden crotchet. As this is done before the descent of the sap, the notch operates like a dam or obstruction to the descending juices, and forces them into a bulbous form and granular substance, whence are emitted a mass of roots necessary to the infant plant. When these are sufficiently formed, that part of the branch which binds them to the stem is severed, and the layer taken up and transplanted.

4. *Of propagation by Suckers.*—This mode is never employed but to obtain a supply of stems, on which to ingraft dwarfs and espaliers, and is, of course, confined to the Paradise and Creeper varieties. All that it requires is to dig up the plants, to give a portion of root to each, to shorten the stems to a fourth or a half of their natural length, and to set them out in nursery rows.

5. *Of propagation by Scions.*—These are parts of living trees, which, when inserted in others of the same nature, identify themselves with them, and grow as if on their parent stems. The objects to

inserted at the sides of pots, so as to touch them, they seldom fail of becoming rooted plants. T. A. Knight succeeded well with the mulberry in this way."—Encyclopædia of Gardening, p. 444

be obtained by this operation (which is called grafting) are four, viz., to preserve and multiply varieties of known and acknowledged merit; to improve
the qualities of the fruit ;* to hasten fructification
in trees slow in bearing; and, lastly, to render barren trees fruitful.† The general rules which guide
in the operation are to unite varieties of the same
nature, as apples and quinces, or apricots and plums,
&c., &c.; to seek a resemblance in the flow of the
juices and the permanence of the foliage, between
the scion and the stock ; to take the scion from lateral shoots, and from the last growth of the wood,
and at a proper season (which is during the winter);
to unite exactly the inner bark of the scion to that
of the stock, and to do this when the sap of the latter is in full motion. The age of the stocks is regulated by the character they are to bear : if intended for full standards, they should not be less than
three years old; if for half standards, two years
old; and if for dwarfs, one year old. The same
rule appears to have determined the elevation at

* Lord Bacon's opinion, that the office of the stem is merely
passive and subservient to the scion, is received with much
qualification by professional horticulturists. Millar asserts that
"crab stocks cause apples to be firmer and sharper, and to keep
longer ; and that breaking pears put on quince stocks give
gritty fruit ; while melting pears, on stocks of the same kind,
give fruit highly improved." Neil thinks "the qualities of the
fruit are partially affected by the character of the stock on which
it is placed." Thouin necessarily holds the same opinion, as he
recommends grafting on a graft as a great improvement of the
fruit; and Loudon, in his Encyclopædia, gives it as the settled
opinion "of all practical men, that the nature of the fruit is in
some degree affected by that of the stock."

† Encyclopædia of Gardening, p. 783; and M'Donald's Ex
periments. If trees comparatively or absolutely barren be
headed down, and receive two or more scions, the roots and
stems, having now less to do, will nourish the grafts well, and
soon enable them to bear fruit. But, besides this effect of increased nourishment, we must remember that grafting, like
ringing, predisposes to the production of fruit-buds by the obstruction it gives to the descending sap.

which the scions are to be inserted ; as it is the
general practice to graft standards at six feet from
the ground, half standards at three feet, and dwarfs
at six or eight inches : but both Millar and Knight
recommend *low* grafting in preference to high, " *in
all cases* where the durability of the tree is an object with the cultivator ;" and our own experience,
though comparatively small, is decidedly with them.

6. *Of propagation by Buds.*—This method is a
modification of the former, and differs from it only
in this, that in grafting we employ a shoot already
matured into wood ; and in budding, a shoot in embryo. The rules which govern in this case are to
select buds from lateral shoots only, and from the
middle of these in preference to either extremity ;
to take them in moist or cloudy weather, or (if this
condition of the atmosphere do not exist) early in
the morning or late in the evening, as at these times
the perspiration of the leaves being least active, the
buds will suffer least by the operation. If, after removing the woody part (which comes off with the
shield), you discover a hole or opening under the
bud, it is unfit for use, having, in technical language,
lost its root. If, on the other hand, the bottom be
sound, lose no time in inserting it in the stock on
which it is destined to grow ; and in doing this, prefer the north to the south side of the stem, and
smooth and shining bark to that which is dry and
spotted ; and be particularly careful to cover the
edges of the shield with the bark of the stem, and
to tie with double ligatures ; the one intended merely to keep the bud in its place, the other, and up-
permost, to obstruct, in some degree, the ascent of
the sap.*

The time for budding is from the first of July to
the last of August ; but the true criterion in this
respect is the condition of the bud, and of the bark

* Encyclopædia of Gardening.

18

adhering to it. When the first is full and verdant, and when the last separates readily from the stem, the operation cannot be ill timed.

7. *Of propagation by mixing the farinas of different sorts.*—This mode (which, by-the-way, is only a qualification of the first) is of late discovery, and has not yet been much practised. We are, however, assured that it has already produced many new and excellent varieties ; and, according to Loudon, it consists "in cutting out the stamens of the blossoms to be impregnated, and afterward, when the stigma is mature, introducing the pollen of the other parent." By this process the discoverer (Mr. Knight) has obtained the *Downton, red* and *yellow Ingestrie, Grange, Brindgwood,* and *Siberian* pippins. The four first named of these were produced by crossing the orange and the golden pippin ; the fifth by crossing the golden pippin and the golden Harvey ; and the sixth by crossing the Siberian crab and the pearmain.* The only important rule laid down for this method is "to select for crossing those varieties whose qualities most nearly resemble each other ;" as many observations show that where the difference between the sorts employed is great (even in

---

* This, and another seedling from the same parents, called the *yellow Siberian,* are, according to Knight's test (the specific gravity of the juices), the best cider apples yet known ; "the gravity of the one being 1079, and that of the other 1085, water being 1000."—Loudon's Catalogue of Apples.*

---

* Subsequent, probably, to Loudon's publication, the specific gravity of the juice of the Downton pippin was ascertained to be 1080. Mr. Knight also produced, in 1807–8, two new varieties, the *Siberian Harvey* and the *Foxley Apple ;* the first affording the heaviest juice ever known, it being 1091 : that of the latter was 1080.—See *Knight on the Apple and Pear ; also* " *Hints,*" &c., *by W. Salisbury.*

The celebrity of Mr. Knight's new varieties of apples induced me to send to England for them in 1823 ; and I have now growing in my garden the *Downton* and *Grange* pippins, the *Siberian Harvey, Foxley Apple,* and some others not named above.— *Fd*

point of size), the new variety produced is not valuable.* We subjoin to these remarks, and in illustration of them, an experiment of this mode, made by a distinguished Scotch agriculturist (M'Donald), as given in the Encyclopœdia of Gardening, page 783. "In 1808 he selected some blossoms of the Nonpareil, which he impregnated with the pollen of the golden and Newton pippins. When the apples were ripe, he selected some of the best, from which he took the seeds, and sowed them in pots, which he placed under a frame. He had eight or nine seedlings, which he transplanted into the open ground in the spring of 1809. In 1811 he picked out a few of the strongest plants, and put them singly into pots. In the spring of 1812 he observed some of the plants showing fruit-buds. He took a few of the twigs and grafted them on a healthy stock on a wall, and in 1813 he had a few apples. This year his seedlings yielded several dozens, and also his grafts; and he mentions that the apples on the grafts were the largest."

Having indicated the varieties of the apple-tree, and the means of continuing these and of producing new ones; the selection to be made among them, and the points in which their management may differ, we proceed to what, in this respect, is common to them all, viz., transplanting, pruning, training, thinning, and, lastly, manuring, or otherwise altering the condition of the soil.†

Of Transplanting.—This process is sometimes repeated twice or thrice before the tree is permanently placed, and, in the opinion of Knight, never

* Mr. Kline, the anatomist, &c., holds the same doctrine in relation to animals.

† The French make a distinction, and justly, between *l'amendement* and *l'engrais*, for which we have no corresponding terms which sufficiently illustrate the distinction. Ploughing, harrowing, irrigating, and leaving in fallow, are among the *amendemens* (improvements): animal and vegetable matter, under some of their many modifications, constitute *l'engrais* (manures).

to its advantage, and often to its injury. Our own practice is to work the stocks as soon as they have attained the diameter of an inch in the seedbed, and transplant once and permanently; believing that, though repeated removals may hasten the production of fruit, they retard the general growth and development of the plant, and sometimes form a crisis in its health from which it never recovers.

The rules which govern in this operation are as follows: Take up the young trees with as little injury to the roots as possible, and replant them without any avoidable delay, in holes not less than three feet square,* and thirty feet apart; give them the same depth and exposition they had in the nursery; bring the earth and the roots into full contact, and water freely till the young trees give evidence of having taken root anew. The time for this operation is during any mild weather in the spring, before the sap has got into motion; or, in the autumn, after its circulation has ceased.†

Of Pruning.—This branch was originally confined to the removal of dead, or diseased, or fractured wood; but the discovery was soon made that branches might do mischief from their position as well as from their unsoundness: and hence the rule, " *to retrench whatever intercepts the rays of light, or prevents a due ventilation of the tree.*" The next step in the art was to take off redundant branches; as frequent experiments proved that, by lessening the quantity of wood, that which was left was made more productive. A third discovery followed: that

---

* For the advantage of this practice, see Cours d'Agriculture, art. Pecher.

† Each of these seasons has its advocates; one set forbidding fall planting, because the high winds of the winter shake and fatigue the young trees; the other spring planting, because a dry and warm spring will destroy them. Our own practice is to employ both seasons indiscriminately, and experience justifies this course.

straight or *perpendicular* shoots gave little and bad fruit; while those pushing at angles less than 45 degrees,* gave fruit abundantly and of a good quality: and hence the rule, "*for rigorously suppressing water-shoots and gluttons,* and *for encouraging side-shoots growing horizontally,*" or nearly so, in relation to the parent stem. An extension of the principle of this rule was found to be usefully applied to *side-shoots* themselves: and hence the practice "*of heading these down, so as to give to the direction of their future growth new and artificial angles ;*" for, by obstructing the flow of the sap, and compelling it to travel more slowly, you compel it also to throw out more blossoms, and, consequently, to give more fruit.

To these remarks we subjoin a few others on this head.

1. Young trees, if of moderate growth, should be pruned early in the spring ;† if of luxuriant growth, later in the season.

2. Established and bearing trees are best pruned in the fall; the operation, performed then, strengthens the tree, and tends to the production of blossom buds.

3. Superfluous and ill-placed buds may be rubbed off at any time; and no buds pushing after midsummer should be spared.

4. The number of shoots to be retained must be limited by the nature of the tree, the size of the

* Cours d'Agriculture, art. Courbure.

† From some years' experience in summer pruning, say late in June and early in July, we are disposed to give it a preference over autumn or spring pruning. At either of the latter periods the tree is divested of foliage, and the wounds are exposed to the drying and corroding influence of the sun and winds; and the accustomed flow of sap in the spring induces the growth of a multiplicity of new sprouts. At midsummer the wounds are shielded by the foliage, the flow of sap is moderate, and the caubium, or elaborated sap, which is then most abundant, soon covers the lips of the wounds, and prevents disease and decay. —J. B.

fruit, and that of the head.   Trees which produce only on young spurs (as the apple-tree), require a larger provision of this sort than those which give fruit for several years in succession on old spurs.

5. In choosing between the shoots to be retained, other things being equal, preserve those which are lowest placed, and, of lateral shoots, those which are nearest to the origin of a branch.

6. The retained shoots should be treated according to the class of fruit-trees to which they belong. If to that which bears on distinct branches and on old spurs, they should be shortened as little as possible, or not at all; if to the class which bears on the last year's wood only (as the apple, apricot, pear, cherry, and plum), they should be shortened alternately, year and year about, so as always to furnish a proper supply of bearers; and if to the anomalous class which bears on both kinds of spurs, the treatment should be of the mixed kind, partaking of the modes severally prescribed for the two other classes, and in proportion as the shoots may indicate a greater or less assimilation to either of these.*

7. Shorten strong shoots one fourth, and feeble ones one half.

Of Training.—Many observations led to the belief that, though the apple tree, when left to its natural form and bulk, possessed its greatest vigour and productiveness, and was in the condition fittest for large and permanent orchards, still that in other forms, and on feebler stems, and under a treatment in all respects more artificial, it may be made to give fruit of an earlier sort, of a larger size, and of better appearance.   Of this important discovery

---

* Some gardeners are in the practice of heading down old and much decayed apple-trees within a few inches of the ground. Forsyth was the first to recommend this practice, on the credit of many experiments made by himself, which prove that trees so managed may be restored to vigour and fruitfulness.—See his work on Fruit Trees.

horticulturists were not slow in availing themselves, and, as in many similar cases, even abused
it; for hence came the whole family of dwarfs and
monsters, so fashionable in the days of La Quinteny
and D'Andilly, and of which some specimens may yet
be found in different parts of Europe. However, as
experiments multiplied, and science and good taste
increased, a medium size, and forms less foreign
from vegetable nature than those of the lion and the
stag, the distaff and the urn, were brought into use,
and established as most proper for garden culture.

In forming these (to which have been given the
names of the half standard, the pyramid, and the
espalier), the labour necessarily begins in the nursery. The stock of the crab, the paradise, or the
quince, is grafted two, three, or four inches from
the earth, with the variety you wish to propagate.
In the spring of the second year after grafting, one
of two methods is employed to form the head; either by shortening the shoots which may have
pushed from the graft, or the graft itself to the third
or fourth eye from its root. In either case, a growth
of more vigorous shoots succeeds, from which you
select your main or leading branches; always taking
care to reject those which are spongy and over-
grown, or feeble and wiry.

The future management of the tree will necessarily be regulated by its destination. If intended for
a *standard*, your labour will be principally confined
to the removal of dead or dying, and redundant
wood; and " to the thinning and shortening the exterior parts of the branches, so that the light may
everywhere penetrate into the head, without anywhere passing through it."* If, on the other hand,
you mean that your tree shall be a *pyramid*, the ordinary mode of giving this form consists in making
the oldest and lowest branches the longest, and in

* Encyclopædia of Gardening.

shortening the upper and younger growths gradually to the top.   But against this practice we are ad-
monished by a British writer of considerable authority,* who says that, " when applied to apple, or
pear, or other trees which produce their fruits at the
extremities of the last year's wood, the conical form
is both absurd and ruinous ; since, to produce or preserve it, we must necessarily destroy a large proportion of fruit-buds."   The terms of this position
are, however, too broad; for, though the objection
be good against the old or ordinary method of producing this shape, it fails altogether against the shape
itself, provided any mode of producing it be found
which shall leave the fruit-buds untouched ; and that
such mode does exist, we learn from another writer
of the same nation, and of equal, if not higher authority.†   "If," he says, " the graft you employ be
inserted with its point (or terminal) bud perfect, the
branches will range themselves horizontally and in
series, and, without violence, produce all the effects
(as to shape) which have hitherto been produced by
pruning and training."   The *espalier* form, if that be
desired, is produced by selecting two healthy shoots
the second year after grafting, which, when spread
out, like the ribs of a fan, against an open frame,
and filled up within by lateral shoots, present two
surfaces, the one in front and the other in rear, for
the production of fruit.   The knife in this case is
only used in keeping these surfaces clear of dead,
or unhealthy, or fractured wood, and in removing all
shoots other than those growing laterally.

   With these several forms may be associated the

---

   * Nicol.
   † Hayward's Principles of Gardening.   An additional authority in favour of the pyramidal form is the practice of those eminent botanists, Thouin and Bosc, in the national gardens at
Paris (the Jardin des Plantes and the Luxembourg).   It is, besides, the form generally adopted, if we mistake not, in the
schools of botany.

artificial shelter of *walls;* which, from many experiments made in the most crowded parts of our cities, are believed to be useful in maturing fruits of many kinds, and especially to such as are of southern origin and delicate constitution, as the peach, the nectarine, the fig, &c. The rules which apply to this branch of the art are few and simple, and will be reserved for a future subject (the peach-tree), as one to which they better apply than to the apple-tree.

*Of Thinning.** —In using this term, we confine ourselves to the removal of *superfluous leaves* and *fruit;* an operation which, though proper and useful, must be cautiously performed; as, in the vegetable economy, the office to which the leaf is destined is very important : being the supply of the plant with that portion of its subsistence derived from the atmosphere. We know of no purpose, therefore, that will justify us in stripping off any considerable part of the foliage, unless it be that of maturing fruit and wood, which, from constitutional defects or a faulty situation, would not otherwise ripen. Peaches, pears, grapes, and some varieties of apples, occasionally come within this description; and though the process may not be equally indispensable to them all, yet all are undoubtedly improved by it. The rule which governs in this case is, " to remove such leaves as shade the fruit, so soon as this has attained its full size, and begins to lose its green colour." To do it earlier would impair the growth of the fruit; and to do it rigorously and at once, would arrest that of the retained shoots : whence it follows that " the thinning must be gradual, and at two or more different times during the space of five or six days."† If the leaves of walltrees hang longer than usual, they should be brushed off, the better to ventilate and ripen the young wood;

* Encyclopædia of Gardening.
† Not applicable, or, if applicable, seldom or ever practised on the farm.—J. B.

but, in doing this, we must be careful to brush *up-ward* and *outward*, and never in the opposite direc-tions, as in that case we could not fail to injure the retained buds.

Thinning the fruit is also an important operation; since, if properly managed, it has the direct effect of improving both the size and the quality of what is left, while, at the same time, it betters the condi-tion of the tree, and adds greatly to its longevity. Few persons have been such negligent observers as not to have remarked the proneness in apricot, nec-tarine, peach, and plum trees, to set more fruit than they are able to ripen. It is true that this exces-sive bearing will in some degree cure itself, but al-ways at the expense of the tree and of the fruit it actually ripens; whence the economy of anticipa-ting nature, and relieving her from the labour of sustaining a useless and abortive progeny. But, as in the case of superfluous leaves, this thinning should be performed cautiously and at different times. "If the fruit be thickly set over particular parts of the tree only, begin by taking off one half from such parts; and if every part of the tree be crowded, take off the same proportion from the whole." Revise it again in June, and finally in Ju-ly; taking off, at each of these revisions, such as may be usefully spared. On healthy and full-bear-ing trees, one apple of large size to every square foot of the superficial contents of the tree, is con-sidered a just proportion; that is, a space of fifteen feet by twelve may be allowed to ripen two hundred apples; and if the fruit be small, this proportion may be increased a third part.* "Many persons," says Nicol, "may think that thinning to this extent will be excessive; but I wish such to be convinced of the propriety of doing so by comparison. If they have two trees of a kind, healthy and well-loaded,

* Encyclopædia of Gardening.

thin the one as directed, and leave the other to itself. It will be found that the tree which has been
thinned will produce an equal or greater weight of
fruit, and this incomparably more beautiful and higher in flavour. The operation should be over by the
time the fruit is half grown; for, if delayed till they
are nearly full grown, and beginning to swell off for
ripening, the mischief will be already done, both to
the tree and to the fruit which is retained."

*Of Manuring, and otherwise altering the condition
of the soil.*—We have said that apple-trees grow
well in a great variety of soils; but it by no means
follows that they affect all soils alike. A substantial loam, whose substratum is dry, is that in which
they thrive best; and a circumstance which is not
discouraging to the agriculturist is, that, should he
not find such ready made to his hand, he can himself make it without much expense of time or
money. Its elements are cheap and abundant,
being sand, clay, and vegetable or animal matter in
a state of decomposition. Equal proportions of the
first and second of these, and a smaller quantity of
the third, will give a soil of great power and durability, requiring only occasional supplies of mould
to reinstate what of that may be taken from the
mass by successive croppings. This mould is itself created by a mixture of various substances, as
dung, ashes, leaves, weeds, lime, marl, &c., frequently turned and thoroughly rotted, and to which,
in this condition, has been given the technical name
of *compost.* A biennial dressing of this, applied to
the whole surface, with an annual and careful culture of some esculent plant between the trees, will
bestow on the latter all the advantages that, in our
climate, can be given by labouring and manuring
the earth.

Apple, like other fruit trees, have their enemies
and their diseases. All excesses of heat or cold,
wetness or dryness, are unfriendly to them; some-

times wholly destroying their fertility for the season, at others seriously injuring it, and occasionally, though rarely, disorganizing the trees themselves. Many insects also prey upon them, attacking their leaves, blossoms, fruit, bark, or roots; of which the Aphis lœnigera,* the curculio, the scarabeus, &c., are the most common and injurious; nor, unfortunately, do we know any specific remedy against these evils.† But, after all, may not our own negligence be considered as the most fruitful source of many others of a similar kind? How often do we find the bark of fruit-trees covered and coloured with parasites, in the form of mosses, and lichens, and smut, which a small degree of labour and a little whitewash would entirely and promptly remove.‡ How patiently do we look on and see the ravages made on their leaves and fruit-buds by caterpillars of different names and appearances, when, if we visited them at daybreak, all would be found at home and asleep, and entirely within our reach? And, lastly, how various and fatal are the wounds inflicted on stems and branches (under the name and pretence of pruning) when left open, as they generally are, to the alternate action of air, and frost, and sunshine, without giving them even the cheap and simple covering of St. Fiacre?§

* The Eriosoma mali of Leach. This insect forms the excrescences called galls on the stems and branches of trees. " W. Salisbury gives an engraving of it, as it appeared through a magnifying glass, eating its way into the roots of a tree; and another of the same insect in the bug state, which he believed to be the male."—Loudon, p. 788.

† Watering, fumigation, &c., are the remedies usually prescribed; but, in our opinion, " a judicious management of the sub and surface soil, culture and pruning, are the things most to be relied upon."—Idem.

‡ The best wash for the apple-tree is a strong ley, to be applied to the trunk and larger branches with a brush, early in June. It destroys both parasitic plants and insects.—J. B.

§ A mixture of cow-dung and clay is called in France (that land of saints) " the ointment of St. Fiacre;" and is, in the

The PEAR-TREE (*Pyrus communis*) was not unknown to the ancient Greeks and Romans, and
grows spontaneously in the forests of Europe as
high as the 51st degree of north latitude. It differs
from the apple-tree in its greater tendency to a pyramidal form, in its being more slow in arriving at
a bearing or productive state,* and, lastly, in its
living to a much greater age.†

The hardiness of the tree and the excellence of
its fruit have recommended it to general cultivation, as might be inferred from the very great number of its varieties. These, which in the time of
Pliny amounted to thirty, have since increased to
three hundred; and, if Van Mons is to be credited,
to even double that number. From this long mus-
ter-roll of names we shall select a few, in their natural order of ripening, which stand highest in public estimation for dessert and culinary uses, and
which may be made to supply our tables from
July to March: The *Green Chissel*, the *Red Musca-
dine*, the *Avorat* or *Muscat Robine*, the *Royale d'Eté*,
the *Green Yair*, the *Beurré Rouge*, the *Messieur Jean*,
the *Crassan*, the *Colmar*, the *Vergoleuse*, the *Wonder
of Winter*, the *Poire d'Auch*, the *Brown Beurré*, the
Muscat l'Allemande, the *Winter St. Germain*, and the
Bon Chretien.‡§

As these varieties do not reproduce themselves
from the seed; as the plants furnished by layers,

opinion of the best horticulturists of that country, a more effi
cient covering for the wounds of trees than the complicated and
much-vaunted mixture of Forsyth.

* Generally from 15 to 18 years.—Cours d'Agriculture, art.
Poirier.

† Knight asserts, that the variety called in England the *Bar-
land* has existed from the beginning of the 17th century, and
conjectures that the *Tanuton Squash* (an older variety) was first
known in the beginning of the 16th.

‡ Du Hamel divides the varieties known in his day into two
classes, and considers them all as proceeding from the fecundation of the wild pear by the quince.

§ See our note on orchards, p. 009.—J. B.

cuttings, and suckers are very indifferent; and as seedlings are slow in giving their fruit, it follows that the pear is principally propagated by scions and buds. These are placed on quince or pear stocks, according as taste or interest may invite to early and small crops of fine quality, or to later and more abundant ones of inferior character. In the former case, the stem of the quince must be employed, and in the latter that of the common pear, and without any material difference in the operation, excepting that "the feebler the stem, the nearer to the earth should be placed the scion or the bud."

Notwithstanding the hardiness ascribed to the pear-tree, we know not any of the kernel class more readily or sensibly affected by particular conditions of the atmosphere. A moist and cold spring, a wet summer, and a rainy autumn, are alike unpropitious to it. In either of these cases, the fruit which does not rot is watery and tasteless, and when all take place, the evil extends to even a second year; as, according to the observations of Coursette, "long-continued moisture rarely fails to convert fruit-buds into wood-buds."

The second year after budding or grafting, the plants may be removed to the places where it is intended they shall stand; and as the manner and time of doing this do not differ from those already prescribed for the apple-tree, we may spare ourselves and our readers the trouble of a repetition of our directions on those heads.

With respect to exposition and soil, though the pear-tree may be made to grow anywhere, still it will succeed badly on the north side of hills or in stiff dry soils, and still worse on those which rest on a wet subsoil. Some of its later and finer varieties require and deserve a deep substantial loam, occasionally refreshed with a dressing of well-rotted dung, and some of the best aspects the garden can furnish.

Cultivated as standards and pyramids, the young trees should be left in a great degree to regulate their own shape ;* and if interference become proper at all, it should be conducted under two rules, "to keep the middle of the head pretty open, and the sides well balanced."† Trees of other forms, and intended for walls and espaliers, require more labour and management, and a degree of both summer and winter pruning; the former of which consists in rubbing off all fore-right, ill-placed, superfluous, or spongy shoots, before they become so hard as to render the use of the knife necessary; while the latter (performed during any temperate weather between November and April) is conducted on the general rule "of sparing all such well-placed and thriving laterals as may be necessary for preserving the form given to the head of the tree, and of cutting away all others close to the branch from which they grow." If the older wood be diseased or redundant, cut this away also, or shorten it down to some healthy and promising shoots. The retained branches, if growing against a wall or trellis, should, after each pruning, be laid down and nailed, with as much extension as can conveniently be given to them.

Mr. Knight's mode of training the pear-tree is to leave on the young stock two lateral branches on each side. When about six feet high, he transplants the tree early in the spring, and inserts grafts on each of the laterals, "so that two of them shall push from the stem about four feet from the ground, and two others from the summit, the ensuing year.

---

* Knight remarks that, in general, very little pruning is required for pear standards or pyramids ; but that there are sorts which form heads resembling those of apple-trees, and that for these pruning may be beneficial.

† To produce a well-balanced tree, shorten the wood of the deficient side, and leave the other to itself. For the reason of this rule, see a note on the art. Apple-tree.

The shoots produced by these grafts, when about a foot long, are to be trained downward, the lower ones almost perpendicularly, and the upper ones just below a horizontal line, and so placed as to distance that the leaves of the one will not at all shade the other. Continue this mode of training the second year, and in the third you may expect an abundant crop of fruit."*

When an old tree becomes unproductive, one of 'wo methods should be adopted: either to cut it down within eighteen inches or two feet from the ground, and train up anew some selected shoots which may have pushed from the stump (which is the method of Forsyth), or "to take off at its base every branch which does not want at least twenty degrees of being perpendicular, and all spurs from such other branches as, by this rule, will be left. Into these (the retained branches), at their subdivisions, and at different distances from their bases quite to their extremities, grafts must be carefully inserted, which, when they attain sufficient length (say twelve inches), must be trained downward between the branches, as directed in the preceding paragraph."†

The enemies and diseases of the pear-tree being those of the apple-tree, we refer the reader to what has been said in relation to them in the preceding article.

The Quince (*Pyrus cydonia*) is a native of the southern and eastern parts of Europe, where it is much cultivated for its fruit, which, though not eatable in a raw state, is readily converted into a mar-

* We have varied Mr. Knight's phraseology a little, having substituted the form of a *precept* for what he has given in that of an *experiment*.

† Forsyth's objection to the practice of cutting off old spurs, viz., "that it brings on the canker, and renders the fruit small and spotted," would admonish us against the employment of this method, had it not been adopted and recommended by Mr Knight.

malade, and an excellent dry paste, to which is giv
en the name of *catignac.* The stem is also employ.
ed for the reception of apple and pear grafts, and
has the property of giving to the fruit it bears great-.
er precocity, an increased size, and an improved
flavour ; but with this drawback, that " the quantity
is small, and the product short-lived, as the age of
the tree seldom exceeds ten or twelve years."

The varieties of the quince are four: the *pear
quince,* the *apple quince,* the *mild,* and the *Portuguese ;*
of which the last should in all cases be preferred,
being hardier, handsomer, and a better bearer than
the other sorts, and, what we consider as no small
additional recommendation, being also more tenacious of its fruit, which rarely falls from mere ri
pening.

Like the other varieties, this is propagated by
seeds, layers, suckers, and cuttings. The first give
the finest plants ; but the process is so slow as of·
ten to exhaust our patience, and thus raise against
it formidable objections. Still, as some may wish
to make the experiment for themselves, it may not
be improper to remark, that, when seeds are employed, they should be fresh and plump, and sown
in a bed of light and moist soil, having a southern
aspect. After vegetating in the spring, the plants
should be thoroughly hoed, and the ground about
them kept clear of weeds till the second year, when
they may be removed to the nursery, where, with
the care ordinarily given to this department of the
garden, they will do well, until transplanted to the
places where they are permanently to stand.

Layers from the quince do not always succeed,
and hence it is that they are seldom employed ; but
his is not the case with *cuttings,* which, placed in
a soil and situation proper for them (moist and shaded), rarely, if ever, fail. Taken in the spring, they
are set out in the nursery at the distance of fifteen
or eighteen inches apart; and, if intended for pear

or apple stocks, are grafted early the ensuing year. In this case the *œil dormant*, within a few inches of the earth, is the species of graft ordinarily employed. But it is not to be forgotten that, from causes not obvious in the present state of our knowledge, some of the varieties of the pear submit quietly to this operation, and even thrive under it, while others will not survive it. Of the former description are the Vergoleuse and the Beurré; and of the latter, the Bon Chretien, Bergamot of England, Salviati, the pound pear, and the Quenois.* The reason assigned by naturalists is the difference of strength between the stem and the graft, or, in other words, the feebleness of the quince stock. But what has a tendency, at least, to lessen our confidence in this theory is, that the Vergoleuse and the Beurré are both placed among the hardy varieties, and yet do well on stems of this kind.

In propagating for stocks, remove the lower shoots, and preserve the stem clean as high as the graft. When the fruit of the quince is the object of culture, train the stem to a rod or stake until it reach the height of four or five feet, or, in other words, till it be able to support itself. The time of planting, mode of bearing, and general culture, are those already described for apples and pears.

The ALMOND-TREE (*Amygdalus*).—Of the six or seven species of this tree known to botanists, there is but one that would at all repay the expense and trouble of cultivation here, and this is the Amygdalus communis, or common almond.† Its varieties, which amount to six or eight, are distinguished by some quality of the shell or of the fruit, as the hard and the soft, the bitter and the sweet; or by names arbitrarily given, as the peach,‡ the pis-

---

* Cours d'Agriculture.
† All the different species are natives of Asia and Africa.
‡ This variety is supposed by Knight to be the Tuberes of Pliny, produced by dusting the stigma of the almond with the pollen of the peach.—Hort. Trans., vol. iii., p. 4.

tachio, the cornichon, and the sultana. Of these,
the last and the sweet almond of Du Hamel and
Forsyth are the sorts most esteemed.

Like the apple, &c., the almond-tree is propagated by seeds when new varieties are sought for, and
by buds when old ones are to be continued. Grafting is rarely practised, and never with good effect,
from the loss of gum inseparable from the wound
it inflicts. Whence it follows that, in moist soils,
the plum stock, and in dry soils, that of the peach
or of the bitter almond, are employed as stocks.

The best time for sowing is in the spring; and
the seeds selected should be those which have been
taken from ripe fruit, and carefully buried in some
dry and cool place, to prevent evaporation. When
put out in the nursery they should be placed with
the sharp ends downward, in rows two and a half
feet apart, and kept free from weeds. As soon as
the young plants show themselves, cover them during the hot weather with straw, and, when four or
five feet high, inoculate; when they are three
years old, transplant them into the fruit garden or
the shrubbery, as you may think best. In either
place, annually labouring the earth around the roots
will be useful.

The cultivation of this tree, under circumstances
favourable to it, is very profitable;* but it must not
be dissembled, that in our climate, whether northern
or southern, it does not succeed. In the former,
the early production of its blossoms (which always
precede the leaves)† greatly expose it to frosts, the
slightest of which are sufficient to destroy it; and
in the latter, from causes not sufficiently explored,
"the fruit falls," as we are informed by Bosc, "be-

---

* "The profits of this culture in the south of France are not
so great, but more certain than those arising from the culture
of the olive."—Bosc.

† There is but one exception to this, the sultana, a sub-variety of the tender shell.

fore it ripens." With us, therefore, the management of the tree, both with regard to soil and exposition, must differ from that ordinarily prescribed;
and, instead of giving to it a dry and warm sand, a
southern aspect, and a wall to reflect the heat, we
must be careful to employ means which shall have
the effect of retarding vegetation.   These are, budding on the plum instead of either the peach or the
almond stock; avoiding a southern aspect; planting
in a soil poor and moist, and always in the open
air, and without the shelter of walls, fences, or hills;
exposing the roots to the action of the frost during
winter; covering them with a thick coat of straw
during the hot days of the spring; and, lastly, an-
nular excisions made in the bark.

The APRICOT (*Prunus*).—The origin of this tree
has been somewhat contested.   On the supposition
that it was a native of Armenia, the botanists have
called it the Prunus *Armeniaca*.   Pallas, however,
claims it for the region of the Caucasus; Grossier
for the barren mountains west of Pekin; Thunberg
for Japan; and Regnier for the banks of the Niger;
while Olivier finds it growing spontaneously, without care or culture, in Asia Minor and in Persia.
The date of its introduction into Europe is not better ascertained than its origin; but the presumption
is that this was very remote, as the tree was known
in Italy in the time of Dioscorides, and was cultivated in France (as we learn from Thouin) when
that country was a Roman province.

As in the case of other fruit-trees long subjected
to cultivation, its varieties are numerous; and many
of them so imperfectly distinguished from each
other, that their imputed differences sometimes escape the observation of even practised horticulturists.   The varieties best ascertained and most esteemed, are,

1. The *early*, principally recommended by its precocity, and by the circumstance that the stones

never fail to give fruit resembling in all respects
that of the parent tree.

2. The *Angumois*, distinguished by the oblong
form of its fruit; by a flesh rich, juicy, and slightly
acid; and by the abundance of its aroma. This
tree attains to great perfection in the southern parts
of Europe, thrives best in a calcareous soil, and in
an open and thoroughly ventilated situation; bears
badly the neighbourhood of walls, and entirely refuses the discipline of the espalier.

3. The *common*, recommended alike by its vigorous growth, its hardness, and productiveness. The
fruit is, howeuer, less rich and less aromatic than
that of other varieties.

4. The *Dutch.*—The stem of this, if left to itself,
is apt to be feeble or diseased; and hence it is that
we generally find this variety grafted on plum
stocks. Its fruit, like that of the Angumois, is
nealy spherical, juicy, and high flavoured, and (when
the tree has a good exposition, and is otherwise
well managed) attains to a considerable size.

5. The *Portuguese.*—The fruit of this sort is small
and round, but abounding in juices, and very high
flavoured.

6. The *Alexandrian* gives a fruit particularly adapted to confitures and marmalades; as its own sugar
is nearly sufficient for its preservation. The objection to the tree is its precocity and tendernesss, as
it blossoms early, and blights under the smallest degree of frost.

7. The *Breda* is an excellent variety, does well in
England, and would probably do better here. The
fruit is large and round, óf a deep yellow colour,
with a pulp soft and juicy. The tree is a great
bearer, especially in the standard form, to which it
seems to be particularly adapted.

8. The *Brussels* gives a fruit of medium size, inclining to an oval form, the flavour fine, and the pulp
not liable to dryness or toughness. The tree is a

great bearer, and, like the apricot of Breda, is well
adapted to the standard form.

9. The *Moor Park* or *Peach*, rarely, if ever, met
with in this country; a fact the more extraordinary,
as many circumstances conspire to give it a decided
preference over all the other varieties. The tree
is large, vigorous, and hardy, and is propagated like
the kind first named, from the stone, without risk
or trouble of grafting or budding; it does well either
as a standard or espalier, and gives fruit in great
abundance and of an excellent quality.*

.The apricot is multiplied in various ways, but
principally by seeds and budding. If we employ
the former of these methods, not a moment should
be lost after the fall of the fruit in placing the
stones in the earth; nor should we omit for a single
day to water them after they are planted. Without an observance of these rules, the pits or seeds
shrivel or become rancid; and in either case, the
power of germination (which in the apricot is naturally feeble) is always impaired and often destroyed. Sow also in the lines and at the distances at
which the trees are permanently to stand, whether
as wall fruit or standards; for, by so doing, the
plants will have more and stouter roots, be better
assured against high winds (which always fatigue
and often destroy them), give their fruit sooner, and
escape the many hazards of transplantation.†

We have just suggested that the stone of the
apricot is slow in giving signs of life; and we may
add that, when it does give them, it requires several
years to render the plant strong, healthy, and productive. This last is probably the circumstance
that has decided nursery-men in favour of the other
(or budding) method of propagation, as by this they

* Catalogue-makers unite in giving this variety the preference.—See Loudon, &c., &c.

† Manage this as we may, still there is a hazard in it, and
particularly so with regard to the apricot.

obtain fruit in half the time necessary in the preceding process. Almond or plum stocks are generally employed for stems; and of the latter, those of the two varieties called the Cerisette and St. Julian are the most approved. Knight, however, prefers budding the Moor Park on the common apricot; and gives as a reason for doing so, that, "thus managed, he finds the trees do not become debilitated or diseased as when budded on plum stocks.*

In selecting plants from the nursery, take those of three years in preference to such as are either older or younger; and those having a single stem to such as have two branches. On this last point Forsyth goes so far as to recommend lopping off one branch where the tree may happen to have two: "as," he adds, "if both be retained, the middle space between them will be naked."

Apricots are often trained against walls (for the general reason of sooner and better maturing the fruit); and, when so managed, will no doubt bear much earlier than in the standard form. But to this process there is a serious objection, arising from the frequent and severe pruning which it renders necessary, and the ill effects of this on the health and longevity of the tree. On the other hand, if set out and managed as standards, though much of this injurious discipline will be avoided, and though in the result we shall have abundant fruit and of fine flavour, still we are compelled to wait long for it, generally *eight*, and sometimes *ten* years. Influenced by these considerations, the well-instructed horticulturist takes a middle course; plants his apricots in a border; leaves them, in a great degree, to regulate themselves as to shape; uses the knife only to get rid of dead or diseased wood; rubs off the fore-right and superfluous buds while in a herbaceous state, and trains the retained shoots to a

---

* Hort. Trans., vol. ii., p. 19.

trellis, so placed as *almost* to touch the south side of the wall. By these means he secures the advantages of both methods, and, at the same time, either entirely avoids or so qualifies their defects, as to render them of little importance.

The fruit is often attacked by flies and wasps, and is best protected against these by nettings. Insects do not appear to do much injury to the tree itself, probably owing to the roughness of its bark and the coriaceous nature of its leaves.

The CHERRY-TREE (*Cerasus*).—This, like most of our other fruit-trees, is a native of Asia, and was first brought to Italy from the town of Cerasunt* by the Roman general Lucullus. Its cultivated varieties are about forty in number,† and are divided by the French botanists into three races, to which they have given the names of the bigarrotier, the griottier, and the guignier. The fruit of the first is distinguished by its hard and fleshlike substance; that of the second by its juiciness and tenderness; and that of the last by its comparative sweetness. Subjoined is a list of such of the varieties (placed in their natural order of ripening) as may be most worthy of attention: The *May Duke*, the *Early Black* (a cross made by Knight between the Graffian and the May Duke),‡ Ronald's *Large Black Heart*, Frazier's *Tartarian*, the *Elton* (another new variety produced by crossing the Graffian and the White Heart), the *Bleeding Heart*, *Harrison's Heart*, the *Cerone*, the *Black Gean*, the *Florence*, the *Amber Heart*, and the *Morello*.

The cherry-tree is propagated both by seeds and

* Hence the generic name of *Cerasus*.
† The Luxembourg Catalogue contains forty-two.
‡ Hort. Trans., vol. iii., p. 212. " The cherry sports more extensively in variety when propagated from seeds, than any other fruit that I have subjected to the experiment, and probably is therefore capable of attaining to a higher degree of perfection than it has yet reached."—Knight *Hort.* Trans., vol. ii., p. 133

suckers when stems are wanted; by seeds alone when new varieties are required;* by scions when you have to work on old subjects; and by buds when your trees are young. If intended for dwarfs, bud your plants at *two*, and if for standards, at *four* years of age. The spring succeeding this operation is the time for transplanting, which should be done carefully, and in the manner prescribed for setting out apple-trees. The fashion or form of the trees will direct the distance at which they are to stand from each other: between standards this should not be less than thirty feet;† and between pyramids and espaliers not less than twenty.

Though in our climate all the varieties of the cherry-tree do well as standards and pyramids, and are, therefore, generally and properly cultivated in these forms, still it may be useful to remark that two of them, the May Duke and the Morello, when trained against walls, give fruit not only of greater precocity, but of much finer flavour; a circumstance in which they differ, not only from other varieties of their own races, but from fruit-trees of all other kinds.‡

As the cherry grows on small spurs, pushing from the sides and ends of two, three, and four year old wood, and as the procession of new buds is constant, it follows, as a general rule, that "the knife must be sparingly employed;" and as a particular one in relation to wall-trees, that "bearing branches are not to be shortened if room can be found for extending them."§ These rules, however rigorously executed, must not prevent *summer* pruning (which,

---

* The seeds employed should be taken from ripe fruit, committed promptly to a bed of sand, and kept in a dry and cool place till the spring, when they may be set out in rows two and a half feet apart.

† Millar thinks the distance should be forty feet.

‡ Nicol.

§ Abercrombie's Art of Pruning.

20

as already stated, consists in rubbing off redundant
or ill-placed buds), nor that of *winter*, if confined to
the removal of fractured or unsound wood, or
branches too much multiplied or crossing each other.*   The nature of the Morello will, however, render it an exception to the general rule here recommended; for, instead of bearing, like other varieties, on two, three, and even four year old wood, its
fruit is generally produced on shoots of the last
year, and rarely, if ever, on even two year old wood.
Whence it follows that, with regard to this variety,
our aim in both summer and winter pruning ought
to be " a removal of old and a provision of new
bearers."

In renovating an old tree pursue Forsyth's method; shorten it to a stump not more than 18 inches
high; remove the old soil from the roots; replace it
with that of upland pasture, on a layer of stone or
some other impervious body, two feet below the
surface, and encourage a single shoot.

Cherry-trees in general are not much affected
by insects. Of this class the red spider is their
greatest enemy in England; and in Scotland an insect called the black beetle, which Naismith found
the means of killing " by burning under the trees a
mixture of pitch, orpiment, and sulphur, and then
giving them a good washing with the garden en-
gine."   Birds are *here* a more potent enemy; and
the best remedy against them are old fishnets
thrown over the trees, clapboards, scarecrows, and
fusees.

The PEACH-TREE (*Amygdalus Persica*) is a native
of Asia, and was first brought to Rome during the
reign of the Emperor Claudius.†   A circumstance
worth remarking in even our short notice of its his-

---

* Caledonian Memoirs, vol. i, p. 427.
† Mentioned by Columella (in his work on Gardens), and also
y Pliny.

tory is, that the product of the species or variety then introduced was believed to be poisonous, and gave to the tree a very bad reputation, which yielded, however, to experiments more carefully made, and to the acknowledged fact that in Egypt, where also it had become an object of culture, the fruit was equally wholesome and delicious.*

The early botanists divided this family into two classes : the one giving a fruit with a downy skin, which they called a peach; the other a fruit with a smooth skin, to which they gave the name of nec-tarine. But as it was soon ascertained that the same tree did occasionally produce both sorts at the same time,† later writers have rejected the distinction, and considering them as the same fruit, have arranged them simply into the downy and the smooth with a free-stone, and the downy and the smooth with a cling-stone.

The sub-varieties of both classes are numerous; and, as they afford much choice, the selection between them ought to be made with care, and under two leading views : 1st, to secure a succession of fruit throughout the season; and, 2d, to do this by employing the sorts which will best adapt themselves to the climate. In making up the following list, we have, therefore, taken only those sub-varieties which, under different modes of cultivation, have succeeded in latitudes even higher than our own. 1st, the *Early Purple* (Pourpre hative of Du Hamel); 2d, *Grosse Mignone;* 3d, *Belle Chevreuse;* 4th, *Royal Charlot;* 5th, *Double Mountain;* 6th, *Bellegarde*

* Knight conjectures, and with great probability, that this first importation to Rome was the *Swollen Almond*, which is known to contain much prussic acid. Olivier brought the Wild Peach of Persia to Paris; where, on cultivation, it gave fruit much resembling the *Avant Peche Blanche*, or what the English call the *White Nutmeg.*

† See Salisbury's short account of nectarines and peaches produced on the same branch, in vol. i., p. 103 of the Hort Trans. ·

or *Galande;* 7th, *Late Violet;* 8th, *Royal Kensington;* 9th, the *Incomparable,* or *Pavie Admirable;* 10th, the *Pavie Rouge de Pomponne;* 11th, the *Yellow Admirable,* or peach having the apricot flavour: and (of the nectarine tribe), 12th, the *Elruge;* 13th, *Fairchild's White;* 14th, *Temple's;* 15th, the *Scarlet;* 16th, the *Early Newington;* 17th, the *Late Newington;* 18th, the *Golden;* 19th, the *Red Roman;* and, 20th, the *Brugnon d'Italie.**

All these varieties are continued by budding, and, as in other cases, new ones are obtained by sowing the stones; in doing which, we ought not to forget that, like oil-giving seeds in general, those of the peach require to be earthed as soon as they are separated from the pulp. In their second year (if wall trees be required), such of them as are destined for stems are budded close to the earth; and if riders or standards be wanted, three, four, or six feet higher. In the spring following, the first shoots from these buds should be headed down to four, five, or six eyes, for the purpose of producing two upright and leading branches, and as many laterals, with which you begin to give to the head the form you intend it shall ultimately take. We need scarcely remark that, on this point, the doctors in horticulture are nearly as far apart from each other as are those of medicine in relation to the origin and contagiousness of yellow fever. But believing, as we do, that our object will be best fulfilled by turning aside from these discussions, we shall content ourselves with a brief notice of two forms, which in our opinion are at once the simplest and most scientific. The first of these (the standard), as we have already observed, is nearly the natural form of the tree: requiring no interposition of art, if we except the removal of dead, or dying, or superfluous

* We have excluded from this list the White and the Red Nutmeg, and the Early Ann, because recommended only by their precocity.

limbs, and an occasional supply of wood (if this be wanted) to keep up a well-balanced head. It is also that form in which the tree succeeds best in hot climates ; and in such it ought always to be employed. But in northern latitudes (where the heat is neither long-continued nor great), the fruit of the standard peach-tree is rarely seen in perfection : it may be large, and juicy, and well coloured, but it will always be deficient in that peculiar flavour, that aroma which is its true characteristic, and without which it is but an ordinary fruit.* To supply, therefore, as far as may be possible, without the aid of fire or glass, that high temperature in which the peach delights, we must resort, first, to the use of walls, which, besides protecting the tree from high and cold winds, concentrate the rays of the sun on its stem and branches, and on the earth which surrounds and nourishes its roots; secondly, to the amelioration of the soil, by giving to it both warmth and dryness, should it be deficient in these qualities ; and, thirdly, to that mode of training " which exposes to the light the greatest surface of leaf in the shortest space of time,† and, consequently, best promotes an equal distribution of the sap." For accomplishing these three objects, the rules are to construct your walls of stone, or brick, or wood, and of a height from 12 to 15 feet; to lay out, on the eastern and southern sides of them, a border 10 feet wide, worked to the depth of three feet, and manured with a mixture of ashes and peat, or bog earth ;‡ to plant in this.(2 1-2 feet distant from the wall) your young trees, furnished with two leading branches, and presenting a figure not unlike the letter Y; to bring down these branches to a position nearly horizon-

---

* To show the effect of climate on this fruit, Bosc says that he has eaten peaches at Verona, compared with which "the celebrated Clingstone of Montreuil (the Pomponne) would be regarded as an abortion."

† Knight.   ‡ Loudon.

tal, and subsequently to train them upward, parallel to each other, as high as the top of the wall, and directly against its side, to which, throughout their whole length, they are to be securely fastened by woollen straps; and, lastly, to encourage side-shoots from these leaders, so as to fill up with bearing wood the intermediate space between them, and such exterior space on the wall as may be thought proper and practicable. To this form is given the technical name of the *Wavy* or *Curvilinear Fan;* and it is obvious that, in preserving as well as in producing it, the use of the knife cannot be dispensed with. Be careful, therefore, in May and June, and occasionally in the succeeding months, to remove water shoots, and all ill-placed, redundant, or diseased buds; and again, at the fall of the leaf, to cut away with a sharp knife, and close to the branches on which they grow, such new shoots as will not readily accommodate themselves to your design, or as may be unnecessary to it, and also all such old wood as may be useless or troublesome.*

The general rules for thinning leaves and fruit (prescribed under a preceding article) must be carefully observed in the treatment of peach-trees and nectarines, as they are known to have an uncommon degree of proneness to overbearing, and as the discipline we recommend will, besides giving an improved fruit, tend directly and greatly to fortify

---

* Knight's method of pruning, in "high, cold, and wet situations," and by which he secures good crops when even the season is unpropitious, may be found useful in our climate. "Instead," he says, "of taking off a large portion of the young shoots in the spring, and training a few only to a considerable length, as is the general practice, I retain a large number of the shoots, and pinch off the minute and succulent points to the length of one or two inches. By these means I obtain spurs which lie close to the wall, and give as strong and vigorous blossoms, in even cold and wet situations and weather, as are produced by the old method under circumstances the most favourable."—Encyclopædia of Gardening, p. 456.

the trees against the attacks of their numerous en emies. Of these the Acarus, Cherines, Aphis, and Thrips (an insect hardly perceptible to the naked eye), are the most common, and are best expelled by water and tobacco smoke. It is, however, the curculio, or grub (as we call it), that may, from its pre-eminence in mischief, be regarded as the de stroyer of the peach. Its attacks ordinarily begin in the stem near the surface of the earth ; and, if not arrested, will soon terminate in the roots, where it riots on the gum exuding from the many wounds i inflicts. The remedies resorted to in this case are, first, the application of boiling water to the roots; secondly, a similar application of unslacked lime, in the proportion of one quart to a tree ; thirdly, re- moving the surface earth, and substituting for it tan- ner's bark; fourthly, removing the earth, as in the preceding case, in the month of November, and ex- posing the roots to the action of the frost during the winter; and, lastly, encircling the lower part of the stem with straw, and thus compelling the insect to begin his attack so far from the ground, that he will be unable to avail himself of its shelter before the coming on of winter.

The diseases of the peach-tree are as numerous, and often as fatal, as the depredators just mention- ed; and are known to horticulturists under the names of the honey-dew, mildew, canker, spots, &c. The first of these yields to the flower of sulphur sprinkled over the tree ; but the most efficient cure for all of them is the removal of the soil about their roots.*

The Plum-tree (*Prunus domestica*) is a native of different parts of Europe, has been long cultivated, and has, of course, many varieties. Of these, the

---

* Kinment's experiments, made in 1811, 12, and 13, show that the last of these diseases is the effect of too much vegetable food, and that, by reducing the quantity of this, the diseased trees will recover.

best recommended are the *Prccoce of Tours.* the *Early Damson of Provence*, the *Green Mirabelle* of Italy, the *St. Catharine*, the *White Perdrigon*, the *Imperatrice*, and all the *Gages, blue, violet,* and *green.*

The St. Catharine, the white Perdigon, and the gages, are propagated by seeds, the products of which never fail to give plants differing in nothing from the parent stem ;* while the other varieties can only be kept up by budding or grafting.† Where trees are of more than four years' growth, the latter of these operations is preferred ; and on all under that age, the former is thought best.

Argillaceous soils, neither habitually wet nor occasionally inundated, and of medium quality, are those which best agree with the plum-tree. Where, from previous culture or accidental causes, the earth has become either very rich or very poor, the tree does not succeed. In the one case, its vigour is directed only to the production of wood and foliage ; and in the other, its growth is feeble and its life short. In favourable climates it should always be cultivated as a standard, and will then require only a little annual labour about the roots, and the removal from the head of dead or dying branches ; but

* This is, at least, a doubtful conclusion. Plants, like animals of the same genus, will mix and produce new varieties, as is amply proved by artificial fecundation ; and the gages, we believe, form no exception to the general law. We have, in several instances, seen and tasted fruits, grown from the pits of the gage ; but we have never seen in any of these fruits an exact resemblance to the female parent. They have been of various colours, shapes, size, and flavour, although grown from pits coming from the same tree, according, as we supposed, to the character of the male parent.—J. B.

† The Muscle, the St. Julian, and the Cerisette, are varieties raised from seeds or suckers, as stems on which to bud and graft other plums, &c. With this exception, all other suckers should be removed as soon as they appear. If you postpone this business till winter, the wounds you then inflict will ensure you a double crop in the spring.

in northern latitudes and cold situations, the espalier form (as practised near Paris) may be not only useful, but indispensable. This differs in nothing from the ordinary mode but in pruning *less severely*. The cultivators at Montreuil, instead of shortening the branches to three or four eyes, leave them fifteen or twenty feet long, and lay them down in such way as shall soonest and most completely enable them to cover the frame to which they are attached.

With regard to product, "*few* and *fine*" is the general maxim. The thinning discipline must not, therefore, be omitted; because it is that which will best fulfil both parts of the rule. (See on this head, article Apple-tree.)

The gum and canker are the diseases most common to the plum-tree, for which heading down is the best remedy.* When wasps attack the fruit they are most effectually kept off by nettings.

The CRANBERRY (*Vaccinium macrocarpum*).—This plant is a native of our own country, and merits more attention than has been given to it, as the experiments of the late Sir Joseph Banks prove at once the facility and the profit of making it an object of garden culture.†

Growing naturally in swamps and bogs, it has been too hastily concluded that it would not succeed but in grounds "often inundated and always wet." But that this belief is erroneous can no longer be doubted, as we learn from Loudon, an eminent practical writer, that "the cranberry can always be made to thrive on the *margin* of a pond;" while the experiments of Salisbury (an amateur of the art) demonstrate that "it will even bear abundantly in pots filled with bog earth, and placed under the

---

* Abercrombie.
† On a bed eighteen feet square, he raised three and a half bushels, Winchester measure.—See Hort. Trans., vol. i., p. 71.

shade of a hedge or fence."* In the first of these cases, enclose a portion of the pond by stakes, fill the bottom with stones, and on these place a stratum of bog earth, raised to the ordinary level of the pond, and upon *this* plant a few cranberries. The runners will soon and completely cover the bed, and your harvests will be both abundant and regular, never suffering either from weather or insects. In the other case, select or make a *hollow*, and within it form a bed of bog earth, set your plants upon this, and shade them on the south and east with some quick growers, as Indian corn, or the butter bean, &c.

The CURRANT (*Ribes rubrum*).—It is only of this sort and its varieties that we shall speak, as the fruits of the other species are rarely, if ever, admitted to the table. This plant is evidently of northern origin and habits, very indifferent to soil or situation, and regardless of weather; growing wherever planted, and never failing, when tolerably cultivated, to give a plentiful crop. The varieties of it are principally distinguished by colour, as the *White*, the *New White*, and the *White Crystal*, the *Large Red*, the *Cluster Red*, the *Champagne Pale Red*, and the *Dutch Pale Red*. These are all propagated alike by seeds, roots, and cuttings, but generally by the last mode, which does not at all differ from that prescribed (in the next article) for the gooseberry. The only farther object of art in the management of this plant, is to keep the head (which is much disposed to become bushy) pervious to the sun and air, the stem clean, and the roots unencumbered with suckers.

The GOOSEBERRY (*Ribes grossularia*).—Though really a native of Piedmont, this plant may be regarded as a British production, as it is only in England and Scotland where its cultivation is well under-

* See Hort. Trans., vol. ii., p. 96.

stood and attended to, and where the fruit is held in high estimation, or deserves to be so.*†

Its varieties are very numerous. In the London nurseries are no less than one hundred different sorts, and in those of Lancashire (where the culture is most general) three hundred; some of which are early, others late; some large, and others small; some abounding in flavour, and others entirely destitute of it. In our brief catalogue we shall be governed altogether by the uses to which the fruit is destined, and shall therefore indicate only *three* sorts, the *Warrington* or *Manchester Red*, employed for the dessert; the *Early Wilmot Red*, famous for tarts and sauces; and the *Walnut Red*, recommended by its quality of keeping or preserving better than any other variety of the family.‡

Like other fruit-trees, the gooseberry may be propagated by seeds, suckers, cuttings, &c., but the last is the mode generally adopted. In this case the cuttings are taken from bearing shoots, placed in the nursery eight or ten inches apart, and trained to the height of a foot with a clear stem, excepting three or four buds at the top, which must be left to form the future head, and which, when they have pushed a few inches, must be radiated at an angle between forty and forty-five degrees. When the roots are sufficiently formed, the plants may be taken up and placed in rows in the border or square intended for them, at the distance of six feet between the rows, and four feet from plant to plant. An annual labour about the roots is necessary, and,

---

* This fruit is also of very large size and fine flavour in some parts of Denmark, Sweden, and Norway.

† In Italy, France, and Spain, the plant is scarcely known, and very little esteemed; nor does it attract much attention in Holland and Germany.

‡ If a larger collection be thought desirable, it may be had on good terms and in excellent order from J. Whalley of Liverpool.

unless the soil be uncommonly rich, a yearly dressing also of stable manure or peat earth.   Too
much shade is oppressive to the plant and injurious
to the fruit, but a degree of it is useful to both, and
is best obtained by sowing rows of the Jerusalem
artichoke between those of the gooseberry.   When
the heads become crowded, all cross and water
shoots growing in their centres must be pinched or
cut off; and if the smaller berries also be removed
early in the season, the result to the crop will be
favourable ; but, in performing the first of these operations, we must remember that the summer
shoots in general must not be touched.

Caterpillars of different names, the white, black,
and green (larva of the Tenthrendinida), are the
worst enemies of the gooseberry.   Most of these,
when full grown, descend into the earth, and remain
there for the winter.   This habit suggests the most
probable mode of destroying them.   Some horticulturists accordingly lay hot lime around the roots
of the plants; others saturate the surrounding earth
with boiling water; others with the urine of cows;
others dig into the earth seaweed or grass, sprinkled
with a solution of salt and water; and J. Tweedie
" pares off three inches of the surface earth, which
generally includes the eggs of the caterpillar, makes
a deep trench, and places this at the bottom, where
the temperature is such as to prevent the eggs from
hatching."   Various washes have also been devised
for destroying the larva while above ground and on
the plants; but, in the opinion of Loudon, with little if any success.   " Hand-picking," he says, " however tedious it may seem, will in the end be found
more certain and cheap than any other mode."

The GRAPE-VINE (*Vitis vinifera*).—This species of
the vine (the only one of which we mean to speak)
is believed to be a native of Persia,* whence it has

* See Michaux, Olivier, and Sickler.   The last of these wri-

been spread over many different regions. Indeed, climate alone appears to have prescribed boundaries to its diffusion; as in Europe we find it successfully cultivated between the 25th and 52d degrees of north latitude, and rarely, if ever, with much advantage beyond these limits. Under favourable circumstances, it attains to a great size and age.*

Having been cultivated at least from the time of Noah, its varieties are so multiplied as to set even enumeration at defiance:† a fact, after all, of little importance to our present object, as it is only a very small class of these varieties, and a still smaller proportion of this class, that comes within the scope of the present work. The following is a list of the sorts which, in our opinion, are best adapted to the climate, and fittest for the only use we mean to make of them, that of the dessert: the *Chasselas of Fontainebleau*, the *White do.*, the *Violet do.*, the *Black Muscat of Jura*, the *Black do. of the Po*, the *White do. of do.*, the *Muscat of Alexandria*, the *Malvoisie of the Po*, the *Red Hamburg*, and the *Sweetwater*.

ters has given a very curious and learned account of the progress of the Grape-vine from Persia to Sicily, by the way of Egypt and Greece, in his work entitled *Geschichte der Obs. Cult.*, vol. i.

* Pliny speaks of a vine 600 years old. Bosc says there are several in Burgundy 400 years old; and Millar, that "a vineyard is young at 100 years." A vine at North Allerton (in England) covered one hundred and thirty-seven square yards; another at Hampton Court, one hundred and sixteen; and a third at Valentines (in Essex) one hundred and forty-seven. "The Hampton vine ordinarily produces 2200 bunches, averaging a pound each; and one of its branches measures one hundred and fourteen feet in length."—Encyclopædia of Gardening, p. 843.

† The most successful attempt yet made at an enumeration of the varieties of the vine may be found in a Spanish work by Don S. Roxas Clemente, Librarian of the Botanic Garden at Madrid. Among the many good things done, or attempted by Bonaparte in France, was the bringing together in a single garden (that of the Luxembourg) all the varieties of the vine to be found in that country. The work began in 1801, under the particular directions of Chaptal and Bosc; and in 1809 three hundred sorts had been collected, cultivated, and classed. We have heard with regret that the work was not completed.

Like many other plants, the vine is propagated :

1st, By *Seeds*, when new varieties are wanted, and most generally by two processes, one of which consists " in approaching two or more sorts so nearly together as to produce a promiscuous impregnation ;"* the other " in cutting out the stamen from the flower of the variety to be impregnated, introducing the pollen of that with which the cross is to be made, and, finally, by dusting the stigma with the ripe anthers."   The former is the method of Speechley, and the latter that of Knight.

2d, By *Layers*.—This method is little practised, because, though plants so raised give their fruit most promptly, they are both feeble and short-lived.

3d, By *Scions*.—These are never resorted to but to correct errors.   When the varieties originally planted are bad or unfruitful, grafting is the remedy ; and though the operation be not uniformly successful, still it succeeds often enough to recommend the experiment.   And,

4th, By *Cuttings*.—This is the mode generally employed, and that which best deserves to be so. The cuttings are of three kinds : the *long* (12 to 18 inches), the *short* (about half the length of the preceding), and the *single eye*.† The first and second have each a portion of the wood of two years ; and the third has but wood enough of the last year to furnish the germe of a single bud.   The first of these methods is that of the Continent of Europe, and has much and long experience to support it ; the last is an English novelty, with little to recommend it, and probably growing out of the easier management of short sets when raised in pots and hotbeds, according to their system.   One quality is, however, indispensable to cuttings of all kinds, whether long or short ; and that is, that " the wood composing them be solid

---

* See Treatise on the Vine.

† Mitchell suggested, and Speechley recommends this species of cutting.

and compact, round and short-jointed, and that the eyes or buds be large and prominent.* Cut in the autumn, they must be carefully buried until the ensuing spring, when they may be taken up and planted where it is intended they shall permanently remain.

Many appearances indicate that the vine is indifferent to the nature of the soil in which it grows, as it is found to live and thrive in limestone clay, in chalk, in gravel, in granite, in schist, in earths charged with the oxyde of iron, in the rubbish of old foundations, and even in the midst of brick pavements and castle walls.† Nor, judging from a first and cursory view, should we suppose it to be more nice with regard to exposition, as it may be found growing under many different aspects, and on every possible variety of surface. Still these appearances are deceptive, and yield to the evidence of many facts, carefully collected by horticulturists, which prove that, notwithstanding this general power of adaptation, the vine is particularly sensible to the influences of soil and exposure, and that, under even slight changes or modifications of these, it becomes more or less fertile, and gives its products earlier or later, or with juices more or less abundant, saccharine, and well-flavoured. In strong, rich soils, its growth in wood and foliage is vigorous; but the fruit ripens slowly, and is comparatively tasteless.‡

* The soils which in France are most generally assigned to vineyards are, 1st, limestone clay; 2d, gravelly clay, as at Nismes, Montpelier, and Bourdeaux; 3d, granitic soil, which gives the wines called *Cotes Rotés*, Hermitage, and Taville, &c.; and, 4th, chalk, as in Champagne.

† See Treatise on Fruit-trees by Hitt, and Laurence on the Fruit Garden. Rozier paved his vineyard at Bezieres. The vine mentioned by Hitt grew in the foundations of Belvoir Castle, and that spoken of by Laurence grew out of the wall of an old castle twenty feet from the ground.

‡ The Clovego estate, famous for the finest description of Burgundy wine, changed masters during the revolution, and was, out of mistaken kindness, or from a desire of doubling the

In soils, whether rich or poor, resting on a hard, impervious subsoil of rock or of hardpan, or on one often or habitually wet, the plant is feeble, difficult to rear, short-lived, and never productive; and on the north sides of hills, and in the neighbourhood of large masses of .wood and water, it does not thrive. It is only under southern and eastern aspects, and in soils light and warm, and of a medium quality as to strength, that the vine attains that degree of perfection of which it is susceptible.*

It is this last-mentioned circumstance that directs us in the choice and application of manures, and which forbids those of a heating quality, or of any quality in large quantities. The fresh mould of old pasture land, the scrapings of streets, and composts composed of stable litter; the leaves of trees, weeds in a green state, and animal remains of all kinds (as hair, skins, feathers, bones, &c., thoroughly rotted), and applied in moderate doses every second year, form the most approved practice on this head.

The vine, from the length and pliancy of its branches, is subjected to very different forms, some of which are no doubt dictated by mere fancy, and others by a long experience of their usefulness. Of the last we shall mention,

1st. The *dwarf standard*, which is that exclusively employed in large vineyards in the northern parts

quantity of the crop, abundantly manured. The consequence, as might be expected, was a larger produce, but a diminished price.

* This delicacy of constitution alone enables us to explain the cause of the great differences found in vines of the same sort, cultivated in the same way, and growing even within sight of each other. The Lafite wine is only found on a farm not exceeding in size 300 acres. The Ostrian, &c., is the produce of a tract not much larger. The Verdelho grape gives genuine Madeira only in the island of that name, &c., &c. An external mark of a soil fitted for the vine is said by Switzer to be the production of brambles. "Where," he says, "*these* grow, the vine never fails."

of France and Germany, and which consists in reducing the plant to a bush of two or three shoots,
and keeping these erect by a stake. The shoots
will each give two or three bunches within fifteen
or eighteen inches from the earth, and are naturally
succeeded by others, which in their turn become
bearers.

2d. The *prostrate* or *creeping* form, by which the
vine is trained over the ground like a melon or cucumber. This was early noticed by Bacon, and has
been since recommended by Vispré, "as least expensive and troublesome, and best calculated for ripening the fruit, by placing it within the sphere of that
heat which is emitted by the earth during the night."

3d. The *espalier form*, by which the leading and
lateral branches are trained against an open frame
or trellis, and in such way "as to expose the largest surface to the action of the sun in the shortest
space of time." And,

4th. The *wall espalier*, which differs in nothing
from the preceding but in having behind it a solid
structure, and the additional heat reflected by it.
This form is often met with in Europe, where the
southern, eastern, and western sides of farmhouses
and cottages are made to supply the walls, and do
it very completely. In gardens, the structures intended to produce the same effect are of two kinds :
the one rising to the height of fifteen and even
twenty feet, made of stone or wood, and meant to
protect the taller kinds of fruit-trees ; and the other,
of similar materials, but not exceeding six feet in
height, and calculated for bushes and dwarfs.
Speechley says the vine does well on the latter ;
and we are instructed by Williams, of Pitmaison,
how best to derive advantage from the former.
"To fill up," he says, "the intervals between the
trees, plant vines, train them horizontally under the
coping of the wall, and, by inverting and inarching
their branches, find means to occupy every vacant

21

space." "I have," he adds, "within a few years
past, gradually trained bearing branches of a small
black cluster grape to the distance of near fifty feet
from the root, and I find the bunches every year
grow larger and ripen earlier, as the shoots continue to advance; for, according to Knight's theory
of the circulation of the sap, the juices become
richer the farther they pass through the alburnum :
whence it follows that trees and vines give blos-
som-buds in greater quantity and perfection in proportion as the branches are long, and that even the
extremities of these are best furnished with flowers and fruit."

As pruning is essential to all these forms, though
not in the same degree, it may be proper to make a
few remarks on this subject. And, first, the knife,
in its application to the grape-vine, is not used till
the second year, when the plant has pushed three
or four shoots. Two of these (generally the lowest) are selected for bearers, and shortened down
to the fourth, fifth, or sixth eye from the root, while
all others are entirely removed. This is done in
the autumn after vegetation is over, and forms the
whole of the first year's pruning. In the subsequent spring, and so soon as the buds have pushed,
follows what the French call *enbourgeonement*, and
the English *disbudding*, and which consists " in rubbing off all fore-right and lateral shoots, which, if
retained, might crowd or cross the bearing branches, or otherwise obstruct the form intended to be
given to the vine." Suckers are also to be carefully removed, and with them axillary buds and
curls, and such of the roots as may run within eight
inches of the surface. The third year's pruning
will be the result of a careful examination, 1st, of
the two leading branches, and the young wood they
have respectively produced; and, 2d, of the surface
(whether of wall or of trellis) which it is your intention to cover. If these be in just proportion to

each other, the knife is unnecessary but to remove dead or diseased branches; but if the growth of the shoots be feeble, or if some be feeble and others vigorous, in both cases the knife is the remedy; shortening all, in the first case, to five or six eyes each; and in the other, the feeblest only. Future prunings will but be repetitions of this; and, as a general rule, every pruning must be followed by a thorough digging of the earth about the roots of the plant.

The insects most injurious to the grape-vine are the red spider, which is best expelled by frequent waterings; and the thrips, and one or two sorts of the cocci,* which may be destroyed by smoke. The best protection against the blue fly is furnished by bottles filled with any kind of sweet liquor, and hung up among the vines; and horsehair bags will completely defend the fruit against the attacks of wasps and garden birds.

The FIG-TREE (*Ficus*), (classed by horticulturists among the berries),† is a native of Asia; and in all hot climates may be made an important object of cultivation. In Greece and in the Ionian Isles it attains to the size of an apple-tree, bears its foliage throughout the year, and is remarkable for hardiness and longevity. Even in climates less propitious to it, it retains the last of these qualities. One brought to England from Aleppo in 1643, by Dr. Pocock, is yet living and vigorous; and another, introduced by Cardinal Pole more than a century earlier (1525), is said to be in the same condition.‡

The species of it are very numerous; but of this long list we shall speak only of the Ficus Carica, or common fig, because it is only from the cultivation of *this* that we may have anything to hope. Nor of its varieties do we know more than six that can probably be acclimated on the banks of the Hudson.

* Hesperidum and Adonidum.
† Loudon.   ‡ Idem

These are, the *Long White*, the *Yellow* or *Angelica*, and the *Violet*, cultivated near Paris ; and the *Black Ischia*, and *Black* and *White Genoa*, which ripen in England.

All the varieties of the fig are propagated by seeds,[*] suckers, buds, scions,[†] and layers ; nor is its propagation by crossing unknown to the horticulturist; but this can only be effected by planting two varieties near to each other, as no means have yet been discovered for extracting the male organ of the fig without destroying the female. Of these different modes, however, those by cuttings and layers are most frequently employed and best recommended. In the first case, select in the autumn eight or ten inches of young wood, with one or two of old attached to it, from the shortest jointed and most fruitful boughs ; bury these during the winter in a bed of sand ; and in the spring, plant them in a border of fresh and warm loam, against the southern or eastern side of a ten-foot wall.[‡] Layering here does not differ from the process of the same name employed in other cases : shoots of two or three years are laid down in the spring, and a single summer will be sufficient for the formation of roots ; after which, sever the young plant from the old, and set it out as directed for cuttings.

In hot climates, as in the case of the peach, the *standard* is the form most approved ; but in climates like ours, the *stellate fan* is that which offers the strongest assurance of success.[§] It is produced by training to a single stem, encouraging lateral shoots, and bringing these down in succession, so as to present a figure nearly circular, and so low as to give it the benefit of a reflected as well as a direct heat.[||]

---

[*] Loudon.   [†] Idem.   [‡] Idem.

[§] "Fan training from two branches is bad, gives only wood and leaves."—Idem. Bosc says, "Keep the branches short, low, and spreading." See also Hort. Trans., vol. iii., p. 307.

[||] Knight's method does not materially differ from this. He

We have already suggested, in relation to other trees, that their mode of bearing ought, in a great degree, to regulate our method of pruning them; nor is the remark more applicable to the apple or the peach than to the fig tree. We need hardly inform the reader that this last blossoms twice in the year; first under the spring, and again under the summer flow of the sap; and, where the climate, &c., is favourable, matures two crops in the season, *on two distinct sets of young shoots.* Whence it follows that the management which shall tend most directly to multiply shoots or bearers, is, in relation to this tree, that which is best. Now many experiments show that, if you shorten a branch of the fig-tree with a *knife*, the tree will exert itself only to recover what it has lost; and, of course, that you will but have a single shoot instead of the one you have removed: whereas, if you substitute *breaking* for cutting, you will, instead of one, have several shoots, and, consequently, a larger proportion of fruit. Hence the rule, "to *cut* when you want to lessen the bulk of the head, and to *break* at ten, twelve, or fifteen inches from the stem, when an increased quantity either of wood or of fruit is your object." These remarks do not, however, supersede the more general rules for removing dead, or diseased, or redundant branches, or for such other use of the knife as may be necessary in giving form to the head; and the less so, as the plant is among those which bear cutting without injury.

Any soil not positively wet, provided it be annually dug and triannually manured with stable litter, will suit the fig-tree. But a more laborious and expensive operation is necessary to protect it against hard and frosty weather With this view, the prac-

encourages lateral shoots from a single stem, and trains them horizontally, or even downward, close to the wall; by which he avoids a too great abundance of wood, matures that which he retains, and escapes injury from frost.—Hort. Trans., vol. iii., p. 307.

tice in France is to bury in the earth all such limbs
or parts of limbs as can be brought sufficiently low;
while in England they cover the tree with matting,
or straw, or branches of evergreens. Either method
may be usefully adopted here, remembering, as a
general principle, to make the covering as light as
may be at all consistent with the object.

We have said above that the natural habit of the
fig is to give two crops in the year; the latter of
which, in hot climates, is found to be the best: but
the result with us will be different. The *spring*
shoots only will give fruit here, and must be retained; while all embryos showing themselves after
midsummer should be carefully rubbed off. The
effect of this will be, not merely to disencumber the
tree of fruit that would not ripen, but to turn the
surplus energy wasted upon it to the preparation of
new embryo figs for the succeeding year.*

We cannot dismiss this article without saying
something on the artificial method employed, even
in hot climates, of improving and ripening the fig,
and to which has been given the name of *caprification*. This process consists in placing on the trees
a few spring figs, in which the Cynips has deposited its eggs. From these multitudes of gnats will
issue, and in their turn puncture the crop of fall
figs, and thus increase their flavour, and quicken,
as is believed, their maturity. Such was formerly the practice in the Levant; while in France
they pricked the fruit with a quill or straw dipped
in olive oil or brandy, and in Italy with the point
of a knife medicated in the same way, on the supposition that any small wound inflicted on the fruit
would have an effect similar to that of the sting of
a gnat. These practices are, however, no longer
as general as they have been, and, like others
founded on doubtful principles, are fast yielding to

* Swayne on the management of the fig in the open air.

a better philosophy. "How," says Bosc, "can the larva of the Cynips improve the fig, otherwise than the larva of the Phalæna improves the apple? And who would be desirous of having a crop of worm-eaten apples, merely for the pleasure of eating them a week or a fortnight earlier?[*]

The fig-tree is liable to few diseases, nor is the fruit much injured by the attacks of insects. In England the red spider, and in France a species of Coccus, to which is given the name of the *fig-louse*, are regarded as its worst enemies. The first is got rid of by watering and smoking the tree; and the last by rubbing the stem, branches, &c., with a coarse cloth.

The MULBERRY (*Morus*).—The species are two, the *White*, cultivated for its leaves only (which form the food of the silkworm), and the *Black*, a native of our own forests, and well meriting our attention for its fruit, recommended as it is by its highly aromatic flavour and cooling subacid juices, which, like those of the strawberry, are not susceptible of the acetous fermentation, and, of course, particularly proper and useful for rheumatic and gouty patients.[†]

This tree is propagated by seeds, suckers, layers, cuttings, and scions. Those from seeds are supposed to give the largest berries, but at such an expense both of time and patience as to deter most cultivators from the experiment. Suckers are liable to the same objection, though in a somewhat less degree; and grafting, except by approach, rarely succeeds.[‡] *Layers* and *cuttings* are, therefore, the modes generally employed; of each of which we shall say a few words: and,

* Olivier, speaking of caprification, says, "It is a tribute paid by man to ignorance and prejudice;" adding, that the practice is going fast into disuse, even in the Ionian Isles.—Travels in the Ottoman Empire.
† Encyclopædia of Gardening. ‡ Hort. Trans., vol. i., p. 60.

1. Of *Layers.*—To obtain these, erect a scaffold under any fruit-bearing tree, and on this place pots or boxes filled with earth, to receive the branches.* These will root sufficiently the first summer; after which, they may be transplanted to the nursery, and trained to a single stem. When four years old, take them up and place them where they are permanently to stand. Plants thus managed will give fruit the second or third year after the last planting.†

2. By *Cuttings.*—These may be eight or ten inches long, with a small portion of the preceding year's wood attached. Plant them in any mild weather of the spring or autumn, in rows nine inches apart, leaving only one or two buds above the ground; cover the bed with half rotten leaves; give it a little water if the weather be dry, and transplant the next season into the nursery. Their future treatment will be the same as that of layers. Millar suggests the rearing of cuttings in pots plunged in a hotbed; but in this experiment Knight and others have failed, and recommend, instead of it, to plant the cuttings in autumn under a south wall, where they remain till April, when they are to be taken up, placed in pots, and transferred to the hotbed. "In this situation," says Knight, "they will vegetate strongly, and emit roots in such abundance, that not one cutting in a hundred, with proper attention, will fail." A mellow, fertile loam is the soil in which the mulberry succeeds best, and the *standard* is the form generally given to it; but the experiments of Williams and Knight give reason to believe that the fruit would be improved were we to train the tree against a south wall, in either the horizontal or stellate form.‡

In pruning the mulberry we ought to aim at two things: diminishing the luxuriant growth of the tree,

---

* Knight.   † Idem.
‡ Loudon. Hort. Trans., vol. ii., p. 92, and vol. iii., p. 66.

and increasing, at the same time, its disposition to bear fruit. . Fortunately, both objects are readily attainable by partial decortication; by tight and long-continued ligatures round the branches; by ringing, as already described; and with better effect and greater facility, by training the branches perpendicularly, or nearly so, downward.* The time for pruning the mulberry is in the spring, because it is then you can best distinguish the blossom buds from others. Pinch off every barren shoot, and shorten every bearing one (not wanted to cover the wall) at the third or fourth leaf; it being well known that the bud immediately below the point where the branch is shortened will give fruit the following year.

The RASPBERRY (*Rubus*).—Of this plant there are two species, subjects of garden culture: the *Ideus*, propagated for its fruit; the *Odoratus*, for its perfume and its rose-coloured flowers. It is only of the varieties of the former that we shall now speak. These are, 1st, the Wood Raspberry, giving a fruit small and sweet, increasing in size, but diminishing in flavour, under cultivation. 2d, the large common Raspberry (both red and white), giving good fruit, and a great deal of it, if favourably situated and well managed. In rich and shaded soils it loses much of its flavour; and in those freely manured with stable dung, becomes disagreeable to the taste. 3d, the *Large Red* and the *Large White Antwerp*, decidedly superior to the preceding sorts, but more troublesome, as they are not productive but when laid down and protected from the winter frosts. And, 4th, the *Cane Stock*, regarded on the whole as the fittest for the main crop.

This plant is a native of cold and mountainous regions, and, of course, succeeds best when placed on the north sides of hills, or in borders a little

* Hort. Trans., vol. iii., p. 63. No tree submits to this form more readily, or to more advantage, than the mulberry.

shaded. A soil loose and moist (not wet), and occasionally and lightly manured with the surface
mould of old pasture land, is most favourable to it.

Like other plants which perpetuate themselves
by suckers, as the Annana, the Jasmin, the Bread
Fruit, &c., the raspberry soon becomes infertile;
and hence the rule for setting out new plantations
every seventh or eighth year.   This is done by seeds
and cuttings, but better and more generally by *suckers*, taken up in the fall or in the spring, and set out
in well-laboured trenches four feet asunder, and at
the distance in these of two and a half feet apart.
If placed nearer together, they crowd and injure
each other; and if farther removed, they lose the
advantage of the shade they would otherwise mu-
tually furnish.

The raspberry, when left to itself, remains long
barren, or productive only in leaves and wood; but,
so soon as it acquires a sufficient number of lateral
branches, its fertility commences.   To hasten this
effect, therefore, is the great desideratum in the culture of the plant ; and the knife is accordingly employed freely and annually, in removing the old
wood, and in shortening the young to one third of
its length.   Of the retained and shortened shoots,
not more than five should be left to a bush;* and if
they be either of the Antwerp races, they should be
carefully covered with earth on the approach of
winter, as otherwise the effect of the frost will
much impair, if it does not entirely destroy, their
fertility for the ensuing season.

We need scarcely add, that, though hardy, the
raspberry, to do well, must be kept from weeds.

* Loudon.   J. C. Kecht (Versuch der Weinbau) produces berries at Berlin much larger than are known elsewhere, by training a single stem to the height of 8 or 10 feet, and vigorously removing all suckers.   This is directly opposed to the theory of
shortening the stems for the purpose of producing side-shoots ;
without which, it has been generally thought that the plant could
not be made productive.

The STRAWBERRY (*Fragaria*).—Of this there are several species, the principal of which are the Pine, the Single-leaf or Monophy lla, and the Chili, natives of South America; the Carolina, the Scarlet or Virginian, and the Wood, natives of North America; and the Hautboy, and Alpine or Prolific, natives of Europe. Of these, the Alpine and the wood are best propagated from seeds, as in this way they never fail to reproduce themselves, and give fruit as soon, and of a finer quality, than the offsets. The other species are more readily multiplied by runners; which, as they take root at every joint, and grow the more vigorously the more they are cut, necessarily furnish a great abundance of plants.

When seeds are used, we must be careful to employ fresh and well-ripened fruit, mashed in the hand, and mixed with a little mellow earth, and sown in rows three feet apart. When, on the other hand, runners are employed, they must be taken off near the ground, divided into sets, planted in rows as in the other case, and occasionally lightly shaded and watered, until they give evidence of having taken root, which they rarely fail to do very promptly. In both processes, the ground must be kept loose and clean, and moderately manured with compost dung.

With regard either to general or special rules in this case, we cannot do better than to make the reader acquainted with the method of Mr. Keans, of Islesworth, an English fruit-gardener, who has cultivated the strawberry with uncommon success. "In preparing the ground," says he, "if new and stiff, trench it; but if the subsoil be of an inferior kind, simply dig it, and place the dung at the bottom: if, again, the soil be good to the full depth, bring the bottom spit to the top, and the top spit to the bottom, and place the dung between the two. The month of March is the best time for planting either seedlings or runners, and remember to make your plantations of *these*, and never from old plants. Sow in beds of three or four rows, with alleys between the beds to walk and work in. When the planting is finished, keep the bed free from weeds, and permit no crops between the rows. When the runners begin to show themselves, cut them away at least three times in the season; and at each cutting dig the ground between the rows; and as often, cover the surface with a sprinkling of clean straw,* for the purpose, principally, of preventing evaporation. One of these cuttings must be done a short time before the fruit ripens, and will have a powerful effect in strengthening the root; and, at the second digging, work into the rows a little half-rotted dung."

To these remarks, which apply to all the varieties alike, Mr. Keans subjoins a few specific notices as follows:

"1. For the *Pine* strawberry the best soil is a light loam, though no other strawberry will bear a strong loam better than this. This is the sort from which it is most difficult to obtain a good crop. Particular care must be taken that they are planted in open ground; for in small gardens they grow strong, but seldom bear fruit, in consequence of being shaded by standard trees, and, under walnut-trees in in particular, they run altogether to leaf. In planting pines I keep the beds two feet apart, and put the plants eighteen inches from each other in the rows, leaving three feet alleys between the beds. The first year of the pine is the best; the second gives a good crop, but the third gives less.

"2. The *Scarlet* must be treated like the Pine, excepting that the rows may be a little nearer together, and the alleys between them a little less.

"3. The *Hautboy* thrives best in a light soil well supplied with dung; for excess of manure does not

* It is from this practice that the plant derives its name

drive it into leaf like the pine. In other respects, the culture is the same as for the pine. There are, however, many different sorts of Hautboys: one has the male and female organs in the same blossom, and bears freely; but the sort I prefer is the one which contains the male organs in one blossom and the female in another. The fruit of this is of the finest colour, and of far superior flavour. Care must be taken that there are not too many male plants in the bed; for, as they bear no fruit, they make more runners than the females. One male to ten females is the proper proportion for an abundant crop.

" 4. The *Wood* strawberry is best raised from seed fresh gathered, sowing it immediately in a bed of rich earth. When of proper size, I transfer the plants to other beds, where they continue till the next March. They are then planted out in beds and rows, and at the distances before described. And,

" 5. The *Alpine* or *Prolific* must always be raised from the seed, sown in a bed of rich earth. When of proper size (which will be in July or August), the plants are put out in rows, at the back of hedges or of walls, in a rich, moist soil; the rows two feet apart, and the plants twelve inches from each other. My Alpines this year, and thus managed, are bearing most abundantly; and so much so, that, in gathering them, there is not room for the women to set their feet without destroying many. In quickness of bearing the Alpines are before all other sorts, as they give their fruit within a single year; whereas the others do not bear under two years."

In gathering the fruit, employ only dry weather. Berries taken early in the morning and late in the evening keep the best, but those picked at midday have the most perfume. Pinch off the calyx and one quarter of an inch of the peduncle with the berry.

The WALNUT (*Juglans regia*).—This tree is supposed to be a native of Persia, and of the southern side of Mount Caucasus, and yields a nut which holds a considerable place among the dessert fruits, and which has been recommended, as far back as the time of Pliny, as a safe and powerful vermifuge.* Its varieties are the Oval, the Large French,† the Tender, and the Thick-shelled.

To obtain these, Millar and Forsyth recommend sowing the nuts in a nursery, keeping them clean, and leaving their maturity to time, without any interposition of art to hasten their productiveness. But Knight and others have succeeded so well by *inarching* and *budding*, that these methods may be considered as having nearly superseded the older and slower modes of propagation. In employing the former (inarching), your young plants, growing in pots, are raised to some branch of an old bearing tree, and grafted *by approach.* A union takes place in the summer; and in the fall you detach the scion from the parent stem. In the other case, the process is equally sure and less troublesome. Many minute buds, almost concealed in the bark, will be found near the base of the annual shoots. These must be taken in preference to those which are fuller and more prominent, and inserted near the summit of the last year's wood, and, of course, near the base of the annual shoots. " Thus managed," says Knight, " they will be found to succeed with nearly as much certainty as those of other fruit-trees, provided the buds be in a more mature state than those of the stock into which they are set."

The walnut-tree grows well in many different soils, but does best in a deep, sandy loam, resting on a dry subsoil. It is often employed as a screen for other and more delicate fruit-trees, in which case it is arranged on the northern and western side

---

* The Spaniards grate the nut into their tarts, &c., probably with a view to its supposed medicinal quality.

† Before 1562 it was called the *Gaul* or French nut

of the garden. Its diseases are generally the result of accident, and it has few, if any, enemies among the insect tribes.

The CHESTNUT (*Fagus castanea*) is a native of Sardis, and, it is said, was first brought to Europe by Tiberius Cæsar. Be this fact as it may, another, of which we are better assured, is, that the tree has been long naturalized in Italy and Spain, and that in these countries it contributes an important article to the food of man.

Like the walnut, it was long propagated by sowing the nut; but the shorter process of grafting (as already detailed under the preceding article) may be advantageously substituted for this. The experiments of the late Sir J. Banks and of Mr. Knight demonstrate that "the Spanish chestnut succeeds readily, when grafted in almost any of the usual ways; and that, when the grafts are taken from bearing branches, the young trees blossom the succeeding year."*

The soil most proper for the chestnut is a sandy loam, on a dry subsoil. With regard to situation, it does well in northern and western borders; but, as its shade is unfriendly to any vegetable growing under it, the better method is to give it a square by itself.

The FILBERT (*Corylus avellana*).—This is the common hazelnut improved by cultivation. Its principal varieties are, the *White*, the *Red*, the *Barcelona*, the *Cosford*, and the *Long Cob*, all of which are propagated alike by suckers, by layers, and by seeds. When the last of these modes is employed, sow the nuts in October or November, and keep the plants in the nursery till they are two years old; after which, set them out, and manure and dress them occasionally. But the better method of propagating them is that by suckers. These are taken up in

---

* Hort. Trans., vol. i., p. 61.

the fall or spring, and planted out in rows, at the distance of ten or twelve feet from each other, where they undergo several severe and successive prunings, for the purpose "of hollowing out the head into the form of a punch-bowl, and of determining the whole nourishment of the tree to the production of the fruit." Williamson is, however of opinion, that the severity of this discipline defeats itself, and is, in fact, the reason why the plants give no fruit three years out of five. Instead, therefore, of a rigid adherence to the Maidstone practice, he recommends "that the trees be left in a great degree to their natural growth and shape."

In some parts of England, the filbert forms an object of very profitable culture, giving, per acre, on an average produce of five years, five hundred pounds' weight of nuts.

The maturity of the fruit is indicated by the brown colour of the nut and the husk, and the readiness with which these separate. Braddick's method of preserving the fruit, by putting it up in airtight casks, is no doubt the best. The filbert is neither often nor seriously attacked by insects. The eggs of the curculio kukans are sometimes deposited in the germen, where, when matured, they subsist upon the kernel. The only cure for this is to destroy the nuts which are so attacked, and with them the larvæ, before they attain the fly state.

THE END.

www.ingramcontent.com/pod-product-compliance
Lightning Source LLC
Chambersburg PA
CBHW030630030726
47497CB00006B/1721